SATAN

Other books by the same author:

Dissent and Reform in the Early Middle Ages (1965)
Medieval Civilization (1968)
A History of Medieval Christianity: Prophecy and Order (1968)
Religious Dissent in the Middle Ages (1971)
Witchcraft in the Middle Ages (1972)
The Devil: Perceptions of Evil from Antiquity to Primitive Christianity
    (1977)
A History of Witchcraft: Sorcerers, Heretics, Pagans (1980)
Medieval Heresies: A Bibliography (with Carl T. Berkhout, 1981)

SATAN ॐ

The Early Christian Tradition

JEFFREY BURTON RUSSELL

Cornell University Press

ITHACA AND LONDON

Copyright © 1981 by Cornell University

First published 1981 by Cornell University Press.
Published in the United Kingdom by Cornell University Press Ltd., Ely House, 37 Dover Street, London W1X 4HQ.

International Standard Book Number 0-8014-1267-6
Library of Congress Catalog Card Number 81-66649
Printed in the United States of America
Librarians: Library of Congress cataloging information appears on the last page of the book.

For Charlotte, Polly, and John

Contents

Illustrations

Preface

This book is the second volume in my history of the concept of the Devil. The history has a twofold purpose: first, to gain a better understanding of the nature of evil; second, to develop a method for the history of concepts and the historical theology of concepts.

The first volume, *The Devil: Perceptions of Evil from Antiquity to Primitive Christianity*, published in 1977, presented a cross-cultural survey of the idea of evil and then traced the development of the concept of the Devil in Hebrew and primitive Christian thought to the first century of the Christian era. The present volume continues the study of the concept's development in Christian thought into the fifth century, by which time the main lines of the tradition had been established. I examine the Christian tradition primarily, with only a brief summary of post-apocalyptic Jewish thought, because the Devil has been much less significant a figure in Judaism than in Christianity. I treat both the eastern and western parts of the Christian community, and thinkers defined as heretical as well as those who came to be considered orthodox.

I appended to the first volume a brief statement of my own beliefs, both because the author's point of view cannot and should not be removed from historical writing, and because I felt that in a matter as important to humanity as the problem of evil it would be disingenuous and cowardly to try to conceal myself. My belief in the importance of candor has not changed, but my view of the Devil has been somewhat modified. I hope that it is the mark of an open mind that it can be moved by investigation and reflection.

At the time I wrote *The Devil*, I drew the line between history and theology too sharply. History can be independent of theology, but theology cannot be independent of history. The least insecure theological statements are historical statements. In this volume I explore the relationship between the history of concepts and historical theology.

In the earlier book I overemphasized the supposed future focus of the concept; my present view is that neither the origins nor the future focus of a concept constitutes the best definition of a concept; rather it must be defined in terms of its entire tradition. I am still inclined to believe that the Devil exists and that his works are painfully manifest among us.

The earliest known Christian depiction of the Devil is in the Rabbula Gospels (p. 102), which date from A.D. 586. Therefore the illustrations in this book, except for the fourth-century Adam and Eve fresco depicting the serpent (not Satan himself), are drawn from outside the period covered by the text. The sixth- to ninth-century pictures presumably represent earlier conceptions quite closely; the four more recent illustrations each make a general point. Why Christian art does not portray the Devil before the sixth century is not known.

I thank the following for their help and advice: Cameron Airhart, Larry Ayres, Carl T. Berkhout, William Donahue, Hal Drake, Abraham Friesen, Richard Hecht, Henry Ansgar Kelly, Ernst Kitzinger, Raimundo Panikkar, Kevin Roddy, Diana M. Russell, Jennifer Russell, Kay Scheuer, Tim Vivian, and Wendy Wright. I am grateful also to the Research Committee of the University of California, Santa Barbara, for its kind assistance.

JEFFREY BURTON RUSSELL

Santa Barbara, California

SATAN

You must one day realize at last of what cosmos you are a part and from what Governor of the cosmos your existence comes, and that a limit of time has been set aside for you, and if you do not use it to clear away the clouds from your mind it will be gone, and *you* will be gone, and it will never return again.

—Marcus Aurelius, *Meditations*

The world is all the richer for having a devil in it, so long as we keep our foot upon his neck.

—William James, *The Varieties of Religious Experience*

1   The Devil

The problem of evil is the theme of this book. Why is evil done to us, and why do we do evil ourselves? No easy answers work; in human affairs the truth is often inversely proportional to the certitude with which it is stated.

Meg Greenfield, writing about the Jim Jones cult, pointed out the dangers of simplifying the problem of evil. Upon hearing of the mass deaths in Guyana, people reacted immediately to rationalize the horror in terms of their own preconceptions. Secularists said that it was the result of religious belief, conservatives that it was the product of left-wing radicalism, and radicals that the right-wing racism of capitalist society had driven the victims to despair. Such quick explanations, Greenfield wrote, make "the night less frightening" and "tame and domesticate the horror by making it fit our prejudices and predilections." But she concluded that in reality the horror arises from "the dark impulses that lurk in every private psyche" and that "the jungle is only a few yards away."[1]

On October 11, 1978, United Press International reported that a father "kept his daughter, Tina Ann, 10, imprisoned in a 3-foot by 4-foot closet in [his small, white frame house] while he slowly beat her to death. He buried her under a dilapidated shed at the rear of the house and the family left town several

---

1. M. Greenfield, "Heart of Darkness," *Newsweek*, Dec. 4, 1978, p. 132.

months later." On January 1, 1980, UPI reported that "Thai pirates held 121 Vietnamese women and children captive on a deserted jungle island for seven days, raping them and hunting them down like animals. . . . One eight-year-old little girl was raped by 100 different men. . . . The pirates took as much pleasure in the hunt as in the capture." Evil—radical evil—exists, and its existence imposes on us the obligation of attempting to understand it and transform it.

Each of the current explanations of evil—for example, genetic inheritance, social environment, class distinction, ignorance, mental illness—may help resolve some individual problems and contribute to our general perception, but we are left with the irreducible fact that the jungle remains within us. Or is it worse than a jungle? A jungle is natural. The core of evil within us may or may not be. We are obliged, as John Hick did in his *Evil and the God of Love*, both to analyze evil and to agonize about it.[2]

This book addresses the problem of evil, but it does not presume to solve it, as if evil were, as Ursula LeGuin expressed it, "something that can be solved, that has an answer, like a problem in fifth-grade arithmetic. If you want the answer, you just look in the back of the book. *That* is escapism, that posing evil as a 'problem,' instead of what it is: all the pain and suffering and waste and loss and injustice we will meet all our lives long, and must face and cope with over and over, and admit, and live with, in order to live human lives at all."[3]

The problem of evil transcends religion. The sincere atheist must also confront evil, as Camus did in *The Plague*. The monist, such as the Hindu, who believes that God encompasses both good and evil, must beware of repressing the problem rather than resolving it, for a divine harmony encompassing napalm and nerve gas surpasses the understanding of even the most enlightened. The problem of evil is particularly acute in the monotheist tradition of Judaism, Christianity, and Islam;

2. J. Hick, *Evil and the God of Love* (New York, 1966).
3. U. K. LeGuin, *The Language of the Night* (New York, 1979), p. 69.

this tradition's efforts to justify God's ways to man are called theodicy.

Four logical options exist in theodicy: (1) God is neither all-good nor all-powerful (an option usually excluded on the grounds that no one would call this God); (2) God is all-good but not all-powerful; (3) God is all-powerful but not all-good; (4) God is both all-good and all-powerful. The last option, usually adopted in the Judeo-Christian-Islamic tradition, is a difficult one requiring some concordance of the existence of God with the existence of evil. A perfect solution still evades us, for we have usually ended up either saving the goodness of God at the expense of his power, or his power at the expense of his goodness.

Theodicy has always been the most difficult task of any monotheist theology assuming the omnipotence and benevolence of the God: if the God is both all-powerful and all-good, why does he permit evil? The problem can be summarized as follows: (1) the world, including matter, energy, and spirit, was created by God from nothing; (2) God is omniscient; (3) God is omnipotent (he can create any world that is logically capable of being created); (4) God is perfectly good (he chooses to create the best world logically capable of being created); (5) but the world contains evil.

No simple solution works, and a number of theodicies have been proposed: (1) What is perceived as evil is really necessary for the greater good. (2) Evil is the necessary by-product of the creation of an essentially good universe. (3) If properly perceived, evil has no real existence: it is nonbeing. (4) The universe is imperfect, but God is drawing it toward perfection. (5) The whole question of evil is semantically meaningless. (6) The meaning of evil is a mystery that God forever hides from our understanding. (7) Suffering tests and instructs us, enabling us to mature. (8) Suffering punishes us for our sins. (9) Evil is solely the result of sin, which arises from the exercise of free will. God permits evil in order to achieve the greater good of freedom. This last has been the most prominent argument of Christian theodicy. But atheists have offered two powerful objections: Why are the degree and the amount of suffering so great? Would it not be sufficient to God's plan for freedom to enable us to slap or kick one another without using knife or napalm? And the second objection: how can natural evils, such as tornadoes and cancer, be the result of free-will sin?[4]

Other lines of argument can be pursued.[5] If we begin with a God who would not permit the innocent to suffer, then obviously that God does not exist. But why assume such a God? What other avenues are open? Any convincing idea of God must account for both the good and the evil in the cosmos. R. W. K. Paterson suggests that in the best of all *possible* worlds as opposed to *ideal* worlds it is necessary that good outweigh evil but not necessary that evil not exist at all. In the cosmos as a whole, good may outweigh evil; indeed, in the life of each individual good may outweigh evil and happiness outweigh suffering, so long as the individual's existence is not limited to this earth but has another dimension. This theodicy requires belief in an "afterlife," however defined. Paterson is well aware that his theodicy is not certain (none is), but he correctly observes that "a solution to the problem of evil is not required to show that the universe is in fact the handiwork of a perfectly good, omniscient Creator, but merely that this hypothesis is logically, morally, and religiously *compatible with* the presence of natural evils in the universe."[6]

4. I discussed arguments for and against (1) through (9) in *The Devil* (Ithaca, N.Y., 1977), pp. 223–227.

5. R. Richman argues that the burden of proof is on the theist to produce an adequate theodicy "on pain of moral skepticism" ("The Argument from Evil," *Religious Studies*, 4 [1969], 203–211). J. L. Mackie claims that there is no valid solution of the problem which does not modify either the omnipotence or the goodness of the God ("Evil and Omnipotence," *Mind*, 64 [1955], 212). W. H. Poteat believes that man's freedom (hence his ability to sin) can be reconciled with God's omniscience if only we use language correctly and "do not mix incomparable models of knowledge" ("Foreknowledge and Foreordination," *Journal of Religion*, 40 [1960], 26). See also D. L. Doig, "The Question of Evil Re-examined," *Theology*, 69 (1966), 485–492; T. Penelhum, "Divine Goodness and the Problem of Evil," *Religious Studies*, 2 (1966), 95–107; F. Sontag, *The God of Evil* (New York, 1970).

6. R. W. K. Paterson, "Evil, Omniscience, and Omnipotence," *Religious Studies*, 15 (1979), 1–23, esp. pp. 1–2 and 23 (quotation from p. 23). A coherent and logical defense of the compatibility of God and evil is P. Geach's

These problems lie at the heart of the concept of the Devil, which this book approaches historically. The bases of the history of concepts are as follows: Truth in the absolute sense cannot be found. Either it does not exist at all or it exists only in the mind of God and is forever hidden from our mortal eyes. All perceptions are human perceptions, and a fact is what we think it is; a fact is not something solid but a proposition of greater or less probability. What is a tree? Is a tree as you see it? Or as a lumberman sees it, or a mystic, or a physicist, or a painter, or a geneticist, or a paper manufacturer? Is it as you perceive it from an airplane, or from fifty feet, or with your face pressed into its bark? Is it as you see it on a sunny noon, or as it appears at dark midnight? Is it as an adult perceives it, or as a child? Is it as a human perceives it, or a dog, or a fly, or a being from another planet with different structures of sense and brain? Does its reality lie in its mass, or in its cellular structure? The "true" nature of the tree is a hypothesis or a myth. Its "objective reality," if it exists at all, exists only in the mind of God. If the objective reality of a tree is difficult to establish, the objective reality of a human construct is even more so. Imagine a conversation between a Baptist, a Catholic, a Muslim, and a Marxist on the subject "What is Christianity?" Absolute truths regarding human constructs cannot be established.

Yet by being intentional toward truth in as sophisticated a fashion as possible, we can obtain truth in a human, rather than an absolute, sense. The purpose of history, as of all disciplines, is a disciplined effort to point the way to truth. History is not merely an intellectual exercise: it is a sacred calling.

History and theology are quite different disciplines, but areas exist where they converge. History is independent of theology: it investigates many other human concerns; and historians do not properly make statements about metaphysical, transhuman realities. Theology, on the other hand, is largely dependent

Providence and Evil (Cambridge, 1977). D. R. Griffin, a process theologian, argues that God's omnipotence is limited by primeval chaos, which he did not create. God is working with the cosmos now, prodding it along toward improvement. See P. Hefner's review article, "Is Theodicy a Question of Power?" *Journal of Religion*, 59 (1979), 87–93.

upon history. Theologians sometimes make metaphysical statements based on a priori assumptions or on revelation, but such statements cannot be validated. Of metaphysical reality we know nothing. What we do know are human perceptions and the history of human perceptions.

I define a concept historically. An individual at any time may have a notion of an entity, such as the Devil or Parliament. Through mutual influence, such notions or views develop into constellations. A variety of such constellations exists at any given time. Through the years some fade and vanish; others gain increasing acceptance. From these latter a tradition is gradually formed. The historical tradition of human perceptions of an entity (the Devil or Parliament) constitutes a concept. A concept may be relatively simple; more often it is manifold and varied. But its boundaries can be located and traced across time. A concept is not simply that which it was in its origins or what it will be or what it is in any given moment. It is a coherent whole transcending time.

The concept may or may not correspond to an objective reality. We do not know what objective reality is. The surest theological statement is the historical statement of a concept. A statement about metaphysical reality may lack meaning in that it is not susceptible of proof or disproof; but a statement about a metaphysical concept is meaningful because it can be tested by the historical evidence. The historian of concepts can thus provide the surest kind of statement for the historical theologian. The boundary between theology and history is not so firm as I had supposed in my earlier book.[7]

7. The historical approach to theology is by no means universally accepted, but it commands increasing attention. The great, standard work is J. H. Newman, *An Essay on the Development of Christian Doctrine* (London, 1845). See also O. Chadwick, *From Bossuet to Newman* (Cambridge, 1957); J. C. Murray, *The Problem of God: Yesterday and Today* (New Haven, 1964); L. Dewart, *The Future of Belief* (New York, 1966); J. Pelikan, *Development of Christian Doctrine: Some Historical Prolegomena* (New Haven, 1969). A fuller exploration of the history of concepts appears in chapter 2 of my *Devil*. Newman's criteria for a valid tradition were: preservation of type; continuity of principles; power of assimilation; logical sequence; anticipation of its future; conservative action upon its past; chronic vigor.

The historical theologian goes further than the historian. He asserts that the concept as defined by its history bears some resemblance to objective reality. The historian treats it as a human artifact; the theologian as a human artifact whose construction is guided by God. For the theologian, the historical concept represents a kind of natural theology, an approach to divine truth by the human intellect without the aid of revelation. The historian perceives the boundaries of the concept as naturally determined and flexible at any time. For the theologian the boundaries are at least partly drawn by God and must be carefully guarded. The historical theologian asks, with John Courtney Murray: "The question is, what is legitimate development, what is organic growth in the understanding of the original deposit of faith . . . , what are the criteria by which to judge between true growth and rank excrescence." Or with Jaroslav Pelikan, "What can it mean for a doctrine to 'become' part of the Catholic faith, which is, by definition, universal both in space and in time?" The historical theologian will argue that doctrines cannot be added to or subtracted from tradition unless for a compelling reason. The historian judges whether an idea fits organically into the pattern of development, not whether it is proper or improper.[8] Though the viewpoint is different, the historian shares much common ground with the historical theologian.

The history of concepts differs from the traditional history of ideas in two ways. First, whereas an idea is intellectual and closely defined, a concept includes the affective as well as the analytical and has hazier boundaries; whereas an idea is rational, a concept draws upon unconscious patterns as well as conscious constructions. To the history of concepts, myth is as interesting as philosophy. Second, the historian of concepts does not consider ideas in a vacuum but rather places them in their social context wherever possible.

The history of concepts is distinct from both sociology of knowledge and social history. At its best, social history has

8. Murray, p. 56; Pelikan, p. 39.

been sophisticated and penetrating, using sources in new and creative ways. At its worst, it has been narrow and unsophisticated in its positivist assumption that "hard," "solid" external realities are more knowable than ideas or concepts. History does not treat objective reality, whatever that may be, but rather perceptions of reality, reflections upon reality. Sophisticated social historians are ready to agree that though the social context of concepts must be considered, the context does not determine the concept.[9]

The history of concepts argues that a phenomenon such as the Devil is best defined through its history. The Devil *is* the tradition of what he has been thought to be. Dangers do lurk in this approach. By studying the history of a concept, whether the Devil or Parliament, we may end by hypostasizing it, considering it a real entity apart from its formulation by humans. This "reification" of doctrines may lead to a search for an approximation of an ideal type, which either does not exist or at least cannot be known, and to unanswerable questions about when an idea "really emerged." When did the concept of Parliament, or the Devil, really begin? Worse, the approach runs the danger of reading back into previous ages ideas that were formulated much later, as if the Anglo-Saxon Witenagemot had been vaguely (and crudely) striving toward the Parliament of Disraeli and Gladstone. Yet so long as historians keep in mind that the concepts they study are man-made (and that whatever other assumptions they may make beyond that they do not make as historians), the value of history of concepts will remain in its expression of the tension between the perceiver and the perceived.

Further, a tradition is only as good as the foundations on which it rests. The tradition must always yield to demonstrable facts. The geographical notion of heaven, for example, ceased to be viable even before Copernicus; it was deprived of its value by a new understanding of geography that had no room for a

---

9. B. Stock, "Literary Discourse and the Social Historian," *New Literary History*, 8 (1976–77), 185–188; and Q. Skinner, "Meaning and Understanding in the History of Ideas," *History and Theory*, 8(1969), 49.

heaven placed in a spatial location. Since the existence and nature of the Devil are not subject to scientific investigation, that particular time bomb is not lurking in this concept. The Donation of Constantine, a spurious document upon which centuries of papal claims to temporal power were based, provides another example of a tradition based on quicksand. Traditions founded upon bases that have been demonstrated to be spurious must be excised in order for a concept to retain its validity. Concepts also are valid only so long as they continue to respond to living perceptions. Thus if, for example, some new social order should be able to eliminate evil (an improbable feat), the concept of the Devil would surely die. A concept must also be internally consistent on central points. Finally, its development must be continuous through time: any chronological break in the development would mean that the concept had ceased to respond to experience and that, if renewed, it would exist on a different basis.

The Devil is the personification of the principle of evil. Some religions have viewed him as a being independent of the good Lord, others as being created by him. Either way, the Devil is not a mere demon, a petty and limited spirit, but the sentient personification of the force of evil itself, willing and directing evil.

Religious tradition has spoken of the Devil, as it has of the Lord, in masculine terms. In English and most other languages the Devil is "he." Tradition suggests numerous subsidiary female spirits of evil but symbolizes the chief of these spirits as masculine. Yet theology does not require a masculine Devil, and in fact Christian theologians have traditionally argued that the Devil, being an angel, has no specific sex. But what to do with language? To pluralize and use "they" for the Devil is misleading, and to use "he/she" is awkward to the point of absurdity, while "it" lacks all sense of personality. I will use the masculine pronoun, with the reservation that the usage is only for convenience.

On the existence of the Devil, history can make no metaphysical judgments. Some nonhistorical arguments for the Devil

The Devil as Tailor, oil on canvas by Jerome Witkin, 1980. Satan craftily sews his plans for the cosmos together. Private collection. © James Palmer.

include: (1) The Devil manifests himself personally: there is a "Devil-experience" as there is a "God-experience." (2) There is a universal human experience of the principle of evil. Some recent writers have spoken of a natural diabology akin to natural theology. (3) The Devil's existence can be demonstrated ontologically. (4) The Devil's existence can be demonstrated a priori from certain theological assumptions. (5) The Devil is accepted on the basis of the biblical evidence.[10]

What history shows is the concept of the Devil, a coherent historical development growing from pre-biblical roots through Hebrew and Christian thought into the present. The essential point of this tradition is that the Devil is a *satan*, an "obstructor" of the will of the good Lord. Satan's basic function is to say, "My will, not yours, be done." In *The Devil* I traced the movement away from initial monism (the belief that the God embraces both good and evil) to dualism (the belief that two opposite divine principles exist, one good and the other evil). I then described the brakes applied to dualism by Judeo-Christian monotheism. The unresolved conflict between monotheism and dualism provides the central tension in the history of Christian diabology: on the one hand the sovereignty of an omnipotent and benevolent Deity; on the other the irreducible fact of evil.

To deny the existence and central importance of the Devil in Christianity is to run counter to apostolic teaching and to the historical development of Christian doctrine. Since defining Christianity in terms other than these is literally meaningless, it is intellectually incoherent to argue for a Christianity that excludes the Devil. If the Devil does not exist, then Christianity has been dead wrong on a central point right from the beginning.

I suggested in my earlier book that the history of the concept may possibly lead to a second merging of the principle of evil with that of good, at a higher and more conscious level than that of traditional monism. William James alluded to such options: "Evil, as an element dialectically required, must be pinned in and kept and consecrated and have a function awarded to it in the final system of truth." He spoke of a possible reconciliation of the two principles: "It is as if the opposites of the

10. See Russell, ch. 7; W. James, *The Varieties of Religious Experience* (Boston, 1902), pp. 63–64; R. Woods, *The Devil* (Chicago, 1973), p. 58; D. and M. Haight, "An Ontological Argument for the Devil," *The Monist*, 54 (1970), 218–220; Sontag, passim.

world, whose contradictoriness and conflict make all our difficulties and troubles, were melted into unity. . . . Not only do
they, as contrasted species, belong to one and the same genus,
but *one of the species*, the nobler and better one, *is itself the genus
and so soaks up and absorbs its opposition into itself.*"[11] And Frederick
Sontag observes, "God is good because he continually controls
evil within his own nature. He is not good to the extent that he
allows unnecessary destruction to rain down on human existence." The problem of evil "prevents us from seeing unity (or
goodness) as the primary divine attribute. A plurality of attributes held together in personality—this now becomes a maximum allowable unity. . . . We are faced with a God whose
attributes are joined more flexibly than in most classical
concepts."[12] The concept of the God, in other words, may integrate good and evil into one, which by virtue of the synthesis,
becomes good in itself. That is, of course, speculation, and the
direction of the concept is in fact different.

It is not speculation that the concepts of the God and the
Devil develop through time. I will speak of the Lord and the
Devil as doing this or that, and as developing and changing.
This is figurative, historical language: "the Devil became" is
short for "the concept changed to represent the Devil as." No
assumptions of process theology (God developing through time)
are made.

The Devil took the concept as far as the New Testament; the
present book moves to the fifth century, at which time almost
all the fundamental points had been made. This volume treats
the development of the concept of the Devil primarily in
Christianity with only a brief summary of post-apocalyptic
Jewish thought, because the concept of the Devil has been
much less significant in Judaism than in Christianity. It treats
orthodox and heretical Christian thought in both western and
eastern Europe. It draws upon theology, history, hagiography,
creeds, canon law, poetry, and mythology.

The New Testament assumes one God, the good Lord, with

11. James, pp. 118, 306.
12. Sontag, pp. 152, 158–159.

whom Jesus Christ, the Son and Word of God, is identified. God is benevolent, but another spiritual power exists that opposes evil to the Lord's goodness and darkness to his light. This spirit is in New Testament Greek *diabolos*, "adversary," a translation of the Hebrew *satan*, "obstructor," and the origin of the English word "devil." The Devil is subordinate to the Lord, but he struggles against him constantly, and the sense and degree of his subordination, unclear in the New Testament, became the subject of theological controversy.

The Devil of the New Testament is the prince of this world of space (*kosmos*) and time (*aiōn*), as opposed to Jesus Christ, whose kingdom is not of this world. To some extent, Satan is the lord of matter and flesh as opposed to spirit. The Gnostic heretics were to exaggerate this point, which was kept in proportion among the orthodox by the insistence that everything was created by the Lord and therefore inherently good. Satan is the prime adversary of Christ. He tried to tempt Christ but failed. He sought Christ's death, yet at the same time tried to avert the act of redemption. Following the death and ascension of Christ, the Devil tries to thwart the Lord's victory by attacking and perverting humanity. Satan tempts people; he causes illness and death. He obsesses and possesses individuals and tempts human beings to sin. He is the leader of a host of evil spirits. He and his followers will be defeated and punished by Christ at the end of the world. The New Testament left a great many questions of diabology open to future theologians, but it affirmed that although the world is full of terrible grief and pain, somewhere beyond the power of Satan a greater power melts that pain in eternal rest and joy.

While the New Testament was giving the Devil considerable importance, Jewish thought was moving decisively in the other direction. The teachings of the rabbis in the Talmud consciously rejected the dualistic tendency of the apocalyptic writers and insisted upon the unity of the one benevolent Lord. Evil results from the imperfect state of the created world or from human misuse of free will, not from the machinations of a cosmic enemy of the Lord. Usually the rabbis rejected the notion of a personified being leading the forces of evil and preferred to speak of the Devil as a symbol of the tendency to evil within humanity. According to rabbinic teaching, two antagonistic spirits inhabit each individual: one a tendency to good (*yetser ha-tob*), the other a tendency to evil (*yetser ha-ra*). The rabbis ordinarily argued that the Lord had created both tendencies but gave humanity the Torah so that we might overcome the evil *yetser* by following the Law. The Devil was perceived as personifying the *yetser*: Rabbi Simon ben Lakish wrote that "Satan and the *yetser* and the angel of death are one."[13] The rabbis discarded the tradition of the rebellion of the angels, since the angels have no evil *yetser* and cannot sin, and they did not identify Satan with the serpent of Genesis or foretell his destruction and punishment. Some of the old traditions persisted in the aggadah—moral stories, legends, maxims, and sermons— where the Devil, known as Sammael more often than as Satan, is a high angel who falls, uses the serpent to tempt Adam and Eve, and acts as tempter, accuser, destroyer, and angel of death. Many Christian demon-tales have their origins in the aggadah. But even in the aggadah, Satan has no existence independent of the Lord, who uses him as a tester of hearts, an agent who reports our sins to the Lord, and an official in charge of punishing them.

The kabbalah, the literature of the Jewish magical/mystical movement that reached its height in the thirteenth century and remained popular into the eighteenth, gives the Devil much more attention than the rabbis did. Influenced by Greek philosophy, Gnosticism and Christianity, the kabbalah taught that all things came forth from the divine being in a series of emanations, each inferior to the one preceding. Originally the God was both good and evil: his right hand was love and mercy and his left hand wrath and destruction. The destructive aspect of God's personality broke away from the good and is known as the Devil. Rabbi Isaac Luria offered the unusual argument that the God contracted into himself (a process called *tzimtzum*) in

13. Babylonian Talmud Baba Bathra 16a.

order to make room for the Creation; the created world thus suffers from incompleteness, the absence of God, evil. Another interpretation of Luria's ideas has it that God contains within him a minute grain of evil called the *shoresh ha-din*, "the root of strict judgment." Jewish legends report details about Satan or Sammael: he has twelve wings, he is covered with eyes, he is like a goat, he can shift his shape at will. He is a rebellious angel who flies through the air causing disease and death. Humanity can defeat him only by following Torah.

The place of the Devil in Jewish thought after the apocalyptic period is slight and is in large part derived from surrounding, non-Jewish thought. As Joshua Trachtenberg put it, the Jewish Devil "was little more than an allegory" of the evil inclination among humans.[14]

14. J. Trachtenberg, *The Devil and the Jews* (New Haven, 1943), p. 19. See also, for example, Trachtenberg, *Jewish Magic and Superstition* (New York, 1939); B. J. Bamberger, *Fallen Angels* (Philadelphia, 1952); E. Langton, *Satan: A Portrait* (London, 1945); L. Ginzburg, *The Legends of the Jews* (Philadelphia, 1938); C. G. Montefiore and H. Loewe, *A Rabbinic Anthology* (New York, 1960); J. Z. Smith, "Towards Interpreting Demonic Powers in Hellenistic and Roman Antiquity," *Aufstieg und Niedergang der römischen Welt* (1978), II: 16.1, pp. 425–439. On the *yetser ha-tob* and the *yetser ha-ra* see E. Urbach, *The Sages: Their Concepts and Their Beliefs* (Jerusalem, 1975), vol. 1, pp. 471–483.

2   The Apostolic Fathers

One of the large questions left open by the New Testament was the degree of the Devil's independence from God. If the Devil was not an independent principle but a created being, what kind of being was he? The church fathers moved decisively in the direction of defining the Devil as a fallen angel. But this definition left other questions open. To what extent was God responsible for the evil actions of this angel whom he had created? To what extent did God order Satan's activities and to what extent merely tolerate them? Was the Devil an agent or an adversary of God? The angel solution did not succeed in reconciling a good and omnipotent deity with cosmic evil, and the basic conceptual options remained: (1) the God is both good and evil; he is not all-good; (2) two gods exist, one good, the other evil: the God is not all-powerful; (3) the God is wholly good as well as all-powerful. Christianity rejected the first two options and adopted the third with all its difficulties.

Though Christianity defined the Devil as a being subordinate to the God, it continued to believe that he was locked in a cosmic struggle with the Lord.[1] The Christians translated the He-

1. I use the term "the God" to designate the monist divine principle, which embraces evil as well as good, and " the Lord" to designate the wholly benevolent aspect of divinity. Since Christian tradition so completely identifies the good Lord as "God," I use the term "God" in the Christian sense as equivalent to "the Lord." However, the distinction between the idea of "God," the

brew stuggle between the Lord and the Devil into a struggle
between Christ and the Devil, and also between Christ and
Antichrist, since the difference between Satan and Antichrist is
often blurred.[2] Finally, it was a contest between the church, the
"community of the faithful," and the Devil.

Other sets of questions inhered in the belief that the Devil
was a fallen angel. What was the nature of his fall? Was it a
moral lapse, a loss of dignity, a physical departure from heaven,
or a combination? The fundamental distinction was between
fall as moral lapse and fall as punishment. What was the geography of the fall? Was it from heaven to lower air; from heaven to
earth; from heaven to underworld; from earth or air into underworld? Where does the Devil dwell now? In the air, on the
earth, or in the underworld? What was the chronology of his
fall? As a moral lapse, did it occur at the beginning of the world
before the creation of humanity, in Adam's time, or with the
Watcher angels at the time of Noah? As punishment, did it
occur at one of those times, at the advent of Christ, at the Passion of Christ, at the second coming of Christ, or a thousand
years after the second coming? What is the role of the Devil in
the millennium? Was his sin the result of a defect in nature or
in will? Did his sin consist of pride, envy, or lust? If envy, was
it envy of the Lord, or of humankind? What was the relationship between the Devil and the other angels; between
angels and demons; between demons and giants; between angels,
demons, and gods? Does the Devil have a body? Is it visible,
and if so, what does he look like? Do angels and demons have
ranks, and if so, is the Devil the chief of the demons? What was
the nature of the Devil's punishment? Can he ever be saved?

What are the Devil's powers? What functions does he per-

---

all-good Lord, and the idea of "the God," who is ambivalent, must be kept in
mind. I use the term "Satan" as the equivalent of "the Devil." The Devil's
name is unimportant: what is important is that he is the origin and focus of
the evil forces in the cosmos. I use the term "cosmos" to designate the entire
economy of existence, spiritual as well as physical, in order to distinguish it
from the merely physical "universe."

2. Victor Maag, "The Antichrist as Symbol of Evil," in *Evil*, ed. Curatorium of the Jung Institute (Evanston, Ill., 1967), p. 65.

form in the cosmos? What functions does he perform in regard to humanity? Is he the cause of natural evils, such as disease, madness, and death? Is he the cause of moral evil? Was it he who tempted Adam and Eve, in the form of a serpent or using the serpent as a tool? Does he dwell within the hearts of human beings as a spirit inciting to evil, like the Jewish *yetser ha-ra*? Does each person have an individual angel and demon warring within him? Does each vice have its own demon? Does the Devil incite sins and foster vice? Can he enter our minds, or only our bodies? Has God put him in charge of temptation? Has he put him in charge of the punishment of sinners?

Before the middle of the second century, Christian thought was Jewish-Christian, expressed in forms derived from Judaism.[3] Most Christians were still of Jewish background, and the influence of Hellenistic ideas still limited. The Jewish nature of early Christianity has been increasingly emphasized in the past few decades; as a result of the Qumran and Nag-Hammadi discoveries, many elements in early Christian thought previously considered Greek have been identified as Jewish. The most important of these is ethical dualism.

Christianity is a moderate dualist religion. The Devil has great power to oppose the work of Christ, but his power is always limited and held in check by God. Some writers still insist simplistically that religions are either dualist or not and that Christianity is therefore not a dualist religion. In fact a spectrum stretches between strongly monist religions and strongly dualist religions, and Christianity is somewhere in the middle of the spectrum, its exact position varying with the individual Christian thinker. Christian dualism derives from Jewish dualism, particularly Essene and apocalyptic thought. The strongest element in Jewish dualism is an ethical dualism ex-

---

3. J. Daniélou, *The Theology of Jewish Christianity* (Chicago, 1964), p. 9. I treated the pseudepigrapha, or apocalyptic literature, in my earlier volume on the Devil, ch. 5. The dates of the pseudepigrapha vary, and most are quite uncertain. Many pseudepigrapha postdate Christianity, and many have Christian additions, also of uncertain date. See J. H. Charlesworth, *The Pseudepigrapha and Modern Research* (Missoula, Mont., 1976).

pressed in a struggle between moral good and evil for, or in, the human soul. Jewish and Christian thought were also strongly influenced by Greek cosmic dualism (the Orphic/Platonic opposition between spirit and matter) and by Iranian cosmological dualism (the struggle between a spirit of light and a spirit of darkness).

The doctrines of the church in the second century were as yet quite unformed. Before A.D. 150 Christians were a tiny minority in the Mediterranean world, an environment that was mostly pagan and secondarily Jewish. Hostility between Christians and Jews grew after the fall of Jerusalem in A.D. 70, when the Sadducees, Zealots, and Essenes were defeated and the Pharisees emerged as the dominant faction among the Jews. The Pharisees, struggling to achieve unity for their religion, excluded Christians from the synagogues and anathematized them. Pressed by hostility from without, the Christian community had little coherent organization within.[4] Nor did Christianity yet possess a body of clearly defined doctrine. In the early years of the second century the Gospels had only recently been composed, and not all of them were generally known. A canon of Scriptures would not be established for two centuries more, and numerous Apocryphal books were widely circulated and accepted as inspired. Standards of orthodoxy scarcely existed as yet.

Of the Jewish Christianity of the early second century only a few texts still exist. The writers who followed the apostles are known as the apostolic fathers. The chronology, authorship, and mutual influence of these early writers are difficult to establish, and it is helpful to take Jewish-Christian thought as a whole rather than to sketch tenuous lines of influence.[5]

About A.D. 94–97, Clement I, bishop of Rome, wrote a letter

4. L. W. Barnard, *Studies in the Apostolic Fathers and Their Background* (Oxford, 1966), p. 155.

5. Generally included among the writings of the apostolic fathers are the works of Clement of Rome, Ignatius of Antioch, and Polycarp, the "Shepherd of Hermas," the "Letter to Diognetus," the Didache, the "Epistle of Barnabas," and the work of Papias.

to the church of Corinth, which had become severely factional-
ized. He expressed his hope that the factions would be reconciled and seek forgiveness for the sins they had committed
"through the promptings of the adversary." Here the Devil is
perceived as a distinct personality urging the Christian community to sin and dissension.[6]

The letters of Saint Ignatius, bishop of Antioch, who was to
be martyred in 107, indicate his sense of approaching martyrdom and his concern for order and unity in the Christian community. Influenced by Paul and showing similarities with the
work of John, Ignatius' thought was the most Gnostic among
the second-century fathers.[7] For Ignatius, the Devil was "ruler
of this age." He made a fundamental assumption of the conflict
between the old and new eons, between the kingdom of this
world and the kingdom of God.[8] This present age or eon, he
wrote, is evil: it has been dominated by evil ever since the fall
of Adam and Eve. The power of this old eon has, however,
been shaken by the Incarnation, and it will finally be shattered
by the Parousia, the second coming of Christ. Christ will introduce the new eon, a new age to be characterized by a radical
transformation of the very nature of the world and its inhabitants. In this new kingdom, age, or eon, evil will have no power. Meanwhile the world has an *archōn*, an evil spiritual prince.[9]

6. Clement 51.1: τοῦ ἀντικειμένου: "of the adversary." *Antikeimenos* is
used in the NT and later Christian writers to mean "enemy" or "adversary."
See F. X. Gokey, *The Terminology for the Devil and Evil Spirits in the Apostolic
Fathers* (Washington, 1961), pp. 68–69; J. Quasten, *Patrology*, vol. 1 (Westminster, Md., 1950), pp. 42–53.

7. Ignatius probably did not know the work of John. Seven epistles of
Ignatius—Ephesians, Magnesians, Trallians, Romans, Philadelphians,
Smyrnaeans, and Polycarp—are now generally regarded as authentic. But
see J. Rius-Camps, *The Four Authentic Letters of Ignatius the Martyr* (Rome,
1979). See M. P. Brown, *The Authentic Writings of Ignatius: A Study of Linguistic Criteria* (Durham, N.C., 1963); Virginia Corwin, *Saint Ignatius and Christianity in Antioch* (New Haven, 1960), pp. 7–10; Gokey, pp. 70–89; Quasten,
pp. 63–76.

8. "Ruler of this age": ἄρχων τοῦ αἰῶνου τούτου. Letter to the Ephesians
17.1, 19.1; to the Magnesians, 1.2; to the Romans 7.1.

9. The Greek ἄρχων can mean leader, chief, general, or ruler. Perhaps the
best translation is the traditional "prince," from the Latin *princeps*, "first
head," "chief," or "ruler." It is clear from the NT use of the term "archon of

Ignatius warned the Ephesians to evade the "stench" of the prince of this world, lest he divert them from the life that Christ wishes for them.[10] The Devil's purpose is to thwart Christ's work of salvation by diverting the Christian people from their proper goal. Ignatius warned the Christians at Rome that the Devil pits himself against each person individually. Ignatius felt himself to be in immediate danger. He begged his friends to support him against the evil prince, who was trying to wrench him away from his steadfast faith and persuade him to shirk martyrdom.[11]

Hosts of angels exist, said Ignatius. Some are evil and follow the Devil.[12] Good and evil humans also exist. The purpose of evil angels and evil humans is like that of their leader: to impede the work of Christ. Ignatius viewed the world as an arena—the image of martyrdom was never far from his mind—in which Christ, the leader of good angels and good humans, is locked in combat with the Devil.

Those evil humans who disrupt the Christian community with factionalism and false doctrines pose the greatest danger. The head of the local Christian community was the bishop, the successor of the apostles. He alone could guarantee organizational stability and doctrinal orthodoxy. A bishop himself, Ignatius said that anyone who acted without the bishop's advice and consent adored the Devil.[13] When, on the other hand, the Christian community unites in peace and harmony, the powers of Satan are enervated.[14] The Devil encourages the schismatics,

---

this age" and from Ignatius' other writings that *archōn tou aiōnou toutou* is to be equated with *diabolos*, "the Devil," and *Satanas*, "Satan."

10. Eph. 17.1: "stench": δυσωδίαν.

11. Rom. 7.1.

12. In the Letter to the Trallians 5.2, Ignatius spoke of the angelic and archontic (ἀγγελικάς, ἀρχοντικάς) powers, which can be either good or evil. Similar terms are used in the Letter to the Smyrneans 6.1. In Eph. 13.1, the angels who follow Satan are called powers of Satan (δυνάμεις τοῦ Σατανᾶ) in echo of Saint Paul. Angels for Ignatius were called *angeloi, archontes, dynameis,* and *exousiai.*

13. Smyr. 9.1: τῷ διαβόλῳ λατρεύει. *Latreuō* means "to serve" or "to be enslaved to"; in Christian usage it also meant "to worship."

14. Eph. 13.1: αἱ δυνάμεις τοῦ Σατανᾶ. *Dynameis* may mean the "powers" of Satan in the abstract, or the angelic (or demonic) powers that follow him.

who divide the community, and the heretics, who teach false doctrines. The fruit of their labors is death, and they will not inherit the kingdom of God.[15] The heretics are pitted against the children of light, who shun both schism and heresy.[16] This division of the world into the children of light and those of darkness is a moral dualism derived from the Essenes and appearing frequently in the works of the apostolic fathers.[17]

The idea that the Devil, the leader of the forces of darkness, pits the heretics against the church has had consequence throughout the ages. If the world is a battleground in a cosmic war between light and darkness, and if the church, the community of light under the leadership of Christ, is at utter war with the community of darkness, it follows that the Christian must give no quarter in battle, for he is at war with total evil. The apostolic fathers did not carry this doctrine to its logical

---

See G. B. Caird, *Principalities and Powers: A Study in Pauline Theology* (Oxford, 1956). The truer translation is usually "angelic powers" or "angels."

15. In Trall. 8.1, the snares (ἐνέδρας) of the Devil seem to refer to his promptings of the disobedient. In the Letter to the Philadelphians 6.2, Ignatius uses similar terms, κακοτεχνίας καὶ ἐνέδρας—"evil devices and snares"—in reference to the Judaizers, a name that may refer to those interpreting the Mosaic law literally or, more probably, to the Ebionites, "Judaizing docetists." See R. M. Grant, *Gnosticism and Early Christianity*, 2d ed. (New York, 1966), p. 178. Phil. 6.2 also refers to the γνώμη of the Devil—his "purpose" or "plan." Eph. 10.3 mentions the weeds sown by the Devil (βοτάνη τοῦ διαβόλου): the reference seems to be to sin in general, though Ignatius may have been thinking of heretics and schismatics in particular. The image, of course, goes back to the NT parable of the wheat and the tares, which became a standard text in the history of heresy. See R. Bainton, "The Parable of the Tares as the Proof Text for Religious Liberty to the End of the Sixteenth Century," *Church History*, 1 (1932), 67–89. Similar references to heresy appear in Trall. 11.1 ("Flee these evil offshoots, which bear deadly fruit"—a different parable, of course) and Phil. 3.3 ("Abstain from evil plants"). The implication for Ignatius is that the evil weeds grow up in the Lord's crop, but at harvest time he will winnow them out and burn them while he gathers the wheat into the barn.

16. Phil. 2.1: "Children of the light of truth, flee division and wrong teachings": τέκνα οὖν φωτὸς ἀληθείας, φεύγετε τὸν μερισμὸν καὶ τὰς κακοδιδασκαλίας.

17. See John 1:4–9; 12:46; 8:12, where Jesus appears as light as opposed to darkness. In 1 John 3:8–10 the children of light war against the children of darkness. For Paul, truth is associated with light and perversity with darkness: 1 Thessalonians 5:5–8; Ephesians 5:8–11; Romans 13:12.

end of violence. For them, the answer lay in passive resistance and martyrdom. But others subsequently employed the doctrine to justify harsh measures against heretics, Jews, pagans, Muslims, and witches. Much of the later intolerance of the church resulted from this concept, which in turn sprang from the basic premise of the New Testament that the world was at issue between Christ and Satan.

In this war martyrdom was an important battleground.[18] The early church perceived martyrdom as a struggle of the athletes of Christ against the servants of the Devil. The Devil was generally believed responsible for the attitude of both the government and the mob. Torture and death were his work, and even kindness on the part of the pagans was a diabolical snare, since it might weaken the martyr's resolution. An ordinary athlete strives in the arena for a material victory, but the Christian athlete strives for a spiritual victory won by preserving his faith to the death. The fathers generally viewed martyrdom as an integral part of the Christian community's struggle to advance Christ's work and the triumph of the saints. The Gnostics held the different belief that martyrdom was a way for an individual soul to ascend and enhance its spirituality. The Roman persecution of Christians (though in fact a very sporadic policy) came to be regarded as a sign that the whole empire was part of the Devil's kingdom. Ignatius did not take such a broad view, but he did see martyrdom as a battle with the prince of this world. "I long to suffer," he wrote, "but I do not know whether I am worthy. . . . I need the meekness in which the prince of this world is undone."[19]

---

18. W. H. C. Frend, *Martyrdom and Persecution in the Early Church: A Study of a Conflict from the Maccabees to Donatus* (Garden City, N.Y., 1965); F.-J. Dölger, "Der Kampf mit dem Ägypter," in Dölger, *Antike und Christentum*, 4 vols. (Münster, 1929–1934), 3:177–191; H. von Campenhausen, *Die Idee des Martyriums in der alten Kirche* (Göttingen, 1936); M. Pellegrino, "Le sens ecclésial du martyre," *Revue des sciences religieuses*, 35 (1961), 152–175. J. Daniélou, *The Origins of Latin Christianity* (London, 1977), cites the early Latin sermon *De aleatoribus*, which presents the image of the Devil as a gladiator attempting to ensnare the Christian in his nets.

19. Trall. 4.2. Cf. Rom. 5.3: "the evil torments of the Devil," κακαὶ κολάσεις τοῦ διαβόλου.

Ignatius believed that God always limited the power and knowledge of Satan. The Lord hid from Satan the virginity of Mary and the birth and passion of Christ. The Devil's strength cannot in the long run prevail. The limitation of such long-run theodicies postulating the ultimate triumph of good was clear to Robinson Crusoe's Friday: why, he asked his master, does the Lord take so long to win? Ignatius did not explore the question, but later fathers would be obliged to.

The "Epistle of Barnabas," the work of an unknown author (who was certainly not the apostle Barnabas), was written about 117–119 in the Jewish-Christian community of Egypt, probably in Alexandria.[20] "Barnabas" was probably a converted rabbi: his rhetoric and use of terms were Jewish. Once having converted, he grew violently to dislike unconverted Jews and Jewish Christians who held too closely to the Old Law. He wrote from the perspective of the Hellenized, allegorical Jewish thought whose chief exponent was Philo but which the Pharisee rabbis after A.D. 70 increasingly rejected. He was also influenced by Qumran, especially in his emphasis upon the Jewish ethical dualism of the "two ways," the way of light and the way of darkness. Barnabas held that the saving remnant of Israel—the *qehel Yahweh*—had been replaced by the *ekklēsia*, the Christian community. In the Old Testament, the Lord elects Israel from among the nations and elects from Israel those faithful to the Law. But in Christianity salvation shifts from the Torah to Christ, and the church replaces the saving remnant of Israel.

Like Ignatius, Barnabas located the struggle between the two ways or two kingdoms at the center of his teaching. The present age is evil and lies in the grasp of the Devil.[21] Though

20. See Gokey, pp. 99–120; Barnard, pp. 41–55; H. Windisch, *Der Barnabasbrief* (Tübingen, 1920); Quasten, pp. 85–92.

21. Barnabas 2.1: ἡμερῶν οὖν οὐσῶν πονηρῶν καὶ αὐτοῦ τοῦ ἐνεργοῦντος ἔχοντος τὴν ἐξουσίαν. The days are evil: *ponēros*, a stronger word than *kakos*. A person who is *kakos* may be content with his own evil, but one who is *ponēros* seeks to undermine the virtue of others (Gokey, p. 114). The Devil is here the ἐνεργόν, the agent or doer of evil, not in the sense of being the agent of a higher power of evil (which would be a contradiction in terms unless God were himself evil), but rather in the sense that it is he who

weakened by the Incarnation, Satan retains his grip on the present age until the second coming of Christ, which is at hand.[22] Since the two kingdoms are at war with one another, each morally responsible being is called to take one side or the other. The angels have already chosen, some taking the Lord's side and others the Devil's. The angels of the Lord are angels of light, the others those of darkness.[23] On the battlefield called earth the children of light struggle against the children of darkness, an imagery common to Qumran and the Gospel of John.

The prince of evil tries to lure us out of the army of light into that of darkness and so lose us to the kingdom of God.[24] For Barnabas the parting of the ways is sharp and clear: the road of light leads to heaven, while the road of darkness, under the

---

actualizes or energizes evil. In Saint Paul, ἐνέργεια is a supernatural power that may be either good or evil, but here the implication is clearly negative. The term ἐξουσία can mean a personified power, i.e., an angel, but here it simply means "power" in general, though again with a negative connotation. Gokey suggests (p. 105) that *exousia* here means the "power" of Satan, which is a kingdom of darkness comprised of all the enemies of Christ. Cf. Luke 22:53: ἐξουσία τοῦ σκότους: "the power of darkness." The fathers also frequently used the adjective πονηρός as a substantive, *ho ponēros*, "the Devil." See Barnabas 2.10. The usage is so established that it lends considerable weight to the argument that the ending of the Lord's Prayer refers specifically to the Devil: ῥῦσαι ἡμᾶς ἀπὸ τοῦ πονηροῦ—"deliver us from the Evil One," rather than "deliver us from evil." The substantive appears in the neuter, τὸ πονηρόν (e.g., Barnabas 19.11), as well as in the masculine *ho ponēros*.

22. In 18.2, the Devil is the prince of this present age of disorder, ὁ δὲ ἄρχων καιροῦ τοῦ νῦν τῆς ἀνομίας as opposed to Christ, the Lord of eternity, ὁ κύριος ἀπὸ αἰώνων καὶ εἰς τοὺς αἰώνας. Here *archōn*, the Devil's title, is contrasted with *kyrios*, "lord," the title of Christ. *Anomia*, "disorder," "chaos," "lawlessness," is the present state of the world and its kingdoms. Later Christian writers referred to the Roman Empire as an *anomia* as opposed to the kingdom of God, where justice reigns. In 15.5, this present era is described as the era of the lawless one, τὸν καιρὸν τοῦ ἀνόμου. Here *ho anomos* is, like *ho ponēros*, a substantive name of the Devil. The Son of God will soon destroy the Devil's *kairos*, his time or age. In 21.3, all things (presumably all things of this evil age) will perish with the Evil One: συναπολεῖται πάντα τῷ πονηρῷ.

23. In 18.1 Barnabas contrasts them: φωταγωγοὶ ἄγγελοι τοῦ θεοῦ as opposed to the ἄγγελοι τοῦ Σατανᾶ. In 9.4 he refers to ἄγγελος πονηρός without the article, so "*an* evil angel" here.

24. ὁ πονηρὸς ἄρχων . . . τῆς βασιλείας τοῦ κυρίου: 4.13.

power of "the Black One," leads to ruin.[25] The equation of evil, darkness, and blackness, a source of later racial stereotypes, occurs here for the first time in Christian literature. The immediate sources of Barnabas' use of the terms "black" and "blackness" are Jewish, Ebionite, and Greek. Behind these is the Mazdaist idea of the darkness of Ahriman, and behind Ahriman is the worldwide, almost universal, use of blackness as a symbol of evil.[26]

In order to seduce us into joining his dark regiments, the Devil seeks to "creep" into us.[27] What this meant to Barnabas is unclear. Later fathers would argue that the Devil can enter only our bodies, not our minds, and that he can tempt us only with externals. Barnabas seems to have intended something more. He said that the heart, symbol of the spirit, becomes a house of demons when it is idolatrous.[28] He was not referring to possession. The Devil or demons were generally believed to be able to attack a person's body by obsession (from without) or by possession (entering into it). Both modes of attack were made against wholly involuntary victims, and though such attacks might cause disease or madness they could not effect the corruption of the soul, since the free will of the victim had not yielded to the enemy. Temptation, on the other hand, assaults the will. It attempts to bend it, though it cannot force it. Temptations were generally regarded as being offered from outside. But Barnabas seems to have had in mind the Devil's cun-

25. ὁδοὶ δύο εἰσιν διδαχῆς καὶ ἐξουσίας, ἥ τε τοῦ φωτὸς καὶ ἡ τοῦ σκότους: 18.1. Cf. 4.10: "hate the deeds of the evil road": τὰ ἔργα τῆς πονηρᾶς ὁδοῦ. ἡ δὲ τοῦ μέλανος ὁδός: 20.1.

26. Russell, *Devil*, pp. 62–88, 141–142, 246–247. Solon, Pindar, Plutarch, Lucian, and other classical writers refer to "black characters" and "black hearts," for example Pindar's μέλαιναν καρδίαν and Lucian's black-haired demon "darker than dusk," μελάντερος τοῦ ζόφου. See Gokey, pp. 112–113. The primary sense of blackness in all these sources is absence of light rather than dark pigmentation, but the transfer of the symbol was later readily made.

27. μὴ σχῇ παρείσδυσιν ὁ μέλας: 4.9. Cf. 2.10: μὴ ὁ πονηρὸς παρείσδυσιν ἐν ἡμῖν.

28. οἶκος δαιμονίων: 16.7. Cf. the Gospel story (Matt. 12:45; Luke 11:24–26) of the man whose house is infested with demons.

Christ resists the temptations of Satan and dismisses him. Satan's black, misshapen wings are contrasted with the graceful, white, full wings of the angels attending Christ. A ninth-century illumination from the Stuttgart Gospels. Courtesy of the Württembergische Landesbibliothek.

ning entry into the mind or soul for the purpose of suggesting sin. Thus the individual soul becomes a battleground between Christ and the Devil. The presence of an evil spirit operating within the soul is closely related to the doctrine of the two ways and to the rabbinic doctrine of the two *yetserim*.[29]

Saint Polycarp, bishop of Smyrna, was martyred about 156. Like Ignatius, he emphasized the importance of martyrdom and the struggle against heresy.[30] Polycarp spoke of the many plots the Devil hatches against the martyrs and his use of prolonged

29. As H. A. Kelly, *The Devil, Demonology, and Witchcraft* (New York, 1974), pp. 70–71, indicates, possession was generally supposed to be effected by demons rather than by Satan himself. In Barnabas 9.4, an evil angel is responsible for the beliefs of the Jews who interpret the Law literally, as opposed to the Jewish Christians, who understand that the law of circumcision is a circumcision of the spirit.

30. The two documents relating to Polycarp are (a) his letter to the Philippians, composed between 120 and 135, and (b) a letter of the church of Smyrna describing his martyrdom, called "The Martyrdom of Polycarp" and written shortly after his death. The documents are very close in tone and content and may have been composed by the same author (in that case obviously not Polycarp himself), so for convenience I treat them both as Polycarp. See Quasten, pp. 76–82.

torture in order to induce them to deny their faith.[31] For Polycarp the Devil has no power over the soul. He can offer intellectual and moral temptations to heresy, or the prospect of fearful agonies as temptations to cowardice, but he has no power to
compel the individual to turn away from God's purpose. And,
if the Devil works in our hearts, so also does the Holy Spirit.
The internal struggle of the two *yetserim* thus becomes the internal struggle of the Holy Spirit against Satan.[32]

The seventh chapter of Polycarp's letter to the church of Phil-
ippi is an attack on heresy. "Anyone who does not believe that
Jesus Christ is come in the flesh is an antichrist, and anyone
who does not believe in the cross's testimony that Jesus really
suffered and died, is of the Devil."[33] This passage was aimed
against the Docetists, who believed that matter was so utterly
unworthy of Christ that his body was only an illusion. Polycarp
added that "anyone who twists Christ's words to suit his own
desires and says that there is no resurrection or judgment is the
first-born child of Satan."[34] The most significant thing in the
letter is the pointed contrast between the Christians, who are
"of God" and the "community of the first-born of God," and
the heretics, who are "of the Devil" and the first-born children
of Satan.[35] Even more clearly than Ignatius and Barnabas, he

31. Martyrdom 2.4; 3.1. Cf. Philippians 7.1, where the term μαρτύριον,
"witness," is used in the phrase "witness of the cross."

32. Polycarp's terms for the Devil are ἀντικείμενος (cf. Clement, note 6
above), διάβολος, ἀντίζηλος ("jealous"), πονηρός, Σατανᾶς, and βάσκανος
("envious"). On *baskanos*, see Gokey, pp. 96–97, and G. J. M. Bartelink,
"Μισόκαλος, épithète du diable," *Vigiliae Christianae*, 12 (1958), 37–44. *Baskanos*
is associated with ὀφθαλμος to mean "evil eye," and Bartelink associates this
with *misokalos*. In classical literature *baskanos* is associated with *daimōn* to mean
an evil, envious spirit. See Phil. 7.1 and Martyrdom, 17.1.

33. Phil. 7.1. "Of the Devil:" ἐκ τοῦ διαβόλου. Cf. 1 John 4:2–3, "of
God," ἐκ τοῦ θεοῦ. The whole passage is similar to 1 John, and it is likely
that here Polycarp and John were drawing upon a similar tradition. Antichrist
—ἀντιχρίστος—could mean simply "one opposed to Christ," but in 1 John
the sense is clearly *the* Antichrist, the man who will come at the end of the
world to aid the Devil in his last assault upon the church.

34. πρωτοτόκος τοῦ Σατανᾶ. Historians used to believe that this passage
was aimed specifically at the heretic Marcion, but in this century the assumption has been disproved.

35. Polycarp's *prōtotokos* of the Devil is meant to be contrasted with Saint

saw the opposition between heretics and orthodox not as a difference of opinion or judgment, but rather as a part of the cosmic struggle between the Lord and the prince of evil. Such a view laid the foundation for the demonization and persecution of heretics and infidels.

The "Shepherd of Hermas" emphasized the struggle between the good and evil spirits within the human heart.[36] There are two paths, one crooked and one straight, and two cities, the city (*polis*) of the Lord and the city of those opposing him—the first known use of the image that Saint Augustine later made famous.[37] Corresponding to the two ways and the two cities are two angels who dwell within the human spirit. It is unclear whether Hermas meant that two cosmic angels do battle within us or whether each of us has his own two personal angels, as in the theory of the *yetserim*. In practice, the concepts are similar. The evil angel within us is either the Devil or a representation or manifestation of him.[38] This angel of evil is ill-tempered, bitter, foolish, and harmful.[39] He enters into our hearts, tempts us, and binds us to sin.[40] Hermas did not mean that the individual could not resist the Devil. Rather, the state of the human soul is *dipsychia*, "double-mindedness": humans possess an innate inability to choose correctly between good and evil. Double-mindedness for Hermas sometimes meant indecision or ambiva-

---

Paul's "community of the first-born of God" in Heb. 12:23: ἐκκλησία πρωτοτόκων.

36. "Hermas" was allegedly a slave, but the identity of the true author is unknown. Probably written about 140, "The Shepherd of Hermas" is the earliest Christian book of pastoral care; in the second half of the second century it was widely circulated as an inspired book. Its emphasis on the two ways marks it as Jewish-Christian. See Gokey, pp. 121–174; Molly Whittaker, ed., *Das Hirt des Hermas* (Berlin, 1956); Quasten, pp. 92–105.

37. Hermas, Mandates 6.2.1–3; Similitudes 1.2–5.

38. Man. 6.2.1–7: one angel is an angel of righteousness, δικαιοσύνης, the other of evil, πονηρίας. The just (*dikaios*) nature of the good angel is worth noting, since some Gnostic thinkers, notably Cerdo and Marcion, opposed the good, loving God to the harsh, just (*dikaios*) God. The angels dwell "with" man: μετὰ τοῦ ἀνθρώπου. *Meta* can mean "with" in a very close sense, almost *within*, and that it has this sense here is clear later in the passage where the angel of evil comes *into* hearts, ἐπὶ τὴν καρδίαν.

39. ὀξύχολος, πικρός, ἄφρων, ἔργα that are πονηρά.

40. Man. 6.2.9: "bound to": δεῖ.

lence, but sometimes he spoke of it as an evil spirit coming from the Devil.[41] Hermas' dualism is Jewish-Christian ethical dualism: the two paths and the two angels are within us, and we have a moral choice to make between them.[42]

The Devil has his own commandments, opposed to those of the Lord. But if we have faith and repent of our sins, we need not fear him. He cannot oppress us if we trust sincerely in God.[43] He can wrestle with Christian athletes but cannot throw them down if they resist him steadfastly. Those who have no faith fear the Devil and become his slaves, but he is forced to shun those who are full of faith, since he finds no passage by which to enter them.[44] As Saint Paul said, we have no merits of our own that can protect us from the Devil's vast power; only faith in Christ can save us by drawing upon his infinite merits. Christ sends an angel of repentance to enable us to withstand the Devil. Faith renders Satan's strength as weak as the muscles of a corpse, for the Lord's power destroys all Satan's power over the faithful.[45]

41. *Dipsychia*: Sim. 6.1.2; Man. 10.2.2–6; Visions 2.2.7, 3.7.1, 4.2.6. In Man. 9.9 *dipsychia* is evil and the daughter of the Devil: καὶ γὰρ αὕτη ἡ διψυχία θυγάτηρ ἐστι τοῦ διαβόλου. (Hermas frequently portrayed the vices as female—hence "daughter.") In Man. 9.11 *dipsychia* is a spirit derived from the Devil. Gokey, pp. 126, 155–161, discusses the meaning of *dipsychia*, relates it closely to ἐπιθυμία, "desire" or "lust," and thinks of both as generally equivalent to the *yetser ha-ra*.

42. That choice must be made by the discernment of spirits. Luke 6:43 advises "by their fruits you shall know them." If a spirit urges us to inflict pain or humiliation, it is an evil spirit.

43. Man. 4.3.4:"subtlety of the Devil"—πολυπλοκίαν τοῦ διαβόλου. Man. 4.3.6: temptation is from the Devil. Man. 12.4.6–7, "commandments of the Devil": ἐντολαῖς τοῦ διαβόλου. "Do not fear the Devil": τὸν διάβολον μὴ φοβηθῇς, ὅτι δύναμις ἐν αὐτῷ οὐκ ἔστιν καθ'ὑμῶν (Man. 7). "He cannot oppress us": διάβολος σκληρός ἐστι: Man. 12.5.1–4. See Kelly, p. 104.

44. Man. 12.5.1–4: "slaves," ὑπόδουλοι, which is to be contrasted with the common appelation of Christians as slaves—δοῦλοι—of Christ. Tertullian later emphasized the struggle between the *servi Christi* and the *servi Diaboli*. "He finds no place to enter": μὴ ἔχων τόπον που εἰσέλθῃ.

45. Man. 12.6.1–4. The δύναμις of the Devil is contrasted with that of the Lord, who will destroy τὴν δύναμιν τοῦ διαβόλου πᾶσαν. "Weak as a corpse's muscles": ἄτονος γὰρ ἐστιν ὥσπερ νεκροῦ νεῦρα. Δύναμις here refers to power in general, not to a personified spiritual power or angel. *Dynamis* is a frequent word in the NT and early Christian thought: it appears at the end of the Lord's Prayer—thine is the "power," *dynamis*.

The angel of repentance has a colleague, the angel of righteous punishment.[46] Of this angel, Hermas said that "he is one of the righteous, but one set over punishment." Several vague assumptions lurk here. The Lord is good, but his goodness embraces justice: he rewards the faithful and punishes the wicked. This punishment often seems harsh, so much so that the Gnostics regarded the God of justice as being in opposition to the God of love. The Lord employs an angel to punish, putting a certain distance between himself and the unpleasant task. The transition from righteous punishing angel to wicked punishing angel is an easy step. Though orthodox Christians never set justice and love in opposition, they wished to relieve the Lord from responsibility for the torments of hell. In this process they eventually placed the Lord's adversaries in charge of punishment rather than the Lord himself. Once this transition was effected, a curious question emerged: are the demons in hell keepers or inmates? Eventually they came to be both.

The writings of Hermas as a whole were allegorical, and the literal and figurative are often mingled. Hermas repeatedly personified the vices as spirits or demons. Sometimes these spirits seem to be taken literally as having "a personal character," sometimes symbolically as representing a "spiritual inclination."[47] Like Barnabas, Hermas used the color black as a symbol of evil.[48]

Papias, bishop of Hierapolis in Asia Minor about A.D. 130, conflated the ancient story of the Watcher angels with another Jewish apocalyptic tradition that held that God had appointed angels to govern the earth and its nations. In late Jewish and early Christian thought, the idea that each person and each nation had its own angel or angels was common. Papias argued

46. Sim. 3.2.4; 6.3.2. Kelly, p. 104, traced Hermas' two spirits to Qumran influence. The positive spirit protects you; the negative spirit both tempts and punishes.

47. These terms are Gokey's (p. 126). For the vices as πνεύματα or δαιμονία see Man. 2.3, 5.2–5.7, 8.3–7, 10.1.1; Sim. 6.2, 9.22.3. In Man. 9.11 double-mindedness (*dipsychia*) appears as a "spirit"—*pneuma* of the Devil.

48. Sim. 9.15.3: the vices as twelve black-cloaked women; a black mountain as the abode of sinners. Vis. 4.1.6–10: Leviathan a huge beast whose head is of four colors: black, flame-colored, golden, and white.

that these angels had abused their authority and come to a bad end. Thus the dominion angels and the Watchers were melded into a general category of fallen angels. Justin Martyr, Irenaeus, and Athenagoras later expressed similar views.[49]

In addition to the biblical books eventually selected as canonical, and the writings of the fathers, a number of apocryphal works were circulating in the second century, some of which commanded considerable respect. At least in their present form, most of these date from later than the mid-second century and reveal influences from outside the Jewish-Christian tradition. Some of them are called *agrapha*, the "unwritten things," meaning alleged sayings of Jesus transmitted orally and later consigned to writing. The agrapha include the statement that this age "of lawlessness and unbelief is under the power of Satan, but the end of the time of his power is at hand."[50] The apocryphal "Apocalypse of Peter" said that in this age Satan makes war against humanity, veiling our understanding of the truth.[51] Things are in flux, the world is unsettled and lawless, and the prince of this world takes advantage of the situation to

49. Daniélou, *Theology*, pp. 188–191. On Papias, see Quasten, pp. 82–85. Papias referred to death as the last enemy and to an angel having dominion over all the earth. Death and the Devil were occasionally, though inconsistently, equated in the writings of the fathers. Other writings generally classified among those of the apostolic fathers have little to say on the subject of the Devil. The *Didache*, written about 150, taught that there is a road of life and a road of death, τοῦ θανάτου ὁδός, and it enjoined against doublemindedness. It forbade idolatry without equating gods with demons. On the *Didache*, see Quasten, pp. 29–39. A. Adam, "Erwagungen zur Herkunft der Didache," *Zeitschrift für Kirchengeschichte*, 68 (1957), 1–48; J.-P. Audet, *La Didachè, instruction des apôtres* (Paris, 1958). The "Letter to Diognetus," written in two sections, the earlier being about 130, speaks of the "deceit of the serpent" and of a warfare between spirit and flesh, but nowhere specifically refers to the Devil. On "Diognetus," see Quasten, pp. 248–253. For a summary of the names of the Devil in the apostolic fathers, see Gokey, pp. 175–180.

50. M. R. James, *The Apocryphal New Testament* (Oxford, 1924), p. 34; E. Hennecke, *New Testament Apocrypha*, ed. W. Schneemelcher, 2 vols. (Philadelphia, 1963), 1:188–189. The lawlessness, *anomia*, of the current age was a commonplace among the fathers.

51. James, p. 519; Hennecke, 1:682. The "Apocalypse of Peter" was written in A.D. 100–150.

work his will with us. But this situation cannot last. The end of the evil eon is near, and soon Christ will come again to break its power forever.

The "Odes of Solomon," a second- or third-century Jewish-Christian document, pitted Christ against Death and Hell. The Odes gave two reasons for Christ's descent into hell: first his death naturally brought him into the underworld, and, second, his descent broke the power of Death so that the baptized might henceforth obtain eternal life. The Odes took Saint Paul's idea that Christ defeated the powers of evil by his death on the cross and synthesized it with Saint John's idea that he defeated them by breaking down the barriers of hell and letting in his life. Paul's view came to prevail in theology, but John's continued in legend and literature. The Odes said that personified Death occupies the deepest and darkest part of hell, the first hint of the conception that the Devil occupies the dead center of the earth.[52]

Much of the fathers' thought developed in reaction to opposing viewpoints. In the Jewish-Christian period before A.D. 150, few doctrinal lines had as yet been drawn, heresy and orthodoxy were not clearly distinguished from each other, and a number of ideas that were later to be rejected competed vigorously for attention in the young Christian communities. The Judaizers, who wished to retain the full and literal interpretation of the Mosaic law, had been defeated by the general consensus among the apostles and attracted relatively little attention in the second century, but other factions—Ebionites,

52. Odes, 42. On the Odes, see J. H. Charlesworth, *The Odes of Solomon* (Missoula, Mont., 1977); Quasten, pp. 160–168. On the descent into hell, see below, pp. 117–122. Dante made the place of Satan at the center of the earth a *locus classicus*. Satan also figures prominently in the Odes as tempter and prince of this world. The "Second Letter of Clement of Rome to the Corinthians" is neither a letter nor by Clement, but an anonymous sermon written before 150, probably in Alexandria. It is Jewish-Christian, possibly Ebionite, and anti-Gnostic, but it shows some Gnostic influence, as do the Odes. The sermon presented Christ as purifying the Mosaic law, taking it back to its pristine form by deleting the interpolations added through demonic influence. It emphasized the two ways and the two ages, but Satan does not play a major role in the document. See Daniélou, *Origins*, pp. 59–61.

Elkesaites, Docetists, and Gnostics—pressed their points vigorously and evoked equally vigorous opposition from the fathers.

The Ebionites (Heb. *ebyon*, "poor"), who emerged by A.D.
70, followed Christ as a great prophet but not as the Messiah or
Son of God. Influenced by the Essenes, the Ebionites taught a
strong ethical dualism that sometmes bordered on Gnostic cosmic dualism, although they never argued that the world was
created by any power other than God himself. Cerinthus, for
example, seems to have been an Ebionite Gnostic, and some
Ebionites went so far as to believe that "God has established
two beings, Christ and the Devil. To the former has been committed the power of the world to come, but to the other the
power of this world."[53] Depending on the interpretation, such a
statement could win approval from Gnostics, Ebionites, and
fathers alike. The Elkesaites, followers of Elkesai, who taught
shortly after A.D. 100, used a kind of baptism to purge the soul
from the Devil, whom they identified with the *yetser ha-ra*.[54]
The Docetists (Gr. *dokeo*, "to appear") argued that matter was
so corrupt that Christ could not have a real physical body; his
body was an appearance or an illusion, and he did not really
suffer or die on the cross. Docetism had strong affinities with
Gnosticism, which emphasized the opposition between soul and
body.

During the first centuries after Christ, Greek philosophical
thought continued to develop ideas that influenced both Christian and Gnostic writers. The Platonists defined demons as
beings intermediary between gods and human beings. Such
beings were readily assimilable to the Hebrew-Christian angels.[55] For the Platonists, demons were a mixture of good and
evil, depending on the degree to which the irrational dominated
their souls. In Homeric and early Greek thought the distinction

53. Epiphanius, *Panarion*, 30.16; Daniélou and H.-I. Marrou, *The Christian
Centuries: The First Six Hundred Years* (London, 1964), pp. 56–57.
54. Daniélou and Marrou, pp. 57–58.
55. Russell, *Devil*, pp. 204–220. The Septuagint translators of the Hebrew
Bible into Greek rendered the Hebrew *mal'ak* by *angelos* rather than by *daimōn*.
Angelos, "messenger," emphasizes the function of the *mal'ak* as the spirit of
Yahweh sent forth, rather than as an independent being.

between a *daimōn* and a *theos* was unclear: "demons," like "gods," were manifestations of the divine principle and, like the divine principle itself, were a mixture of good and evil. Socrates' famous *daimōn* was a guardian spirit whose influence was apparently for the good. By the time of the Christian era, the term *daimōn* was frequently replaced by *daimonion*, which had a more negative connotation, and the Christians connected the *daimonia* with the evil angels.

Philo of Alexandria (30 B.C.–A.D. 45), the greatest of the Hellenistic Jewish thinkers, influenced the Christians more than he did the rabbis, who rejected his allegorical approach to the Scriptures. Philo distinguished between gods and demons, equating the demons of the Greeks with the angels of the Jews. These angels/demons lived in the air, probably in the ether—the upper air near heaven—but they moved back and forth between heaven and earth as intermediaries between God and man. The angels/demons are arranged in twelve companies.[56] Some are benevolent: they help and guide individuals and nations. Others are "employed by God to inflict punishment upon all who deserve it."[57] But Philo also indicated the existence of a third class, which he called evil angels. It is not clear whether he meant these beings allegorically or literally, but apparently he identified them with the Watchers, who fell because of their lust for mortal women.[58] Elsewhere Philo referred to the two *yetserim*. Because of the presence of the evil *yetser* in humans, God did not create men and women directly, but rather through intermediaries, so that "man's right actions might be attributable to God, but his sins to others . . . for [God] ought not to be the cause of evil."[59] Plutarch (A.D. 45–125), a Middle Platonist, argued that the demons were torn between goodness and spirituality on the one hand and imperfection and matter on the other. They struggled to enhance their spirituality and to rise in the cosmic order. Those who failed sank lower and were

56. H. A. Wolfson, *Philo*, 2 vols. (Cambridge, Mass., 1947), 1:377.
57. Wolfson, 1:382.
58. Wolfson, 1:383–384.
59. Wolfson, 1:273; 2:279–303.

contaminated by matter, caught and entrapped in the cycle of birth. Demons and human beings therefore have similar natures, since both strive to shuffle off this mortal coil and ascend to spiritual realms. The demons circle everywhere in the lower air between earth and moon, some hurting us and some helping us. Under Iranian influence, the idea that demons were of mixed nature, each fighting a spiritual struggle of his own between good and evil, was more and more replaced by the idea that some demons were inherently good and others inherently evil. In this form, Greek demon-belief became markedly congruent with Judeo-Christian ideas about good and fallen angels.[60]

60. G. Soury, *La démonologie de Plutarque* (Paris, 1942).

3   The Apologetic Fathers and the Gnostics

In the mid-second century Christianity underwent a significant change. The mythical and intuitive thought that had prevailed among the apostolic fathers began to be accompanied by theology—analytical and logical reflection upon revelation. The "apologetic fathers," such as Justin and Irenaeus, recognized that when Christianity claimed universality it had to compete intellectually with both rabbinic thought and Greek philosophy. Christians also faced the hostility of the Roman state and of the established Roman pagan religion (which was, however, already in deep decline). Dissension within the Christian community was an increasing problem. The canon of the New Testament was still in flux. Under such circumstances radical differences of opinion arose within the community during the second century. The party that eventually won became orthodox—"right-thinking"—by reason of its victory, and its writers were given the name "apologetic fathers." Their defeated opponents came to be called heretics.

> Heresy never prospers.
> Why? I daresay
> If heresy prosper
> None dare call it heresy.

By far the most significant opposition to the emerging consensus among the fathers was Gnosticism, one of the most important movements in the history of Western religion. Modern scholars employ the term "gnosticism" in a variety of senses. Simply speaking, Gnosticism used to be regarded as a Christian heresy arising from a radical Hellenization of Christianity. But scholars writing since the Qumran and Nag Hammadi discoveries recognize that nearly all the ingredients of later Gnosticism were already present at Qumran. Gnosis is now seen as a general attitude drawing from a number of sources: Iranian Mazdaism, Greek philosophy (especially Middle Platonism), Hebrew tradition, the Essenes, and Christianity. This general attitude gradually found expression in a movement, first in the Jewish-Christian community and then in the Greek-Christian community. In the Jewish-Christian milieu, little distinguished Gnostic thought from that of the more dualist apostolic writers. Then, after about A.D. 150, Gnosticism became more dualistic, more mythological, and more Hellenized. As early as 120 or 130, some Christian writers, perceiving Gnosticism as a dangerous doctrine, began to think of it as a heresy.

Some important facets of the thought of the second-century fathers developed in reaction to Gnostic beliefs. Many of their ideas, for example on the Devil's relationship to matter, must be understood largely in that context. The orthodox insistence that matter is good and created by a good God was a turning point in Western civilization, enabling future scientific and technological progress—and disastrous ecological exploitation—to occur.

Gnosticism took so many diverse forms that defining the term is still difficult. Most scholars now distinguish (1) a wide, vague movement called "Gnosis," whose tendencies can be found in Jewish, Greek, and Christian thought, from (2) "Gnosticism," the complex system invented by the second-century Christian Gnostics. "Gnosis" may have been an alternate faith to Christianity, but Gnosticism is certainly Christian, though it existed on and beyond the borders of what came to be defined as Christian tradition. The Christian community was still young and unformed, its boundaries still vague, but the conflicts between Gnostics and fathers helped define these boundaries. Gradually a consensus arose that excluded Gnosticism.

Gnosticism failed to achieve dominance or even respectability within the Christian community, partly because of the orthodox effort to set the boundaries of the community, but more because of weaknesses inherent in Gnosticism itself. Gnostic thought—despite some artificial recent efforts to revive it—was a dead end. The mythologies of Gnosticism became overburdened, complicated, unbelievable; its appeal was elitist, its social organization incoherent, its institutional organization ineffective. Gnosticism faded in the West by the end of the third century, though it endured in the Near East in the fourth, and its influence continued to appear sporadically among Manicheans, Paulicians, Cathars, astrologers, Mandaeans, and Rosicrucians. The theologies of Gnosticism were enormously varied and complex, but their identifiable central themes are important both in themselves and in the responses they evoked from the orthodox. Gnosticism's appeal lies in its continued championship of the radical dualist alternative in theodicy: God is not responsible for evil, because evil arises from an independent, malevolent principle.

The importance of Gnosticism in the history of the concept of evil lies first in the reactions it provoked. By bringing the question of theodicy front and center, the Gnostics forced the fathers to devise a coherent diabology, which had been lacking in New Testament and apostolic thought. Gnostic emphasis upon the power of the Devil caused the fathers to react by defining his power carefully; Gnostic stress upon the evil of the material world elicited their defense of the essential goodness of the world created by God. Second, the fathers shared many Gnostic ideas. A strict line between orthodoxy and Gnosticism was not drawn until the third century; until then a wide range of ideas and attitudes were held in common, with the result that some Gnostic ideas became permanently embedded in Christianity.

Gnosticism was focused on *gnōsis*, a "knowledge" obtained not by study or meditation, but through revelation. Gnosis was essentially knowledge of self: *Gnōthi seauton*: "know thyself." Gnosticism was a spiritual, self-centered religion of psychological depth and sophistication, whose purpose was to raise the spiritual level of the self through gnosis. The Gnostic believed that through revelation he became privy to secrets not shared by the uninitiated and that these secrets could be passed on to and by only a chosen few. Gnostic theologians devised elaborate cosmological speculations and mythological structures whose effect, if not purpose, was to mystify and impress. But Gnosticism did not exist for show. The Gnostics were striving almost desperately for a convincing theodicy, to the point that a later Christian writer argued that their central error had been to torment themselves past reason with the problem of evil.[1] What united the various Gnostic sects was the belief that the world is completely evil and cannot be redeemed.[2]

The Gnostic concern with evil began with experience, the "feeling of man that he lives in a world that is alien to him, in which he must be afraid." This world is so riddled with evil that it can only be an inferior world, a shadow of something better and beyond.[3] The Gnostics melded the Mazdaist view of a cosmic battle between spiritual powers of good and evil with the Orphic view of a struggle between spirit, defined as good, and matter, defined as evil. The human body, being matter, is

1. Epiphanius, *Panarion*, 24.6. For editions of Epiphanius, see the Essay on the Sources. Early Gnosticism has attracted a great many writers and given rise to a number of still current scholarly disputes. Some of the more important or accessible works are J. Daniélou and H.-I. Marrou, *The Christian Centuries: The First Six Hundred Years* (London, 1964), pp. 56–66; W. Schmithals, *Gnosticism in Corinth: An Investigation of the Letters to the Corinthians*, 2d ed. (Nashville, 1971); Schmithals, *Paul and the Gnostics* (Nashville, 1972); H. Jonas, *The Gnostic Religion: The Message of the Alien God and the Beginnings of Christianity* (Boston, 1958); E. Yamauchi, *Pre-Christian Gnosticism: A Survey of the Proposed Evidences* (Grand Rapids, Mich., 1973); H. Leisegang, *Die Gnosis*, 4th ed. (Stuttgart, 1955); G. Quispel, *Gnosis als Weltreligion* (Zurich, 1951); K. Rudolph, "Gnosis und Gnosticismus: Ein Forschungsbericht," *Theologische Rundschau*, 38 (1973), 1–25; R. M. Grant, *Gnosticism and Early Christianity*, 2d ed. (New York, 1966); Grant, ed. *Gnosticism: A Sourcebook of Heretical Writings from the Early Christian Period* (New York, 1962); W. Foerster, *Gnosis: A Selection of Gnostic Texts*, 2 vols. (Oxford, 1972–1974); G. Widengren, *The Gnostic Attitude* (Santa Barbara, Calif., 1973); R. Haardt, *Gnosis: Character and Testimony* (Leiden, 1971); E. Pagels, *The Gnostic Gospels* (New York, 1979). Overall, the best account is K. Rudolph, *Die Gnosis* (Göttingen, 1977).
2. Grant, ed., *Gnosticism: A Sourcebook*, p. 15.
3. Schmithals, *Gnosticism in Corinth*, p. 27.

an evil, wretched prison in which our souls are languishing. The material world, base and dark, is ruled by a malicious prince, as opposed to the spiritual world of light, ruled by a benevolent deity. This good God would never have created the gross world in which we live. He is remote and hidden from this world, which is the artifact of one or more inferior spirits who are evil or blind or both. These evil spirits the Gnostics called archons or eons, recalling the apostolic doctrine of an evil archon of the *aiōn* or *kosmos*, but with the great difference that the apostolics never even hinted that the cosmos could have been created by any spirit lesser than God or God's word, which is God himself. The Gnostics usually distinguished the archons, often seven in number, from the angels; the archons were higher than the angels, possibly even their progenitors. In concept, however, they differed little, since both were created, spiritual beings inferior to God.

Orthodox Christianity and Gnosticism are both in part dualist. But orthodox Christian dualism found a strong counterweight in the omnipotence of God and the basic goodness of what he had created. Gnosticism was much closer to the dualist pole of the spectrum, where the entire created world is evil.

The Gnostics disagreed among themselves as to the nature of the subsidiary, evil creator. The most extreme dualists among them claimed that two independent spiritual principles existed in eternal opposition to each other, that the evil spirit was independent of and wholly different from the good Lord. The more moderate Gnostics assumed that the creator of the world was a spirit who had originally been good but who had devolved or fallen into evil. This ignorant, blind, corrupt spirit they often identified with the Devil. In Hellenistic Gnosticism he was often called "demiurge," "partial mover," as opposed to the prime mover, God—a concept deriving from Platonism. Remnants of monist thought persist in the idea that the evil spirit begins as part of God and then somehow becomes alienated from him. "The Demiurge of Gnostic theory," writes Robert McL. Wilson "is simply the Satan of Jewish and Christian theology . . . transformed by the dominant Gnostic pessimism

into the creator of the world, its present ruler."[4] The ultimate
monism lurking behind the apparent dualism appears in the
third-century "Gospel of Philip": "The light and the darkness,
life and death, right and left, are brothers one for another."[5] It
is even clearer in the doctrine, attributed to the Elkesaites, that
Christ and the Devil are brothers.[6] The tendency of the Gnostics to think of the creator spirit as evil led some of them to
identify the God of the Old Testament with the Devil.

Gnostic anthropology was depressing: a human being is a
spirit trapped in a gross body, like a pearl buried in mud. Mankind is the microcosm: both the small world of humanity and
the great world of the cosmos are battlegrounds in the war between the good spirit of light and the evil spirit who rules matter. Originally humans were pure spirit, but, entrapped by the
evil eon, they became earthly creatures imprisoned in matter.[7]
It is therefore our duty to liberate our spirits from our bodies.
We are able to do this when the grace of the good Lord teaches
us to know our being, origin, and destiny. The divine process
of redemption is, in the words of Mircea Eliade, "tantamount to
collecting, salvaging, and consigning to heaven the sparks of the
divine Light which are buried in living matter, first and foremost in man's body."[8] Evil spirits feel it to be their opposite
duty to tempt us to abandon our spiritual heritage and to pursue gross material pleasures.

The thought of one of the leading second-century Gnostics,
Marcion, illustrates a typical Gnostic approach to theodicy.
Marcion, a Syrian, came to Rome in A.D. 139–140 and was ex-
pelled by the Roman Christian community in July 144 as a

4. R. McL. Wilson, *The Gnostic Problem* (London, 1958), p. 191.
5. Foerster, 2:79.
6. Epiphanius, 30.16. Δύο δέ τινας συνιστῶσιν ἐκ θεοῦ τεταγμένους, ἕνα
μὲν τὸν Χρίστον, ἕνα δὲ τὸν διάβολον. καὶ τὸν μὲν Χρίστον λέγουσι τοῦ
μέλλοντος αἰῶνος εἰληφέναι τὸν κλῆρον, τὸν δὲ διάβολον τοῦτον
πεπιστεῦσθαι τὸν αἰῶνα: "They say that two entities were brought forth from
God, Christ and the Devil. And they believe that Christ is the head of the
good age to come, but the Devil is the ruler of this present evil age."
7. Widengren, p. 15.
8. M. Eliade, "Spirit, Light, and Seed," *History of Religions*, 11 (1971), 23.

heretic, though his ideas in many ways resembled those of Paul and John. Later, Tertullian would accuse him unjustly of failing to cope adequately with the classic question, "Whence is evil?" In fact, Marcion and the other Gnostics struggled with the question more fiercely than the orthodox. Marcion seems to have been shocked into a search for the answer by the contrast he perceived between the harsh God of the Old Testament and the loving God of the New. They could not, he thought, be the same. The God who tempted people to sin and punished them for what he tempted them to do, the God who hardened hearts and laid cities waste, could not be the merciful Lord revealed by Christ. Deeply disturbed by this discrepancy, Marcion asked how, in a world in which evil is manifest, God can be all-good and all-powerful. His answer was that two gods must exist. Saint Paul had seen a tension between Law and Gospel but had never dreamed of setting up an opposition between the God of the Law and the God of the Gospel. Marcion did. He carried this and other dualist tendencies in Christianity to their extremes.

For Marcion, one god is just, but also harsh and warlike, hewing to the letter of a stern law. This is the God of the Old Testament, the Demiurge, the creator of the material world. He is the *conditor malorum*, the "author of evils." He and the material world he created are evil. The good God is kind and merciful. But before the mission of Christ this God was wholly unknown to us and even now remains mostly hidden.[9] The wonder of the New Testament is that it for the first time gave us a glimpse of the true God. The true God is the father of Jesus Christ, whom he sends to us for the purpose of revealing the truth about the cosmos as opposed to the lies spread by the evil God. Though each of the two gods is an independent principle, one is nonetheless assumed to be inferior, for the evil god's days are numbered. His time has been curtailed by the mission of Jesus Christ, and in the end he will be defeated by the good God and will disappear along with the cosmos he cre-

9. Unknown: ἄγνωστος, *ignotus*; hidden: *absconditus*.

ated. The material world, the evil imposition of the evil god, imprisons, defiles, and corrupts our spirits. The body in particular does these evil things, so Christ's earthly body must have been a mere illusion. Most Gnostics were Docetists, believing that Christ's body was only appearance, though not all Docetists were Gnostics. Christ's mission was to reveal the saving gnosis that we need to liberate our spirits from our bodies and from the entire material cosmos. Marcion apparently conceived of Satan as a creature of the evil god rather than as the evil god himself, but this, like many other elements of his thought, is not clear and he probably never worked it out consistently.[10] If Marcion did view the Devil as a helper of the creator of evil, he introduced one of Gnosticism's unnecessary refinements and complications. If Satan has a superior in evil, then that superior is really the Devil. The only useful definition of the Devil is the principle, or at least the prince, of the forces of evil. In fact the evil creator god is Marcion's true Devil.

The unnecessary complications of Gnosticism multiplied also, for example in the system of the Valentinians. Valentine was an Egyptian who came to Rome about the same time as Marcion. Believing that he was restoring Christianity to its true meaning, he gradually constructed, with the help of his disciple Ptolemy, a complex, cluttered, emanationist mythology aimed primarily at the problem of evil. In Valentine's mythology, to mention only a few of its convolutions, Being emanates eight "higher eons," called the Ogdoad, and at least twenty-two lower eons. The eons form the divine "pleroma," the fullness of the divine nature. To greater or lesser extent, these emanations are all part of the divine, but each succeeding emanation is farther removed from its source and therefore more imperfect. Such imperfection, as in the thought of Plotinus, produces ignorance and, consequently, error and fear. Sophia, the lowest emana-

10. Tertullian, *Adversus Marcionem*, 2. 10, said that Marcion regarded the creator god as the *auctor diaboli*, "maker of the Devil," and in 2.28 reported Marcion as holding that the creator allowed the Devil, the author of sin, and all other evils, to exist: "auctor delicti diabolus et omne malum creator passus est esse."

tion, being farthest from the Father, is most deficient, and the void of her deficiency is filled with pride, *hybris*, which causes her unlawfully to seek to learn the essence of the Father. Her effort is frustrated, but it has disturbed the serenity of the pleroma, which rejects her pride and thrusts it out into the void, where it becomes hypostasized as the Lower Sophia, or Achamoth, wandering miserably in the emptiness. The fruitless longing of Sophia produces *psychē*, spirit. Her anguish produces *hylē*, matter. Christ's pity for her produces *pneuma*, soul. She now brings forth the Old Testament God, who in turn creates the material world out of the three elements of matter, spirit, and soul. The beings who inhabit this world, including humans, are therefore a mixture of good and evil. In each person, however, one of the elements prevails. Three classes of people exist. Some are *sarkikoi*, imprisoned in *sarx* (flesh) and *hylē*; these can never be saved. Some are *psychikoi*; they can be saved only with difficulty. Some are *pneumatikoi*; these attain salvation by receiving the gnosis bestowed upon them by Christ.

Valentine's eager efforts to address the problem of evil had become mired in unnecessary complexities. He valiantly tried to preserve the goodness of the God by buffering him from this gross world with a bewildering multiplicity of emanations. But emanationism always fails to relieve the God of responsibility, for it cannot avoid the assumption that he chooses to permit the ignorance and evil that result from the emanations.

A view such as Valentine's had radical implications for all Christian theology, especially original sin. Since the creator god is not the true God at all, but a subsidiary and corrupt being, Adam and Eve's revolt against Yahweh takes on a reverse moral meaning. Rebellion against the creator becomes a virtue, and the serpent a benefactor of humanity who teaches us the principles of good and evil that the creator has been trying to hide from us. The Gnostic Sethians, Naasenians, or Ophites venerated the serpent (Heb. *nachash*; Gr. *ophis*, "serpent") as liberating humanity from the evil archon and imparting to men and women the first saving gnosis. This idea is similar to the incipient Christian tradition of the fortunate fall or *felix culpa*, the

notion that original sin enabled humanity to rise above its childish innocence and grow in wisdom; it also was the cause of the
central moment of the cosmos, the incarnation of God as Jesus
Christ. In most Gnostic systems, however, the serpent of Eden
remains negative and is identified with the dragon, the Devil,
and evil.[11]

The difficulty with the Gnostic effort to shift blame for evil
from the supreme God to the subsidiary creator god was
observed by Tertullian, who inquired why the supreme God
would permit the inferior god to do wrong. Against the extreme
dualism of the Gnostics the apologists insisted that the spirit of
evil was in no way equivalent in power or eternity to the good
Lord, nor did his evil derive from imperfection introduced by
emanations. Rather, he was a creature of God, and as such he
had a nature that was created good, a nature that he deformed
through his own free will. The fathers did not thereby solve the
problem of evil, for they did not explain why God permits his
creature the Devil as much power to do evil as in fact exists in
the world. Indeed, some modern authors have argued that the
fathers warped the Christian message by exaggerating the importance of the Devil in their newly developing theology.[12] But
in fact, given the prominence of the Devil and demons in the
New Testament and the Gnostic tendency to exaggerate the
Devil's powers, the fathers took a cautious, moderate line.

Along with Gnostic dualism, the Jewish-Christian dualism of
the two ways found earlier in Barnabas continued into the
second century, finding expression in the Pseudo-Clementine
homilies ascribed incorrectly to Saint Clement of Rome.[13] In
these homilies the two kingdoms, two eons, and two powers are
constantly at war. The demons, followers of the king of dark-

11. In my summary of Gnosticism I follow Kurt Rudolph; see also Grant,
Gnosticism and Early Christianity, pp. 128–131, on Valentine and the Valentinians.

12. For example, Kelly, *The Devil, Demonology, and Witchcraft*.

13. See the summary by J. Daniélou in the *Dictionnaire de spiritualité
ascétique et mystique*, vol. 3, cols. 165–170, and Daniélou, *Theology of Jewish
Christianity*, pp. 189–191. The Clementines arose from an Ebionite background. The homilies have been dated as late as the early third century.

ness, attack both body and mind, inciting us to passion so that we may lose control of our rational faculties and fall under their power. Against these temptations to demonic enslavement we rely upon faith in Christ, fasting and using his name in exorcism and in baptism. The formula of baptism in the second century reflected the importance of demons: before baptism, our body is a house of evil spirits; in baptism Christ expels the demons, releases us from our sins, and takes up his abode in us.

The apocrypha of the second and early third centuries occupied the wide borderland between orthodox and heretical thought. The struggle within the Christian community to establish a common theology was accompanied by a less dramatic, but even more important, effort to establish a commonly accepted canon of the New Testament. The canon remained very fluid in the first half of the second century: there was no general agreement as to what writings were divinely inspired. By about A.D. 150, a body of scriptures existed which Justin Martyr called "our writings," and which included some gospels and epistles (it is not certain which ones). About 170, Papias objected to the "masses of books" generally accepted and circulated as being part of the New Testament—books such as the Gospel of Nicodemus, the Gospel of Thomas, the Gospel of the Hebrews, and the Apocalypse of Peter. The first formal effort to establish a New Testament may have been made by the heretic Marcion about 160: his canon consisted of the Gospel of Luke and ten letters attributed to Saint Paul. The orthodox party later in the century added Mark and Matthew to the accepted gospels and worked to exclude some widely accepted books as apocryphal. The term *apocrypha* means "hidden" and was first applied to the "secret" books of the Gnostics, materials that the Gnostics themselves often wished to reserve to the *pneumatikoi*, those saved on account of their understanding of gnosis. By the early third century, a consensus on what belonged in the New Testament was growing, and the canon we have today was set by the middle of the fourth century. By that time all the books rejected from it, whether Gnostic or not, were categorized as apocryphal. But their wide previous acceptance meant that many of their ideas found their way into tradition.[14]

One apocryphal book, for example, "The Ascension of Isaiah," told a story about Belial (Beliar) that entered medieval popular tradition. The anterior part of "The Ascension," written in the first century in a Jewish milieu, described King Manasseh, who abandoned Yahweh and served Satan, also called Beliar. Manasseh became "a servant of Beliar, for the prince of unrighteousness who rules this world is Beliar." Beliar urged Manasseh to witchcraft, magic, divination, adultery, and persecution of the just, as well as to the prime sin of forsaking the true God. Beliar was furious at Isaiah because he had revealed and prophesied the coming of the Messiah, but Beliar/Satan cannot prevent the triumph of the Lord, who "will come with his angels . . . and will drag Beliar with his hosts into Gehenna; and he will bring rest to the pious." The latter part of "The Ascension" is a Christian addition dating from the second century and identifying the Messiah with Christ. "Sammael Satan" and his hosts are locked in a confused struggle arising from their envious hatred of one another; soon Christ will come, force Satan to worship him, and destroy the Devil's power forever.[15]

In "The Acts of Peter," a semi-Gnostic work dating from about 180, Peter blames Satan for the ills of the world. Satan, the devourer and waster of eternal life, snared Adam in lustful desire and "bound him by . . . ancient wickedness and with the chain of the body." The Devil shoots "at innocent souls with . . . poisoned arrows," but in the end "the devouring wolf" will have its "blackness" turned against it by Christ, who will pack him off to be burned.[16]

The orthodox fathers often drew upon these ideas even while opposing them. Many—Tatian and Tertullian, for example—

14. On the apocrypha, see especially James, *The Apocryphal New Testament*, and E. Hennecke, *New Testament Apocrypha*, ed. W. Schneemelcher, 2 vols. (Philadelphia, 1963). On the Devil in the apocrypha, see Hennecke, 1:189, 470–481; 2:245, 254, 258, 290–291, 312, 316, 383, 411–415, 644–653, 662–663, 682, 760, 793.

15. Hennecke, 2:645–663. The confusion of the fallen angels became a commonplace and appears dramatically in Milton's *Paradise Lost*.

16. Hennecke, 2:290–291, 316.

spent part of their lives in heresy, and the fathers seldom constituted a united doctrinal front. Nonetheless a number of second-century theologians, notably Justin, Tatian, Athenagoras, Irenaeus, and Tertullian, eventually gained general acceptance, and the effect of that acceptance was gradually to draw boundaries beyond which ideas could no longer be considered Christian.

Justin Martyr, the first apologetic father, was one of the earliest Christian theologians. Since Justin was the first to discuss the problem of evil in theological terms, he was enormously influential for centuries. Justin saw no conflict between philosophy and Christianity, for Christianity was the full fruit of the mature philosophical tree. He was born about 100 in Samaria. A brilliant thinker questing for truth, he received a Greek education and adopted Platonism. Eventually finding all secular philosophies insufficient, he converted to Christianity.[17] He went to Rome about 150 and between 152 and 154 wrote his "First Apology," whose purpose was to defend Christianity against the accusations and ridicule of both Greeks and Jews and to demonstrate the consistency of Christian thought with what was true in philosophy. His "Second Apology," composed between 154 and 160, is a long appendix to the first, written in response to the sentencing of Christians to death. The charge against the Christians was atheism; Justin turned the argument back against the pagans. His third work is the "Dialogue with Trypho the Jew," written about 160. He was martyred by the Romans between 163 and 167.[18]

The "consciousness of the demonic element in the universe was central to Justin's world view," writes one of his recent biographers.[19] For Justin and the other second-century fathers, as for the apostolic writers, Christ and the Christian commu-

---

17. See A. D. Nock, *Conversion* (London, 1961).

18. On the Devil and demons in the apologetic fathers in general, see H. Wey, *Die Funktionen der bösen Geister bei den griechischen Apologeten des zweiten Jahrhunderts nach Christus* (Winterthur, 1957). Justin's extant works are the two "Apologies" (1 Ap.; 2 Ap.) and the "Dialogue with Trypho" (Dial.). See the Essay on the Sources.

19. L. Barnard, *Justin Martyr: His Life and Thought* (Cambridge, 1967), p. 107.

nity were locked in a cosmic struggle with the Devil and his followers. Justin had no doubt about the existence of angels.[20] The angels are created beings. Since only God is pure spirit, the angels must have tenuous bodies; they eat manna, which is heavenly food. The fallen angels have grosser bodies than do the good angels, and the evil angels devour the smoke of pagan sacrifices.[21] Angels live in heaven or in the air.[22] For the early fathers, the air was a geographical region between earth and heaven. Some fathers followed the Stoics in distinguishing the lower, denser air between the earth and the moon from the higher, finer air, or ether, between the moon and heaven. Those who assigned demons or angels ethereal bodies thus thought of them as having finer and more spiritual bodies than those made of air. Heaven is located beyond the sphere of the fixed stars. (See the diagram.)

God appoints a number of angels to rule the world for him, assigning each a nation, region, or person. The angels are duty bound to do God's will: if they fail, they sin. Justin was original in combining this late Jewish doctrine of the angels of the nations with the apocalyptic idea of the Watcher angels who sinned through lust. For him the sinful Watchers were angels of the nations who were derelict in their duty.[23]

God created angels with free will to choose between good and evil.[24] Some of them fell from grace as a result of misusing

20. Dial. 85: καὶ ἄγγελοί εἰσιν ἐν οὐρανῷ, καὶ δυνάμεις: "both angels and powers exist in heaven." The *angeloi* can be good—ἀγαθοί—or evil—φαῦλοι, πονηροί. 1 Ap. 6: ἀγαθῶν ἀγγέλων στρατόν, φαῦλοι ἄγγελοι καὶ δαίμονες, Dial. 105: πονηρὸν ἄγγελον. In Dial. 85 and 102, δύναμις—"power"—has a positive connotation, but it is evil in Dial. 78 and 105. The terms ἄρχαι, ἐξουσίαι (Dial. 41, 49) have a bad connotation.

21. Dial. 128 seems to assert creation and reject emanationism, though the passage is far from clear. On the bodies of angels, Dial. 57; on the demons eating pagan sacrifices, F. Andres, *Die Engellehre* (Paderborn, 1914), p. 23.

22. Here the influence of both Platonism and Apocalyptic Judaism appears. Later, the implication would be drawn that the demons, occupying the air between heaven and earth, obstruct our way to God. See Daniélou, "Les démons de l'air dans la 'Vie d'Antoine,'" *Studia Anselmiana*, 38 (1956), 136–147.

23. 2 Ap. 5. See Kelly, p. 29.

24. 2 Ap. 7: αὐτεξούσιον τό τε τῶν ἀνθρώπων. Dial. 140–141; 102:

Cosmological conception of the early fathers

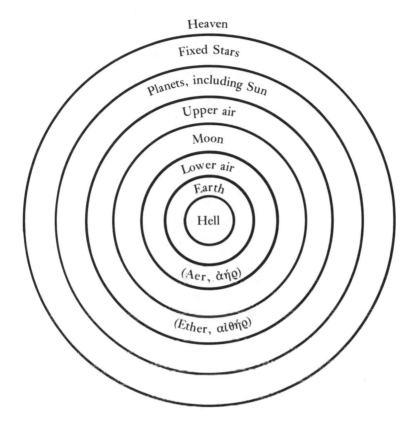

their free will. Justin was unclear as to the nature of their sin, but he leaned strongly to the theory of the lustful Watchers.[25] He was also uncertain about whether Satan induced the angels to fall, or whether they sinned on their own; in any event they followed the Devil's example, and their fall assimilated them to

αὐτεξουσίους πρὸς δικαιοπραξίαν καὶ ἀγγέλους καὶ ἀνθρώπους, God has created "both men and angels free as regards the practice of righteousness."

25. 2 Ap. 5: οἵ δ'ἄγγελοι, παραβάντες, "the angels, falling away," mingle with women and "produce children," παῖδας ἐτέκνωσαν. Elsewhere Justin calls the angels ἀποστάντας, πονηπευσαμένους, "apostates," "evil-doers": Dial. 76; 79.

him so that they came to share in his evil labors.[26] Justin repeated the apocalyptic story that the Watchers fathered children
on human women. At least two categories of evil spirits other
than the Devil therefore exist: the fallen angels and the children
that they engendered.[27] Justin's distinction between fallen
angels and demons, though shared with the apostolic fathers,
was based on a dubious interpretation of Genesis. The threefold division among Devil, fallen angels, and demons had no
function and eventually disappeared from the tradition, along
with the whole Watcher story, by the fifth century.

Justin showed ambivalence about the relationship of the Devil to the demons. He does not treat the Devil dualistically as
an independent principle; chief, prince, or general of the fallen
angels, the Devil probably is to be considered one of them.[28] Yet
if he is an angel, he differs from the other angels in his power
and in the time of his first sin. For whereas the Watchers sinned
with women at the time of Noah, the Devil sinned at least as
early as the time of Adam and Eve, because Justin identified
him with the serpent.[29] Although he accepted the biblical description of Satan as a liar, deceiver, and sinner from the beginning, Justin, like the New Testament, was unclear as to what
the "beginning" meant.[30] Did it mean the beginning of time?

26. Dial. 45, 100. See Andres, p. 22.

27. Justin seems to have inclined to this view, for on several occasions he
distinguished between fallen angels and demons, equating the demons with
the children of the fallen angels. 2 Ap. 5: παῖδας . . . οἵ εἰσιν οἱ λεγόμενοι
δαίμονες, "the children . . . are those who are called demons." 2 Ap. 7: οἱ
φαῦλοι ἄγγελοι καὶ δαίμονες . . . τῶν φαύλων δαιμόνων.

28. 1 Ap. 28: ὁ ἀρχηγέτης τῶν κακῶν δαιμονίων ὄφις καλεῖται καὶ
σατανᾶς καὶ διάβολος: "the leader of the evil spirits is called the serpent,
Satan, and the Devil." The Devil is also called ἀκάθαρτον πνεῦμα, an "unclean spirit." See also Dial. 131.

29. Dial. 45, 79, 100, 124. In Dial, 103 Justin offered the false etymology
that the word "Satan" derived from the Hebrew *sata*, "apostate," and *nas*,
"serpent." Actually Hebrew for serpent is *nachash*, but Barnard observes
(*Justin Martyr*, p. 108) that Justin as a Samaritan might have pronounced the
word *nas*. The etymology is also found in Irenaeus, but if the Samaritan explanation is correct, it follows that he derived the idea from Justin.

30. Dial. 45; 1 Ap. 5. Cf. John 8:44.

When, in that event, was the Devil created, if indeed he was created at all? Did it mean that he sinned in the very origins of his nature? In that event, was he created evil? Justin did not face these questions systematically. He seemed to argue that Satan fell as a result of tempting Adam and Eve, but he did not address the question whether Satan's adoption of the role of tempter in Genesis presupposed a previous internal sin, a previous motion of the will away from God.[31]

The Devil is apparently created by God, and he is certainly inferior to him. The Devil's power lasts "only for a time," and his knowledge is limited: for example, he had no foreknowledge that Christ's advent would be his ruin and damnation.[32] Justin followed the Book of Revelation in equating the Satan of the Old Testament with the serpent of Genesis; Revelation 12:7–9 describes the archangel Michael's war with the Devil, "and the great dragon was cast out, and that old serpent, called the Devil, and Satan which deceiveth the whole world: he was cast out into the earth, and his angels were cast out with him." Though he failed to account coherently for the Devil's origin, nature, or sin, Justin confirmed that Satan is the tempter of Adam and Eve, the tempter of Jesus, the serpent, and the prince of demons.[33] Christ's power is pitted against that of the Devil, and for Justin a primary function of Christ's work is the destruction of that power.[34] The Devil held full power in the world for a time, but Christ has broken that power through his Incarnation and Passion. Yet the diabolical power will not be fully destroyed until the second coming. The Devil's kingdom *has been*

---

31. Dial. 124. The association of the fall of Satan with that of humanity is found in apocalyptic literature, e.g. Syriac Baruch 56, dating from the end of the first century A.D. (J. H. Charlesworth, *The Pseudepigrapha and Modern Research* (Missoula, Mont., 1976), pp. 83–86; Life of Adam 15, a haggadic midrash of the first century A.D. (Charlesworth, pp. 74–75); Ascension of Moses, first century A.D. (Charlesworth, pp. 159–166).

32. Irenaeus, *Adversus haereses*, 5.26, reporting Justin's opinion.

33. Andres, p. 20.

34. Dial. 78, 116: the power—*dynamis*—of the Devil versus the *dynamis* of Christ.

Satan was thought by many of the fathers to have used the serpent as a tool in his temptation of Adam and Eve; later it was more commonly believed that Satan himself had assumed the form of the serpent. Fourth-century fresco from the Catacombs. Courtesy of the Ponteficia Commissione di Archeologia Sacra.

broken and *will be* broken.[35] But Justin's argument leaves a big question unanswered. Why should Christ, once having come, delay his demolition of Satan's power? That dilemma derives directly from the ambivalence of the New Testament teachings of the old and new eons. The old eon, the age dominated by the

35. See G. Aulén, *Christus victor* (Paris, 1949). Christ's passion redeems us from three evils: sin, death, and the Devil. 1 Ap. 14, 28, 45, 60; 2 Ap. 6, 8; Dial. 30, 41, 45, 91, 94, 121, 125. Dial. 121 illustrates the confusion: Christ broke the demons, he is breaking them, and he will break them.

Devil, began to come to an end with the Incarnation. The new eon began with the Incarnation, but the final replacement of the old with the new age will not occur until Christ comes again. Of course the delay seemed less important to Justin than it did later, because he shared with the apostles the conviction that the second coming was going to occur very shortly.[36] He also suggested that the delay or destruction of Satan's kingdom was being postponed so that the number of the just might be filled up.[37]

Satan knew from the moment of Christ's passion that his doom was sure, but he still strives viciously and vainly against that fate by trying to undermine Christ's saving work in the church, the Christian community. His work is unremitting, for he is incapable of repentance.[38] The Devil's punishment is as certain as his defeat. He and his angels have already been cast down from heaven and doomed to final ruin, yet at present they still roam the world, and their suffering in the flames of hell is reserved to the end of time. (Tatian, Irenaeus, and Tertullian agreed with Justin that punishment was reserved, but other fathers disagreed, and the opposite teaching came to prevail. Yet an apparent contradiction remained between the demons being punished and at the same time free to roam the world.)

The Devil and the fallen angels will suffer in eternal fire when Christ comes again. Thus consumed, they will perish. God foreknows the sin of the angels, but he does not will it, for he wishes all beings to be good.[39]

The Devil tempted Christ but failed to corrupt him, so his present plan is to obstruct his work by disrupting the Christian

36. Dial. 49.
37. 1 Ap. 45; 2 Ap. 7. A certain span of time is necessary for all the human souls to be born who are going to be saved. A notion not found in Justin but expressed by later writers was that the just were needed to fill up the angelic ranks depleted by angelic sin.
38. Dial. 141. See Barnard, *Justin Martyr*, pp. 109–110.
39. 1 Ap. 28; 2 Ap. 7, 8; Dial. 45. God's foreknowledge: 1 Ap. 28; Dial. 141.

community and leading Christians into sin.[40] The Devil plays upon our weaknesses, our irrational living, our attachments to worldly things.[41] The chief ploy of the demons is to persuade people that demons are gods. Justin's grim insistence on that idea reflected his personal loathing of paganism. He argued that the demons dwelt in idols and consumed the offerings that the pagans sacrificed to the idols.[42] The pagan gods were not mere illusions but actual demons, servants of the Devil devoted to blocking Christ's work on earth. This explains their cruel and adulterous behavior. Such a point of view, widely held in the church, accounts for the stubborn refusal of the Christians to offer sacrifice. Sacrifice to an idol was not a silly foible, but an act of worship of the Devil, a blasphemy against Christ, a deed worthy of damnation. The serpent is involved in the idolatrous rites of the pagans.[43]

Myths were inspired by demons to mock Christ and to make people believe that Christians were merely copying the pagan gods. The demons knew in advance what the Christians would teach and so invented similar myths and rites, such as the story that Perseus was born of a virgin, or the Mithraists' use of baptism. Nowhere in pagan myth, however, did Justin find a story of a god dying for his people on a cross (he ignored the similar symbolism of the mysteries of Attis, who suffered on a tree). The demons did not copy the cross, he wrote, because Christ's passion was hidden from them by divine providence.[44] Justin reconciled his respect for Greek philosophy with his hatred of Greek religion by excepting the philosophers from condemna-

---

40. 1 Ap. 58.

41. 1 Ap. 5, 10, 14, 58. The use of the adverb ἀλόγως, "irrationally," is an indication of Justin's effort to wed Greek moral philosophy to Christian moral revelation. Justin did not raise the question, debated by later fathers, whether the demons can interfere with human free will.

42. This idea derived from the Septuagint Psalm 95:5: οἱ θεοί τῶν ἐθνῶν εἴδωλα δαιμονίων εἰσίν. See also Deut. 32:17 and 1 Enoch 6–9.

43. Gods and demons equated: 1 Ap. 5 (they defile women and boys); 12, 25–27, 62 (sacrifice—λύτρον—to gods is sacrifice to demons); 2 Ap. 5; Dial. 55, 73, 79, 83. Serpent: 1 Ap. 27.

44. 1 Ap. 21–22, 54–56, 62–69; 2 Ap. 13; Dial. 67, 69. Cross: 1 Ap. 5–6.

tion and suggesting that the demons hated such virtuous pagans as Socrates and Herakleitos.[45]

The Devil uses many other means to defeat our love of Christ. He stimulates dreams and visions to confuse and control us. Demons cause us to muddle bad laws with good. They teach us the use of magic and other vain arts.[46] They try to seize the souls of the dying: before the time of Christ they could do this readily, but now they have to struggle against his power. Demons possess us, cause illnesses, and inflict other bodily and mental ills. They teach us sins and urge us to them.[47] They invent and promote heresies. Justin claimed that the Gnostic leaders Simon, Menander, and Marcion were under the suggestion of demons and asserted that the miracles imputed to Menander were worked by evil spirits. Besides promoting Gnosticism, the demons also cleverly spread the fantasy that the punishments of hell do not exist.[48] Miracles done by orthodox Christians are, of course, worked by God.

The most fearful engine of the demons, in Justin's view, is persecution. Demons provoke hatred, lies, and false accusations against the Christians, and they devise and encourage the pagan persecutions. Judges and rulers who prosecute Christians are in the service of the Devil.[49] After Justin, Christians commonly blamed the persecutions on the demons and held them responsible for the dungeons and the arenas. The demons provoked both the government and the mob and were even behind acts of kindness, which they used to undermine the martyr's determination. The Roman Empire came to be seen as a kingdom

45. 1 Ap. 5, 44, 2 Ap. 7–8. But Justin believed that Plato plagiarized from Moses: Jewish thought, being inspired, had to be both prior and superior to Greek.

46. 1 Ap. 5, 14. Later Christian theologians tried to discern which dreams come from God and which from demons. Laws: 2 Ap. 9. Arts: 1 Ap. 14, 18, 56. This doctrine was taken from the myth of the Watchers.

47. Dial. 105. The idea that a demon and a good angel struggled for the spirit of a dying person became a topos in Christian literature and art. Illness: 1 Ap. 18, 57, 63; 2 Ap. 6. Sins: 1 Ap. 5, 26; 2 Ap. 5, 12; Dial. 78.

48. 1 Ap. 26, 56–58; Dial. 35, 56–58. Jews are associated with demons in Dial. 31.

49. 1 Ap. 5, 11, 57; 2 Ap. 1; Dial. 39, 131. Judges: 2 Ap. 1.

ruled by the Devil. The martyrs were "athletes" imitating Christ who, himself an athlete, had on the cross wrestled Satan down.[50] Christians were to take no violent action in their own defense; such an act would be a moral capitulation to the Devil. Rather, by suffering fear and death without renouncing their faith, they could strike a powerful blow against the Devil. To help Christ in his struggle against Satan, then, the most telling action a Christian could take was to be a martyr, though it was traditional that no one should seek martyrdom if it could be avoided without sin. Justin proved true to his idea of martyrdom by dying a martyr himself.

Justin's diabology, though sometimes vague, was decidedly less dualistic and less Gnostic than the "two ways" of some of the apostolic fathers. Justin's Devil is important, but he is not the almost independent prince that the apostolics described. Justin and the other apologists diverted Christianity from belief in the cosmic struggle between almost independent powers and the total opposition between spirit and flesh. The Devil's inferiority to God is absolute: God's existence is essential; the Devil's is contingent. God is eternal; the Devil will perish. God's destruction of Satan and his elimination of evil are certain, but his reasons for tolerating evil in the meanwhile are not evident. The apologists did not solve the main problem: why does God create a cosmos such that the Devil, who God knows will sin, and terrorize the world, exists? Why does God permit the old eon to continue, and why does he delay in causing the new eon to triumph? But although these questions have eaten like worms at the rose of Christian theodicy, they are quite different questions from those posed by dualism. The Christian tradition affirmed *one* ultimate power in the universe, and that one ultimately benevolent.

50. Justin's attitude, reflecting that already expressed by Ignatius, became standard among Christians. In the "Passion of Saint Perpetua," for example, Perpetua is represented as understanding the truth in a dream—this one a dream sent to her by God: "Intellexi me non ad bestias, sed contra diabolum esse pugnaturam," (I understood that I was going to fight, not against the beasts, but against the Devil: *Passio Perpetuae*, 10.1–14). See Dölger, "Der Kampf mit dem Ägypter," pp. 177–178, and Frend, *Martyrdom and Persecution in the Early Church*, for this and other examples.

Tatian, a disciple of Justin, was born in Assyria about 120. He had a Greek education and studied philosophy, making his living as a traveling sophist. He converted to Christianity and then went to Rome, where he studied with Justin and became influential in the Christian community. He died about 180. Going further than Justin in his distaste for Greek religion, he ridiculed Greek philosophy as well, though unconsciously drawing upon it. Tatian's cosmos was filled frighteningly with demons, who inhabit everything from the stars to our bodies. Tatian lived in the border country between orthodox and Gnostic theology, and elements of Gnostic dualism were present in his theology to such an extent that he eventually became alienated from the Christian community, rejecting marriage as a work of the flesh and the Devil. His "Discourse against the Greeks," written early in 177, gave the Devil and the demons an important part in the cosmos.[51]

Tatian believed that God created angels before humans.[52] Angels have fine, spiritual bodies. Demons, alienated from the true spirit (*pneuma*) of God, have grosser more material bodies. He contrasted the material spirit (*pneuma hylikon*) of the demons with the true *pneuma* of God. Demons received their structure from matter, which is evil, but they have no flesh, their bodies being similar to fire or air.[53] They can be seen only by those who, protected by the spirit of God, are on a relatively high spiritual level. Unlike Justin, Tatian insisted that the demons are identical with the fallen angels and rejected the troublesome story of the Watchers and the giants.[54] He also rejected the belief that the demons were the souls of dead humans, mere spirits of nature, or otherwise allegorical.[55]

51. For Tatian's "Discourse against the Greeks" (Dis.) see the Essay on the Sources.
52. Dis. 7.
53. Dis. 12: ἐξ ὕλης. Dis. 15: they have no flesh (σαρκίον), but they do have bodies (σώματα). Their bodies are like fire or air, ὡς πυρὸς, ὡς ἀέρος. See Daniélou, "Les démons de l'air." The fiery or aerial nature of the demons' bodies is derived from Stoicism.
54. Dis. 7, 9, 20.
55. Dis. 16, 21. Justin had spoken of possession by ghosts, but Tatian ignored such a belief.

The Devil is one of the angels: in this belief Tatian took an un-Gnostic stance. The Devil is also the first-born of the demons and their chief and prince.[56] His position as first-born means only that he was the first being to sin and therefore the first angel to become a demon. A liar and a deceiver from the beginning, he fell through willful ignorance of the *pneuma* of the true God.[57] Other angels fell because of stupidity, vice, and vainglory.[58] They fell soon after the Devil, imitating him, and so became the host of demons. The fall of the Devil and demons was closely associated with that of Adam and Eve, but not with sexual intercourse with women. The true *pneuma* had lived in Adam's breast, but in consequence of his sin it departed from him, and he became mortal. As a result of their fall, the Devil and his demons were expelled from heaven and plunged into the lower air, where they now wander about in confused commotion.[59] The demons, once thrown down, were demoralized, but their power is not as yet wholly broken, and they are allowed for a while to range the earth to our harm.

Though Christ's mission weakened them, the demons continue until the last judgment to pursue their purpose of obstructing his plan of salvation. All evil and misery come from demons, who wish to subjugate and corrupt humanity. Tatian identified the demons with the pagan gods, claiming that Zeus

56. Dis. 7: "the first-born demon," ὁ πρωτόγονος δαίμων. Dis. 8: "military leader," ἡγούμενος.

57. This teaching bears some resemblance to the progressive ignorance of the Gnostic archons. Dis. 7: διὰ δὲ τὴν παράβασιν καὶ τὴν ἄγνοιαν, "through his fall and his ignorance."

58. The idea of pride as motive for the angelic lapse does not specifically appear in Tatian, but it is implied in his description of the demons as robbers who attempt to steal the divine nature: Dis. 12: λῃσταὶ θεότητος, "thieves of divinity." The idea that the demons are robbers derives from John 10:8. Later fathers would tie these robbers to those of the parable of the Good Samaritan. Then the demons would be the robbers, the victim the Christian, his wounds his sins, and Christ the Samaritan who cares for him. See G. J. M. Bartelink, "Les démons comme brigands," *Vigiliae Christianae*, 21 (1967), 12–24; Daniélou, *Origins*, p. 52, for the image of the Devil as trespasser in the Lord's vineyard.

59. Dis. 7: δαιμόνων στρατόπεδον. Adam and Eve: Dis. 7. Lower air: Dis. 7, 9, 20, 29. In 9 they are πλανῆται, *planētai*, wanderers and so associated with the planets, the "wandering stars." Tatian followed Justin here.

Demons inflict storm, plague, and fire on the world. A ninth-century illumination from the Stuttgart Gospels. Courtesy of the Württembergische Landesbibliothek.

was their leader and equating the king of the gods with the Devil. For this reason Christians must despise the Greeks and Romans as demon-worshipers. The demons employ a number of tricks and deceptions in order to hold us in thrall. They persuade us to trust fate rather than divine providence or our own free will. They predict the motions of the heavenly bodies and make us think that the stars guide our courses. They delude us into believing in astrology and divination.[60] They teach magic. All these things they do in order to weaken our faith in God and to make us believe that they control the cosmos.[61] They

60. Tatian followed Justin, adding some Gnostic coloring. Dis. 8–9, 12, 16: the purpose of demons is to keep us from the true *pneuma*. Subjugate: Dis. 8, 15. Dis. 18: demons as so-called gods, νομιζόμενοι θεοί. Dis. 18: Zeus as their leader: οἱ δαίμονες αὐτοὶ μετὰ τοῦ ἡγουμένου αὐτῶν Διός. Dis. 22: pagan festivals and games honor demons. Dis. 13: the demons ape Christ by promoting pagan cults that resemble Christianity. Greeks and Romans: Dis. 14. Fate: Dis. 8–9, 14–16, 18–19.

61. Dis. 17. Tatian indicated that since God does not design the world in such a way that it is controlled by magic, whatever magic is worked is worked

occasion visions, dreams, erotic fantasies, disease, and possession, and they invented medicine, a magical art, in order to
deceive us as to the true, demonic origin of illness. Their
twisted approach to medicine is to cause people to become ill
and then, when the physician has been summoned, withdraw
from the invalids in order to persuade people that the physician's magic is curing them. Demons want us to be like them in
evil and misery, so they teach us to sin. But they have power
over us only because of our own attachment to the world and
the flesh. As material spirits (*hylikoi*), the robber demons use
our own material attachments against us.[62]

For protection against the Devil and his minions we have
only Christ as a shield. Baptism, by incorporating us into his
mystical body, sets us free from the demons' power. Exorcism,
prayer, and trust in God help. God never cheats or errs, and
demons always cheat us; even when for their own purposes
they try to tell us the truth, they err through ignorance. Tatian's emphases were much more Gnostic than Justin's: as a result of original sin, we have lost the higher soul (*pneuma*) and are
ruled by the lower soul (*psychē*) and so wander in ignorance,
easily tricked and deceived by demons, who are skillful in playing upon our material desires. To be saved, therefore, we must
renounce matter and the flesh, overcome our ignorance with
saving knowledge, and rise to reunite outselves with God's
pneuma.[63]

With God's help we can break away from evil matter. But
the Devil and his demons are doomed, for they cannot repent
or be saved. Unlike humans, who are made in the image of
God—however much we distort it—the demons are made in

---

with the help of demons. This idea, quite removed from the prevailing Platonism of the times, came to dominate later medieval thought and provided
the theory for the prosecution of witches as demonolaters. See J. B. Russell,
Witchcraft in the Middle Ages (Ithaca, 1972), pp. 142–143.

62. Dis. 16, 18. Teach sin: Dis. 8, 14. Using matter against us: Dis. 16:
ὕλη δὲ τῇ κάτω, πρὸς τὴν ὁμοίαν αὐτοῖς ὕλην πολεμοῦσιν.

63. Dis. 9. Salvation: Dis. 12–13, 15–16.

the image of matter and are forever bound to their sin.[64] They were cast down from heaven at the time of their sin and presently range the air and the earth. Living in the air, they attempt to bar the soul's progress from earth to heaven and from matter to *pneuma*.[65] The demons will suffer in fire, which they can feel in their aerial bodies even though they lack real flesh. Tatian painted himself into an odd corner here: humans are closer to God than are demons, since they are in the image of God and capable of salvation, while the demons are in the image of matter; nonetheless, humans have grosser material bodies than do the demons and in this sense are ontologically further from God. The demons' suffering is not eternal, because they are not eternal, but they will live to the end of the world, and their torments will endure as long as they do.

Athenagoras, who wrote his "Plea for the Christians" in 177, had a good command of Greek philosophy and literature.[66] Like Justin and Tatian, he confronted pagan religion, although with more tolerance. Athenagoras argued, as Justin did, that there were three classes of evil spirits—the Devil, the fallen angels, and the souls of the giants whom the fallen angels had begotten upon women.[67] The angels were created by the Logos, the Word of God, for the purpose of serving the Lord. The Devil is one of the angels. Like the other angels, he was created by God

64. Again this reflects Gnostic ideas. The demons made in the image of matter and iniquity: Dis. 15: τῆς γὰρ ὕλης καὶ πονηρίας εἰσὶν ἀπαυγάσματα. There is no way that they can repent: οὐκ ἔχει μετανοίας τόπον. An apparent conflict exists with Tatian's free-will theology here, but it might be resolved by saying that once the angels had sinned of their free will, they became demons, and at that point were made in the image of matter and iniquity and barred from repentance by their material nature.

65. Dis. 16: the path to heaven: τὴν ἐν οὐρανοῖς πορείαν.

66. On "The Plea for the Christians" (P.) see the Essay on the Sources.

67. P. 25: three classes of evil spirits. No distinction exists between their functions, but the giant-souls do evil according to their base natures, while the angels do evil because of their own free will. P. 26: Athenagoras, unlike Tatian, adopted the Euhemerist view that the pagans' alleged gods were really dead heroes. The result is the same as with Justin and Tatian: the demons now hide behind these names and occupy the idols, so that whatever sacrifices are made are made to the demons, who eagerly lick up the blood of libation.

and has an intrinsically good nature.[68] God entrusted him with the governance of matter.[69] Some of the angels remained good, but the Devil fell through his free will, abandoning his duty to God and so violating both his office and his nature.[70] Cast out of heaven, the Devil and the angels can no longer rise, so they roam through the air between heaven and earth. Under the Devil's leadership, they attack us internally and externally, using their power over matter to tempt us.[71] Athenagoras was the first Christian theologian to use the term "anti-God," which he himself did not specifically apply to Satan, though it was used by later theologians in that sense.[72]

Theophilus, bishop of Antioch from about A.D. 169, was a Greek theologian influenced by Platonism; he died after 180. His "Discourse to Autolycus" emphasized monotheism and human responsibility much more than demonic influence, but he cannot be assumed to have downplayed the role of Satan, since in the Discourse he referred to a work, now lost, that he had written on the Devil.[73] Theophilus was even more explicit than Athenagoras in defending the Devil as an angel, and this view from that time was fixed in tradition.[74] The evil-doing demon, also called Satan, used the serpent to tempt Eve because he envied the happiness of the first couple. When he saw that they were not totally miserable even after their fall, his envy was unabated, and he therefore urged Cain to attack Abel, thus intro-

68. P. 24: γενόμενον μὲν ὑπὸ τοῦ θεοῦ, καθὸ καὶ οἱ λοιποὶ ὑπ' αὐτοῦ γεγόνασιν ἄγγελοι.

69. P. 24–25: the Devil is *archōn* and *logos* of matter. P. 25: ὁ δὲ τῆς ὕλης ἄρχων. P. 25: κατὰ τὸν τῆς ὕλης λόγον. But he is not an independent principle; he rules matter as a creature of God with God's permission.

70. P. 24. The specific sin of the other angels was lust. Thus Athenagoras adopted the Watchers story rejected by Tatian.

71. P. 25–26.

72. The term ἀντίθεος did not mean "opposed to God" so much as "non-God," the power that derives from and rules matter as opposed to spirit. See G. Ruhbach, "Zum Begriff ἀντίθεος in der alten Kirche," *Texte und Untersuchungen*, 92 (1966), 372–384. Later, Lactantius used the term to mean "opposed to God," and at that point it became an epithet of the Devil.

73. For Theophilus' work "To Autolycus" (Aut.), see the Essay on the Sources.

74. "Originally he was an angel," ἄγγελος γὰρ ἦν ἐν πρώτοις: Aut. 2.28.

ducing death into the world.[75] Theophilus was the first to follow Wisdom 2:24 in emphasizing envy as the motive in Satan's fall. Irenaeus and Cyprian later did the same, but Origen preferred pride, and that explanation came to prevail.[76]

75. Envy: φθόνος. Cain's sin as the beginning of death: καὶ οὕτως ἀρχη θανάτου.

76. See I. M. Sans, *La envidia primigenia del diablo según la patrística primitiva* (Madrid, 1963), and H. A. Kelly, "The Devil in the Desert," *Catholic Biblical Quarterly*, 26 (1964), 190–220.

4   Human Sin and Redemption: Irenaeus and Tertullian

Toward the end of the second century two theologians with a deep concern for morality, sin, and atonement brought these ideas to the forefront of the discussion of evil. Irenaeus, born about 140 in Asia Minor, became bishop of Lyons, where he laid the foundations of the church of Gaul. He died about 202, possibly a martyr. His foremost concern was to defend the unity of the church against internal dissent. In this cause he wrote "Against the Heretics," a work attacking the Gnostics, especially Valentine and his pupil Ptolemy.[1] Though Irenaeus, like most of the fathers, shared some dualist tendencies with the Gnostics, he made a sharp distinction between orthodoxy and Gnosticism, and the Christian community began in his day to relegate the Gnostics to the status of heretics.

Irenaeus totally rejected the Gnostic contention that the world was the product of an evil creator. Rather the creator was the Logos, the Word of the good God.[2] The angels are part of the cosmos that God has created; the Devil is an angel, so, like the other angels, he was created good.[3] The Devil is a creature, inherently and forever inferior and subordinate to God. This

1. For the works of Irenaeus, see the Essay on the Sources. References below are to "Against the Heresies" unless preceded by "P." for "Proof of the Apostolic Preaching."
2. Heresies 1.5; 4.pref. and passim.
3. 3.8; 4.41; 5.24.

idea, now firmly established, moved Christianity radically away from cosmological dualism.[4]

The Devil apostasized and fell from heaven.[5] Irenaeus granted Satan less power than did the Gnostics or the other fathers, emphasizing human responsibility for sin instead. The Devil deceives our minds, darkens our hearts, and tries to persuade us to worship him rather than the true God. But his powers over us are limited, for he is only a usurper of authority that legitimately and ultimately belongs to God, and he cannot force us to sin.[6] The Devil fell from grace because he envied God, wishing to be adored like his maker, and even more because he envied humanity. Satan could not tolerate the favor that God showed us by making us in his own image and likeness and by placing the universe under Adam's authority.[7] This scenario affected the chronology of Satan's fall. Since his envy was directed primarily against us, he must have fallen *after* God created humans (the more common explanation) or at least after having got wind of God's intention to create humans. But since he entered Eden with his heart already corrupted with the desire to ruin our first parents, his own sin clearly preceded their temptation. This argument, by the way, runs counter to the later notion that God created humans in order to make up for his loss of the fallen angels. The other angels fell later, at the time of Noah, Irenaeus said.[8]

4. Not a principle: 3.8, 5.22. "He himself is one of God's creatures"; the Devil has created nothing himself. Irenaeus' terms for the Devil are similar to those of the other fathers: he is a liar (5.22–24), our adversary (3.18), a serpent (4.40), a murderer and a "strong man" (3.8, 3.18, 5.22); an apostate (5.25), and a thief (5.25).

5. 4.37; 4.41; 5.21; 5.24. In 5.21, Irenaeus followed Justin's false etymology of Satan as "apostate serpent."

6. 4.41; 5.24.

7. Satan wishes to be adored as God: 5.22, 5.24; pride, 5.21; envy of humanity: 3.23, 4.40, 5.21, 5.24, P. 16; falsehood: P. 16.

8. The Devil is an angel, and the Devil and the other evil angels were expelled from heaven on account of their sin: 4.40. But Irenaeus usually distinguished the serpent from the apostate angels. Irenaeus accepted the canonicity of Enoch and in 4.16, 4.27, and 4.36 implied the story of the Watchers: God sends the Flood to destroy and purify the human race, corrupted as it was by the sinful angels who had polluted themselves with hu-

Irenaeus was less concerned with the mythology of demons
than with the alienation of humanity from God, a concern that
led him to tie the sin of the Devil closely to the sin of Adam
and Eve. Irenaeus worked out the first fully developed theology
of original sin. God created Adam and Eve and placed them in
Paradise to live happily in close relationship with him. But
Satan, knowing their weakness, entered the Garden and, either
taking the form of the serpent or using the serpent as a tool,
tempted them.[9] Satan's spite could have had no effect had God
not given humanity freedom to choose between good and evil.
Satan did not compel the first man and woman to sin; they
chose their sin freely. But God had not only made them free,
he had made them weak enough to yield to Satan's importuni-
ties. Irenaeus attributed a degree of responsibility for original
sin to God himself, who could have made Adam and Eve
stronger.[10]

---

mans. In P. 18 the whole story of the Watchers is recounted. Sometimes
Irenaeus spoke (3.23) as if the Devil and the angels fell at the same time. For
his own part, Satan blamed God instead of himself for his apostasy: 5.26.

9. 3.23; 4.pref.; 5.22–23.

10. Hick took this suggestion of the imperfection of Adam and Eve and
made it the hallmark of an "Irenaean theology." Hick meant to illuminate
modern theological speculation rather than to study Irenaeus himself, and he
did not intend to attribute the views of those whom he called "Irenaeans" to
the church father. Nonetheless, his modern theological preoccupations led him
to make too much of the weakness theory in Irenaeus. According to Hick,
"Irenaean theology" argues that God created men and women imperfect and
that we are gradually developing in the direction of the moral goal set by
God. Original sin, in this view, is no catastrophe, but rather "an under-
standable lapse due to weakness and immaturity" (*Evil and the God of Love*, p.
221). This world is a mixture of good and evil, where suffering exists so that
we can learn virtue. Hick ascribes the purpose of the terrible suffering of the
world to God's purpose in leading us to the good through "soul-making and
mystery" (p. 363). Without the sense of suffering in the world, he argues,
there can be no compassion. Hick's presentation of the "Irenaean" view can be
summarized as follows: (1) the human race was created imperfect; (2) God is
therefore responsible for sin and evil; (3) evil makes sense in terms of the
overall purpose of God; (4) in the end everyone will be saved. Such a view is
more compatible with some modern theologies than with the fathers. See
Clark's critique, especially pp. 121, 124. As F. M. Young points out in her
brilliant article "Insight or Incoherence: The Greek Fathers on Good and
Evil," *Journal of Ecclesiastical History*, 24 (1973), 113–126, this argument is
theodicy rather than redemption theology and is inconsistent with the ransom
theory of redemption that Irenaeus himself emphasized.

All humans participate in the sin of Adam and Eve. By our own free choice we became slaves of the Devil, powerless to free ourselves from him.[11] Subject to Satan, we distorted the divine image and likeness and thereby doomed ourselves to death. The happiness of Eden was shattered.[12] Because we turned our backs on God through our own free will, we delivered ourselves into the power of Satan, and it was right and just that Satan should hold us until we were redeemed. In strict justice God could have abandoned us to Satan's power forever, but his mercy led him to send his Son to save us.[13]

In Irenaeus' view, the suffering of Christ, his Passion, saved us. The Passion began with the Devil's temptation of Christ, the second Adam, a recapitulation of the temptation of the first Adam, except that this time the Devil failed.[14] It culminated in the trial, condemnation, and execution of Jesus. Here the Devil thought, briefly, that he had won, but he soon learned that he was deluded.

Christian tradition has interpreted the saving work of the Passion in three main ways. According to the first interpretation, human nature had been sanctified, dignified, transformed, and saved by the very act of Christ's becoming man. In the terms of the second, Christ was a sacrifice offered to God in order to bring about reconciliation between man and God. The third, the ransom theory, found its first strong proponent in Irenaeus, and its basis is as follows. Since Satan justly held the human race in prison, God offered himself as ransom for our freedom. The price could be paid only by God. Only God could freely submit. No one else could choose freely, because original sin had deprived us all of our freedom. By submitting to Satan's power of his own free will and choice, Christ liberated us from the Devil's power. God handed Jesus over in order

11. 3.23; 4.33; 4.37; 5.23.

12. 3.23; 5.23.

13. 4.37–38; 5.12; 5.14; 5.22. See J. N. D. Kelly, *Early Christian Doctrines* (London, 1958), p. 174. Hick contrasted Irenaeus' free-will argument with the predestination later emphasized by Augustinians.

14. 3.17–18; 3.20; 3.31: secundum Adam; 3.32; 5.21. The emphasis upon the Passion rather than the Incarnation as the most important saving act of Christ is based on New Testament teaching: cf. Hebrews 2:14.

to release the hostages. The Devil accepted Jesus. But when he seized him and put him to death, he overstepped the boundaries of justice, since Jesus himself was without sin and could not justly be held. The Devil had held us justly in the past, but when he broke the rules of justice himself, he lost his rights and could no longer hold either Jesus or us.[15] Christ's suffering crippled the Devil, freeing us from death and damnation.

The theory of sacrifice, the chief alternative theory in Irenaeus' time, argued that Christ, man as well as God, took all the sins of humanity upon himself, and by offering himself to death of his own free will he made compensation acceptable to God. In the one theory, Christ is offered up to Satan, but in the other, God demands the victim for himself. The ransom theory, although sometimes crudely expressed, did reflect the apostolic emphasis on the cosmic battle between Christ and Satan and in general fitted the moderately dualist assumptions of early Christianity well enough. It was left to Saint Anselm in the twelfth century to formulate a more coherent soteriology.

For Irenaeus, Christ was the second Adam, who lifted the chains of death laid upon us because of the weakness of the first Adam.[16] The notion of "recapitulation," of Christ the Second Man undoing the damage done by the First Man, was the center of Irenaeus' Christology. His ransom theory sprang from his controversy with the Gnostics, who claimed that the Devil had

15. The ransom theory was followed by Origen, Ambrose, Augustine (to some extent), Leo the Great, and Gregory the Great. Some of the fathers went so far as to call the transaction a trick that God played upon Satan, since Satan did not know that Jesus was God when he seized him. See 1 Corinthians 2:8, Origen, below, p. 140, and Irenaeus, 5.26. Gregory of Nyssa drew upon Job for a notorious image derived from angling: Christ was the bait and the hook upon which the old dragon was landed by God. This metaphor, introduced to the West by Rufinus of Aquileia about 400, was adopted by Gregory the Great and because of Gregory's wide influence passed into common use. See below, p. 193. Ransom: Irenaeus, 2.20, 3.18, 5.21. Irenaeus referred to Genesis 3:15 and Matthew 12:29 for his ideas about Christ's triumph over the Devil. From Matthew 12:29 comes the use of the term "strong man" for the Devil.

16. 3.18; 3.23; 5.21–23. Christ thereby defeated the "serpent," the "enemy," the "adversary," the "apostate angel," who in retribution will himself be chained.

rights over mankind because he was the creator of our bodies and of the entire material world. Firmly denying that the material world was evil and that Satan was the creator, Irenaeus insisted that Satan's rights resulted solely from the First Man's misuse of free will. And now the free-will suffering of the Second Man canceled these rights.

The discussion of the Passion begun by Irenaeus opened up new difficulties for the concept of evil. The theology of atonement requires quite a different approach from that demanded by theodicy. Theodicy is philosophically oriented and often aimed at convincing pagans and agnostics. The theology of atonement can convince only believers. The fathers often used both approaches together, but in fact they are inconsistent. Theodicy is monist in tendency, explaining evil as a necessary part of the God's cosmic plan; atonement recognizes the existence of an irreconcilable evil so radical that God himself must die in order to draw its sting. On the one hand God is the source of everything; on the other, he is opposed to evil.[17] Later Christian writers usually failed to grapple with the inconsistency, and when they did they often introduced even greater complications, such as the nonbeing of evil. For many of them, writes Frances Young, "theodicy and atonement were virtually consigned to separate compartments, and their paradoxical relationship went unobserved."[18]

The differences of approach between theodicy and atonement are reflected in the two theories of sacrifice and ransom. Those more interested in theodicy tended to the sacrifice theory because it emphasizes the basic goodness and harmony of God's cosmos, which has been distorted by humanity's sins, but which can also be straightened out by reconciliation between God and the human race. Those more concerned with salvation tended to the ransom theory, which pitted God against the powers of radical evil. The fathers oscillated, as Young put it, "between theodicy and atonement doctrine, varying suggestions

17. Young, p. 123.
18. Young, p. 121.

Christ heals a demoniac while Satan, with black wings on his head, looks on in horrified astonishment. A ninth-century illumination from the Stuttgart Gospels. Courtesy of the Württembergische Landesbibliothek.

employed side by side, and consistency between them neither sought nor demanded."[19]

Defeated by Christ, the Devil nevertheless exerts himself vigorously, though vainly, to thwart salvation, according to Irenaeus. He encourages paganism, idolatry, sorcery, blasphemy, and especially heresy and apostasy.[20] Heretics are members of Satan's army, his agents in the cosmic war against Christ.[21]

19. Ibid. Young concludes, "We see here the response of groping believers, not a coherent answer to a philosophical problem." But the concept of evil, like most broadly-based concepts, advances more through such groping than through coherent analysis.

20. 1.25; 4.pref.; 1.15: evil magic, "which Satan, your father, enables you to accomplish with the help of the mighty angel Azazel."

21. 1.25: the Carpocratian Gnostics "were sent forth by Satan to bring dishonor upon the church; 1.27: "the serpent inhabiting Marcion"; 4.pref.; 4.41; 5.26: apostates as "full of the spirit of the Devil; 5.26: Gnostics as "agents of Satan."

This doctrine, latent in the New Testament and fully developed by Irenaeus, had a baleful effect. It was used as a justification for holy wars, crusades, and the persecution of heretics and non-Christians; revulsion against the doctrine is one of the main reasons for the decline of belief in the Devil since the eighteenth century. For if in fact the Devil is at war with Christ, and if in fact he summons evil angels and evil men to fight under his banner, then those who oppose the saving work of Christ are indeed soldiers of the Devil. The question was how the Christian community defined itself, how it separated the heretics from the orthodox. Irenaeus and the majority in the church found the answer in apostolic succession, the doctrine that the bishops of the church were the successors of the apostles and were to some degree guarded from error by the Holy Spirit. For Irenaeus, heresy was defined as that which the bishops condemned as heresy. From the eleventh century the growing power of the papacy allowed heresy to be defined as opposition to the see of Rome, but this idea had not been thought of in Irenaeus' time, when the power of the Roman see was still inchoate. Irenaeus' definition is a pragmatic one: a heretic is one who is designated by the bishop as a heretic. Since no objective definition of "heretic" is possible, this definition was almost inevitable.

Like the other fathers, Irenaeus argued that the Christian's defense against the Devil is Christ. The Devil flees Christian prayers and the uttered name of Christ. Only those fearful and weakened by sin can be destroyed by demons; those fortified by baptism and loyal to their faith are protected by the Lord.[22] Nonetheless, the battle is by no means over. The demons, doomed though they are, continue to torment us. Near the end of the world the Antichrist will come, an apostate, murderer, and robber, who will have "all the Devil's power." Those who now follow Satan will then flock to Antichrist, worshiping the two together. But Antichrist will be defeated, and the world will then come to an end. At that time Satan and the demons will go to hell, where, since they are immortal, they will suffer

22. 2.32.

eternal death in the flames.[23] Though the Antichrist is a human rather than a demon and therefore appears only at one point in time, at that point his function and that of Satan are almost indistinguishable. Both represent the last, desperate effort of the powers of evil to thwart God's saving plan.

The diabology of Tertullian was even more influential than that of Irenaeus. Born about 170 into a wealthy, literary family at Carthage, Tertullian spent most of his life in that city. He converted while still young, took a Christian wife, and became bishop of Carthage, dying about 220.[24] The first great Latin

23. 3.23; 4.37; 4.40–41. In 5.25–30 is the first prolonged discussion of Antichrist in patristic literature. For a view of the Johannine precedents, see R. Yates, "The Antichrist," *Evangelical Quarterly*, 46 (1974), 42–50. Hippolytus, a Roman father who wrote against the pagans, Jews, and heretics and who was martyred about 235, wrote a "Treatise on the Antichrist" about 220 (MPG 10, 725–788) and may also be the author of the "Chapters against Caius," which dealt with the Antichrist and the millennium. Hippolytus set the tradition that there would be one Antichrist as there was one Christ, and that Antichrist would ape and imitate Christ in every possible way in order to deceive us. He also identified the Antichrist as a member of the tribe of Dan, thus paving the way for the firm identification of the Antichrist as a Jew. Hippolytus' work "is the most complete summary of early patristic traditions on the final enemy of man," writes B. McGinn (*Visions of the End* [New York, 1979], p. 22). In ch. 56, Hippolytus called Antichrist "the son of the Devil and the vessel of Satan," υἱὸν ὄντα τοῦ διαβόλου, καὶ σκεῦος τοῦ Σατανᾶ, and in ch. 63 he says that the Antichrist's advent will occur in accordance with Satan's activities, with all his power in signs, prodigies, and lies, and in all of his deception and injustice, οὐκ ἐστιν ἡ παρουσία κατ' ἐνέργειαν τοῦ Σατανᾶ ἐν πάσῃ δυνάμει καὶ σημείοις καὶ τέρασι ψεύδος, καὶ ἐν πάσῃ ἀπάτῃ τῆς ἀδικίας ἐν τοῖς ἀπολλυμένοις. I avoid prolonged discussion of Antichrist in this book, since the tradition is very complex and is tangential to the central problem of evil.

24. On Tertullian's life and works, see T. D. Barnes, *Tertullian* (Oxford, 1971), and the Essay on the Sources. The relevant works and the abbreviations used here (I follow Barnes's chronology) are: A.D. 196–197: *De spectaculis*, "Shows"; *De idololatria*, "Idolatry" (Idol.); *De cultu feminarum*, "Women's dress" (Women), part two. 197: *Ad nationes*, "To the Gentiles" (Gent.); *Adversus Judaeos*, "Against the Jews" (Jews); *Ad martyras*, "To the Martyrs" (Mart.); *Apologeticum*, "Apology" (Apol.). 198: *De testimonio animae*, "The Soul's Witness" (Witness). 198–203: *De baptismo*, "Baptism" (Bapt.); *De oratione*, "Prayer"; *De paenitentia*, "Penitence" (Pen.); *De patientia*, "Patience" (Pat.); *Ad uxorem*, "To My Wife" (Wife). 203: *De praescriptione haereticorum*, "The Outlawing of Heretics" (Her.). 203–204: *Scorpiace*, "The Scorpion's Sting" (Scorp.). 204–205: *Adversus Hermogenen*, "Against Hermogenes" (Herm.). 205:

theologian, Tertullian helped establish Latin theological vocabulary and in many ways anticipated Augustine, laying the groundwork for his fellow African's great theological synthesis. Tertullian firmly rejected the cosmological dualism of the Gnostics, yet the old strain of Jewish ethical dualism was very strong in his own thought. A practical writer stressing the application of theology to everyday affairs, he insisted that a strict and disciplined moral life was part of the campaign against the Devil, whereas an immoral, worldly life was enlistment in Satan's army. "No man," he quoted Scripture, "can serve two masters. What do light and darkness have to do with one another?"[25] His moral rigidity grew with age, and by about 212 he was taking an extreme position, associating himself with Montanism, an ascetic movement that by the fourth century came to be considered heretical by the majority. The practical Tertullian judged that the Gnostics had fallen into error by being too theoretical and especially by brooding over the problem of evil.[26] In his own way, Tertullian had as great a concern with evil as they had. His moral bent led him to devise a demonology that is less a description than a frontal attack upon paganism. The pagans are citizens of the old eon, the evil age, soldiers in the army of Satan.

Creation is good. Tertullian remained unbudging on this point against the Gnostics.[27] But as we look around us we see a

De pallio, "The Christian's Robe" (Robe). 205–206: *De culta feminarum*, part one. 206: *De carne Christi*, "The Body of Christ" (Body). 206–207: *Adversus Valentinianos*, "Against the Valentinians" (Val.); *De anima*, "The Soul" (Soul); *De resurrectione mortuorum*, "The Resurrection of the Dead" (Res). 207–208: *Adversus Marcionem*, "Against Marcion" (Marc.). 208: *De corona militis*, "The Chaplet" (Cor.). 208–209: *De exhortatione castitatis*, "Exhortation to Chastity" (Exhort.); *De fuga in persecutione*, "Fleeing in Time of Persecution" (Flee.). 210–211: *De monogamia*, "Monogamy" (Mon.); *De jejunio*, "Fasting" (Fast.); *De pudicitia*, "Modesty" (Mod.); *Adversus Praxean*, "Against Praxeas" (Prax.). 212: *Ad Scapulam*, "To Scapula" (Scap.).

25. Shows 26. Tertullian drew from Matthew 6:24 and 2 Corinthians 6:14.

26. Her. 7; Marc. 1.2.

27. Marc. 1; 5.13. Here Tertullian firmly rejected Gnostic monist dualism. See E. P. Meijering, *Tertullian contra Marcion: Gotteslehre in der Polemik Adversus Marcionem I-II* (Leiden, 1977). Tertullian suggested (Marc. 5.13) that if the creator is evil, then we are left, not with a problem of evil but with a

far from perfect world, one in fact full of pain and misery. Why? Because of sin. This emphasis on sin is the key to Tertullian's diabology, and it is also, as with Irenaeus, a basis for future Christian moral theology. Tertullian's refutation of dualism against Marcion typified the views of the fathers. Sin deforms the world; everything bad in the world is the result, not of God's action, but of the action of sin. And sin is not the work of an evil creator or demiurge, as the Gnostics say. Such a being does not exist, for it is inconceivable that there should be more than one god. God could not be two. The definition of God is an all-powerful being. Two unequal, all-powerful gods could not possibly exist, because both would not be all-powerful. The principle of parsimony also makes it impossible that two equally powerful gods exist—there is no logical need for two. Further, the cosmos cannot be in strict balance between two opposite forces, for if it were, there could be no motion. And if the slightest imbalance between the two forces existed, one side would have superiority. And if superiority, immediate victory, for if in eternity the scale begins to tilt to one side it will tip forever. Nor could the two opposing forces wax and wane with time; this too in the context of eternity is impossible. Since the powers proper to each would be fixed in eternity, there would be no reason for them to change. If Being exists, it must be one; any multiplicity must be subordinate to Being, because the alternative to Being is not another being but nonbeing. Dualism cannot therefore be the answer to the problem of evil.

Evil is not an independent principle. Yet it exists. Where does it come from? From two sources: the sin of Satan and his angels, and the sin of humans. God granted us freedom, which is in itself a great good, but of our own free will we misuse

---

problem of good. Instead of the question "Whence is evil?" we would be baffled by the question "Whence is good?" If the creator were evil, how could there be any good in the cosmos? J. Quasten, *Patrology*, 3 vols. (Westminster, 1951–   ), 2:318, says that in a lost work against Apelles, Tertullian attacked the Gnostic view that an angel created the world and then regretted it.

freedom, bringing about evil. The source of all the evil in the world is free-will sin. Thus the Devil and sinners "have perverted [God's] gifts."[28]

"The world comes from God, but worldliness comes from the Devil."[29] This statement transposes the latent cosmic dualism of the New Testament into an ethical dualism centering on the question of sin. Saint Paul and Saint John had spoken of the Devil as the lord of this world (Gk. *kosmos* or *aiōn*; Lat. *saeculum*), and both saw "this world" as an entity divorced in time and space from God. The precise meaning of "this world" for the apostles and apostolic fathers is unclear.[30] They may have meant the entire created world of space and time, including matter, energy, and spirit; or they may have meant our own attachment to this world. Tertullian might have condemned the cosmos as evil in itself. But he moved decisively away from the cosmic explanation to the moral one, redefining the terms as he did so.

Saeculum, the cosmos, is good. The evil is not *saeculum*, but *saecularia*, worldly affairs, not the world itself, but attachment to the things of this world more than to God. "The world" can now be a metonymy for "the sinful attachments of this world;" most subsequent writers would use it in this way. It was now possible for Christians to love "the world" in the sense of God's cosmos, beautiful, good, and true, and at the same time to hate "the world" in the sense of attachment to sin.[31] Though Tertullian's morality was sometimes so extreme as to appear dualistic, he flatly rejected the Gnostic idea that the body was bad. The body is a good creature, and Christ had further dignified the

---

28. Shows 2.
29. Shows 15: "Saeculum Dei est; saecularia autem Diaboli."
30. See ch. 2 above and Russell, *The Devil*, ch. 6.
31. The ambiguity left its mark in all western languages, e.g., the double meaning of *monde* in French, with the moral ambiguity of *mondain* and *siècle*. The same ambiguity persists in the English "man" and "man of the world." In Latin and English, *saecularis*, "secular," always denotes this world as distinguished from God's but often has a morally neutral meaning, as in the phrase "secular princes," as well as the negative connotations Tertullian gave it.

flesh by taking it on himself in his Incarnation. Only abuse of the body is evil. The creator God of the Old Testament is one and the same as the redeeming God of the New.[32]

Tertullian never shirked the question of the real evil in the world. Indeed, he said that the evil in the world is so patent, so obvious, that people can grasp the existence of the Devil by experience. The mind knows the Devil directly by virtue of its observation of evil, just as it knows the existence of God directly by virtue of its observation of beauty and goodness. "We learn and understand the Lord and his rival, the Creator and the Destroyer, at one and the same time."[33] When people call upon Satan's name in cursing, it is as if they respond to some intuitive knowledge of the Devil arising in their soul. We have direct and unmediated experience of certain events as evil and as proceeding from an evil source.[34]

The Devil is not an independent principle, nor is he the creation of some other independent principle, evil creator, or demiurge.[35] Tertullian rejected Marcion emphatically on this point. The Devil, for all his vast power, is creature, not creator. But God, though the creator of the Devil, cannot be blamed for evil. God created the Devil good in his nature. God created an angel; that angel made himself into the Devil. By his own act he became corrupt.[36] "He was created in the presence of God as a good being is created in the presence of a good Being; but afterwards he was transformed by his own free choice into an evil being."[37] Before his fall, he was not only an angel but the fore-

32. See E. Evans, ed., *Tertullian adversus Marcionem*, 2 vols. (Oxford, 1972), 1: xiii–xiv.

33. Shows 2: "Nos igitur, qui domino cognito etiam aemulum eius inspeximus, qui institutore comperto et interpolatorem una despeximus." For the use of *aemulus* and *interpolator* as terms for the Devil, see below, p. 94.

34. Apol. 22: "Proinde de propria conscientia animae"; Witness 3; Soul 57.

35. Nor is he an emanation from the Pleroma: Val. 12.4 and passim.

36. Marc. 2.10: "Tam institutione bonum angelum illum quam sponte corruptum" (an angel created good but corrupted by his own free will).

37. Marc. 2.10: "Apud deum constitutus qua bonus apud bonum, postea vero a semetipso translatus in malum." *Apud* implies a close relationship between the Devil and God; cf. the relationship in John 1:1 of the Father and the Word: "Et Verbum erat apud Deum," "and the Word was with God."

most angel.[38] Some fathers shared this view that the Devil was the greatest of the angels, but others rejected it on the grounds that the lowest, not the highest, orders of angels were most susceptible to sin. The objection is illogical, since all the angels had been granted freedom, real, autonomous freedom, which made the highest angel as free to sin as the lowest.[39] Satan did not fall with the other angels, who sinned at the time of Noah because of lust, for Satan was a liar "from the beginning."[40] Tertullian did not mean that the Devil was created bad or that he was bad from the beginning of the cosmos. God had created angels and humans with free will so that they might have the potential for moral good instead of being mere automatons. But the potential for good entailed an equal opposite potential. God created Satan without reproach and made for glory, but he opted to corrupt himself; he made a free choice for evil.[41] Since he was the first of all God's creatures to sin, it was by him that sin and evil entered the cosmos, and thus he was a liar "from the beginning."[42]

Satan fell because of envy and jealousy. He was furious that God had created humans in the divine image and had given them governance over the world. In his envy, he turned his will away from God's and entered Paradise to tempt and deceive Adam and Eve, later urging Cain to slay Abel.[43] The motion of his will against God just preceded his entry into Eden. Thus

38. Marc. 2.10: "eminentissimo angelorum . . . sapientissimus omnium editus ante quam diabolus" (he was the most eminent of angels, created the wisest of all of them, before he became the Devil).

39. One does not generally observe among humans that the stupid sin more readily than the brilliant. Tertullian based his view in part on the apocalyptic tradition and in part on the widely held view that after his fall the Devil was ruler of the fallen angels: Soul 6.17. Augustine and Gregory the Great followed Tertullian's view, with the result that it came to be generally accepted in the West.

40. See below, p. 96. Satan a liar from the beginning: Cor. 7: "Diabolus . . . a primordio mendax." Cf. Prax. 1. Tertullian's view, shared by most of the fathers, derived from John 8:44.

41. Marc. 2.10.

42. Marc. 2.10: "auctor delicti" (the author of sin). Cf. Pat. 5.

43. Pat. 5; Marc. 2.10; Soul 39. Marc. 5.17 also refers to pride. Pat. 5 refers the sin to the Devil's impatience: he viewed the power and grace

Tertullian, like Irenaeus, set the time of Satan's fall not before but after the creation of man and woman. As a result of his sin—whether the original motion of the will or the actual temptation of the first humans—Satan was cast down from on high.[44]

The Devil's function in the cosmos is precise. As God creates the cosmos, the Devil destroys it. As God has created things good, the Devil distorts and perverts them. Thus Tertullian thought the Devil's function similar to that of the shadow of God, the destroying *mal'ak Yahweh* of the Old Testament, with the fundamental distinction that the Devil was a creature rather than a manifestation of divinity. The Devil has taken God's beautiful creation and filled it with lies.[45] The author of all evil, he has become lord of this world, not in the sense that he controls the cosmos, but in the sense that he dominates the part of it that he has corrupted, and he is lord of that part not absolutely but only insofar as he has permission from God.[46] The Devil is the rival and ape (*aemulus*) of God and the corrupter and perverter (*interpolator*) of God's world.[47] God plants a field with

---

granted Adam and Eve impatiently; this caused him to grieve, which caused him to envy, which caused him to sin.

44. Shows 16: "Diaboli ab alto praecipitati."

45. Cor. 6; Marc. 5.17: he has filled the world with his pretense of divinity, "ita enim totum saeculum mendacio divinitatis implevit."

46. Soul 57: "Totius erroris artificem." Marc. 5.17: "Diabolus quem . . . deum aevi huius agnoscemus." Here *aevus* is a direct translation of *aiōn*, the evil period of time before the triumph of Christ. Satan's power over the pagans is an important part of his lordship over this world. Bapt. 9; Idol. 18; Flee. 2.

47. Shows 2; Women 1.8; Pat. 5, 16; Idol. 18. See J. Fontaine, "Sur un titre de Satan chez Tertullien: *Diabolus interpolator*," *Studi e materiali di storia delle religioni*, 38 (1967), 197–216. Witness 3: "Satanam . . . quem nos dicimus malitiae angelum, totius erroris artificem, totius saeculi interpolatorem" (Satan, whom we call the angel of evil, is the creator of every error and the corrupter of the whole world). Shows 2: "Multum interest inter corruptelam et integritatem, quia multum est inter institutorem et interpolatorem" (a great gulf separates corruption from what is whole, just as a great gulf separates the Creator and the Corrupter). Here again the Devil is the shadow. It was this corrupting force that tempted the human race to ruin. Shows 2: "illa vis interpolatoris et aemulatoris angeli ab initio de integritate [hominem] deiecerit (the power of that corrupting and envious angel debauched the wholesomeness of humanity right from the beginning). Fontaine shows that the verb *interpolare*

wheat, and the Devil strews it with weeds. In every way the Devil acts as God's opposite, seeking to destroy the truth, corrupt virtue, and pollute beauty.[48] As perverter of the cosmos, he is the foremost enemy of Christ and of humanity. All injustice comes from him.[49]

The greatest harm that Satan could do to God's world was to

---

has no equivalent in Greek and that this concept of the Devil as corrupter is original to Tertullian. Tertullian used *interpolare* and *interpolatio* in a number of contexts, but he used the personalized noun *interpolator* only six times, five of which denote the Devil.

48. Women 1.8: "Deo . . . auctore naturae . . . Diabolo interpolatore naturae." The literary parallelism is forceful. God, the author of nature, is contrasted with the Devil, the corrupter of nature. The image is applied colorfully and directly to women's custom of "falsifying" their beauty with ornament and makeup. Soul 16: the Devil as "superseminatorem et frumentariae segetis nocturnum interpolatorem" (the one who comes along at night and corrupts the crops by sowing weeds into them). The connections of this idea with the idea of heresy are twofold. First, the later fathers continually referred to the parable of the tares (weeds) as an illustration of heresy, arguing that the heretics were the weeds that the Devil had introduced into the harvest of the just. Second, Tertullian himself used the verb *interpolare* in connection with the heretics, claiming that they *interpolant* (corrupt, adulterate) the Scriptures. This helped tie heresy ever more closely with the Devil. See below, p. 98, and Fontaine, pp. 206–208.

49. Flee. 2: the Devil has the right to tempt us; the Devil is placed in power over the Gentiles. Tertullian used many names and phrases to describe the Devil: Pat. 5: adversary (adversarius), angel of ruin (angelus perditionis); Her. 31: the enemy (inimicus); Soul 1: creator of error (artifex erroris); Soul 35: accuser (criminator); Soul 35, Marc. 2.10: Destroyer (delator); Soul 39: bird-catcher (auceps). The most common word is "envious ape" (aemulus), which appears in Soul 2, 8, 20, 43; Bapt. 5; Women 1.8; Cor. 6; Marc. 1.26, 5.17, 5.19; Shows 2; Pat. 5, 16; Apol. 2, 21, 23, 27, 48. G. M. Lukken, *Original Sin in the Roman Liturgy* (Leiden, 1973), lists similar names appearing in baptismal rites of the third and fourth centuries: "the ancient destroyer" (vastator antiquus), p. 23; "guilty against God, guilty against his Son, and guilty against the human race" (reus Deo, reus Filio eius, reus humano genere), p. 26; "the accursed one, the damned one" (maledictus, damnatus), p. 29; "the author of ruin, sin, and death" (auctor perditionis, peccati, at mortis), p. 35; "clever enemy" (hostis callidus), p. 36; "ancient serpent, dragon, seducer" (serpens antiquus, draco, seductor), p. 42; "deceiver" (deceptor), p. 44; "author of lies" (auctor praevaricationis), p. 47. Though Satan can take on the appearance of an angel of light, he cannot alter his corrupted nature: Marc. 5.12; Res. 55. The anonymous treatise *De montibus Sina et Sion* called the Devil *contrarius*, "the opposing one," a direct translation of the Greek ἀντικείμενος. See Daniélou, *Origins*, p. 40.

corrupt those beings whom God had created in his image and likeness. Unlike Irenaeus, Tertullian believed that Adam and Eve were strong enough to resist temptation successfully if they freely willed to do so, but they chose to follow the Devil.[50] Having first corrupted humanity, Satan turned his attention to his fellow angels. Angels are inferior to humans, since they are not made in God's image.[51] Ministers or messengers of God, they have bodies of a marvelously refined corporeal substance. Though naturally imperceptible to any of our senses, they may choose to take on form and even shift their forms as they please.[52] Some of the angels, tempted by women, "corrupted themselves" and were cast down from heaven. At that point Satan became their prince.[53] The commerce of angels with women produced a "brood of demons yet more corrupt."[54] Together the fallen angels and giants constitute the demons.[55] Over all evil beings—fallen angels, giants, and corrupt men and

50. Marc. 2.5–10; Shows 2: "Cum ipsum hominem, opus et imaginem Dei, totius universitatis possessorem, illa vis interpolatoris et aemulatoris angeli ab initio de integritate deiecerit" (the power of the corrupting and lying angel from the very beginning destroyed the integrity of man, who was the work of God and his very image, and the possessor of the entire world). Women 1.1–2; Pat. 5: Eve singled out for special blame. Of Eve, and women in general, Tertullian exclaimed, "Tu es diaboli janua" (you are the Devil's doorway): Women 1.1–2. But F. F. Church, "Sex and Salvation in Tertullian," *Harvard Theological Review*, 68 (1975), 83–101, has said that, taken as a whole, Tertullian's thought was not unusually misogynistic. The story of Genesis interpreted as original sin readily lent itself to an attack on women, as did the story of the Watchers. Tertullian's exaggerated moralism blamed women for their vanities of dress and for the temptation they offered to men. To modern eyes Tertullian appears misogynistic, and even in the context of late classical society his views were strong. In fact no good reason existed for blaming Eve for original sin any more than Adam.

51. Marc. 2.9–10. Most fathers did not follow Tertullian in placing angels lower on the ontological scale than humans.

52. Marc. 2.9, 3.9, 5.12; Her. 6.

53. Apol. 22; Idol. 9; Prayer 22; Virg. 7; Idol. 5.6: here and elsewhere the term *diabolus* may be a general term for all hostile spiritual powers. Marc. 5.17: the Devil as prince of the power of the air (princeps potestatis aëris). Here Tertullian followed Ephesians 2:2.

54. Apol. 22.

55. Apol. 22; 39. Tertullian sometimes separated the two and sometimes treated them as one group. Their functions, in any case, are identical. Apol. 32 specifically repudiates the pagan notion that the term "demon" can designate a benevolent spirit.

women—Satan is chief. Though accepting the Watcher story, Tertullian clearly believed that the Devil was an angel and not a different variety of being. The earlier fathers had tended to see the Devil as different from the angels. The following logical options were open: Satan and the angels had different natures and different sins; Satan and the angels had the same nature but different sins; Satan and the angels had the same nature and the same sins. The movement of the tradition was clearly from the former toward the latter; in this sense Tertullian's espousal of the middle choice was a step forward.

The Devil and demons have filled the entire world in their lust to destroy it. Each individual has an evil spirit abiding in him to tempt him.[56] The Devil and the demons dwell in the lower air, where they range about on wings with incredible swiftness.[57] Until Christ's Passion, God allowed the demons to work against humanity within the limits that he had set, acting as his agents to test us and punish us. Their power was a corollary of Satan's just power over us as a result of original sin.[58] Christ's Passion has weakened and doomed the demons, placing them within our power, for we can now repel them by faith in Christ; yet they still remain free to attack us until the last judgment, and presently they still exercise wide authority in the world under God's permission. God has two purposes in allowing the Devil power over a person—to tempt and to punish.[59]

56. Apol. 22, 47; Soul 1; Shows 8: "totum saeculum Satanas et angeli eius repleverunt" (Satan and his angels have filled the whole world). Individuals: Soul 57.

57. Apol. 22: "Momento ubique sunt; totus orbis illis locus unus est" (they are everywhere in an instant; the entire world is like one place to them). Apol. 22: "Omnis spiritus ales est. Hoc angeli et daemones" (every spirit is winged; this is true of both angels and demons). This statement set the future course of the iconography of the Devil. Wings were a symbol of divine power throughout the ancient Near East, and the Book of Revelation offered Christians ground for belief in winged angels. In early Christian art angels and the Devil were not always winged, but Tertullian's view gradually gained full acceptance, and later wings became almost obligatory. Often angels and demons were shown as having different kinds of wings, the angels' being like those of feathered birds, the demons' like scaly bats' wings.

58. Flee. 2; Prayer 8.

59. Apol. 27; Soul 46; Flee. 2; Idol. passim; Marc. 5.17–18. Idol. 18.3: "daemonia magistratus sunt saeculi huius" (the demons are the magistrates of

In the beginning, the Watcher angels taught women magic, metallurgy, and other arts in order to rouse our vain curiosity.[60] When Christ came to earth, the Devil tempted him. Satan and the demons cause natural ills such as disease, crop failure, storms, evil dreams, and death itself. But some disasters and sufferings are sent directly by God in punishment for our sins, and the demons derive their power over natural evils from God. As for moral evils, Satan uses tricks, temptation, and fear to drive our minds to fury, lust, delusion, and madness.[61] The demons pose as gods and promote paganism and idolatry.[62] They encourage pagan myths and rites and introduce false versions of Christian ideas into the minds of the pagans, whose fables weaken the credibility of the real truth. The demons stir up persecutions, but they do this too according to God's will, for God knows that the persecutions bring martyrdom, and martyrdom is a triumph over evil and an example to others: "the blood of Christians is the seed of the church."[63] Persecution comes "not from the Devil but through him."[64]

Almost as bad as paganism is heresy, which Satan also invented and encourages. "The spiritual unrighteousness from which heresy comes was sent by the Devil. . . . Heresy is not far from idolatry, since both are of the same author and craftsmanship. . . . Every falsehood about God is a kind of idolatry."[65] If the heretics appear to worship God and to be

---

this world). Here *saeculum* has a sharp negative connotation and seems to be equated with the apostolic *kosmos* and *aiōn*.

60. Women 1.2, 2.10; Soul 57. This is taken directly from Enoch.

61. Apol. 22–23, 37; Soul 46–47, 50, 57; Scap. 4. Disasters: Marc. 2.14; Flee. 2. Moral evils: Apol. 22, 27.

62. Idol. passim. Idol. 9: astrology and magic; Soul 57: magic; Shows 10: soothsaying. Tertullian followed Justin and Tatian here. The gods are really demons, who devour the smoke and blood of sacrifices. Shows 4, 8, 9. Shows 8: "spiritus diaboli" infuse paganism. Scap. 2; Apol. 22–24; Soul 39. Pagan myths and rites: Apol. 47; Her. 40; Bapt. 5; Cor. 15; Wife 1.

63. Apol. 50: "Semen est sanguis Christianorum." Flee. 2; Scap. 5: "Your cruelty is our glory"; Scorp. 6; Apol. 27; Pen. 7.

64. Barnes, p. 179.

65. Her. 40. Also 3–6, 21, 34, 38–39 and passim; Soul 35; Prax. 1; Mod. 13.

virtuous, this is only a snare of the Devil, who can transform himself at will into an angel of light. Tertullian raised again the dangerous doctrine characterizing certain people as soldiers in Satan's vast army. Not only that. He moved a step back from the discernment of spirits, the idea that one can distinguish between God's work and the Devil's by their fruits. By insisting instead that good lives lived by heretics and infidels cannot actually be good but are always disguised works of the Devil, Tertullian and the other fathers laid the basis for centuries of persecution of Jews, heretics, and witches.[66]

Tertullian, with his moralistic emphasis, paid great attention to the activities of the Devil in daily life. Astrology, necromancy, magic, and all the arts are by nature demonic.[67] Tertullian's work on "Shows" has for its theme the diabolical nature of entertainments—including horseraces, baths, taverns, and theaters (not to mention brothels), and even entertainment in private homes. In the first place they are idolatrous; in the second they provoke passions that cause us to lose our reason; in the third they are empty lies. Women's makeup and elaborate dress distort the truth. Tertullian did not intend these statements as metaphor or hyperbole; he meant quite literally that the Devil was present in such activities. It was a lie for a woman to make herself up to look different from what she was, a lie for an actor to play a part. Shows are an integral part of the Devil's plan to corrupt the world. Those who participate even as spectators are actually servants of the Devil. The theaters are the congregation of Satan.[68] "Whoever enters into communion with the Devil by

66. The dangers of abuse in such a doctrine are evident. Even those convinced that the Devil exists and is active in the world nonetheless can never have sufficient evidence to assert that any individual person is controlled by the Devil completely, and so damned. On this doctrine in Tertullian: Her. 34: Valentine and the other heretics receive honor and grace from the Devil, who uses them as tools in his war against God. Her. 31: the image of the Devil as the sower of weeds.

67. Shows 10; Soul 57. Daniélou, *Origins*, pp. 162–167, argued that Tertullian had first-hand familiarity with the Book of Enoch.

68. For example, a woman who goes to the theater comes home possessed: Shows 38; Theaters: Shows 25: "Diaboli ecclesiam."

going to shows separates himself from the Lord."[69] The Devil also provokes other immoralities such as lust, impatience, and anger, though he can never compel, but only prompt, us to sin.[70]

Against the constant temptations of the Devil and his demons, who swarm through the air in vast numbers, the Christian has but one protection: Jesus Christ. Even more bluntly than Irenaeus, Tertullian argued that the primary function of Christ's Passion was to redeem us from the Devil. "If the Son of God has appeared, it is to destroy the works of the Devil." It was Christ's suffering on our behalf that crushed the Devil and sent him sprawling for the second time. Christians thus can use the name of Christ and the sign of the cross to rout demons. But the most efficacious way, in fact the sole necessary way, of obtaining Christ's protection is through baptism. "If the Son of God has appeared . . . to destroy the works of the Devil, he has destroyed them by delivering the soul through baptism." Baptism resembles the miracle worked for Moses at the Red Sea. Believers pass through the dangerous waters of this world by means of the grace of baptism, but the Devil drowns like Pharoah in the flood.[71]

"When we have entered the water" of baptism, "we confess our faith according to the words of divine law, and we declare that we have renounced the Devil, his pomp, and his angels." Infidels do not have this advantage. Unbaptized, we remain the

69. Shows 26: "De his qui cum diabolo apud spectacula communicando a domino exciderunt." Tertullian's view of the theater no longer seems absurd, given the quality of contemporary cinema and television.

70. Pat. 5; Mod. 13. Women 1.2: lust comes from the "angels that we renounced in baptism."

71. Mod. 19; Flee. 12: "Et Dominus quidem illum [hominem] redemit ab angelis mundi tenentibus potestatibus, a spiritalibus nequitiae, a tenebris huius aevi, a judicio aeterno, a morte perpetua" (*sic*; the syntax is unclear): and the Lord has truly redeemed humanity from the angels of this world who hold power over it, from the spiritual forces of iniquity, and from the shadows of this world (*aevus*, used as the equivalent of *aiōn*), from eternal judgment and perpetual death": Idol. 5.6; Marc. 3.18: "The cross, by which the serpent, the Devil, was degraded" (crucis qua serpens diabolus publicabatur). Cross: Apol. 23. Baptism: Mod. 19. Pharoah: Bapt. 9. Saint Paul had already (1 Corinthians 10:2) made the analogy, but Tertullian introduced the image of the Devil drowning in the waters of baptism.

prey of demons; baptized, we have the power of Christ over them and can repel them with his help. Tertullian did not invent the word "pomp," but he was the first Latin writer to use it pointedly. "Here is what the pomps of the Devil are," he explained, "worldly dignities, honors, solemnities, and, at the heart of them all, idolatry. Shows, luxuries, and all the vanities of this world are rooted in idolatry, the veneration of the works of Satan instead of the works of the Lord."[72] If one's ultimate concern is money or some other worldly value more than God, then one is an idolater, worshiping something in God's place. Tertullian wrote at the time that baptismal procedures were just becoming standardized. Until about A.D. 200, baptism was often preceded by a rite of exorcism. Beginning about 200, the exorcism and formal renunciation of Satan were incorporated into the baptismal rite. Possibly this change was a result of Gnostic influence. Tertullian and his contemporary Hippolytus helped standardize the practice. From their time onward, the renunciation of Satan was the first important act of baptism.

By the third century, three distinct elements occurred in the Christian's confrontation with the Devil at baptism, according to a study by H. A. Kelly: (1) the expulsion of demons from the candidate by exorcism; (2) the voluntary renunciation of the Devil on the part of the candidate; (3) prophylactic measures against future demonic assaults upon the new Christian. Exorcism was employed in two ways: first, the exorcism of the water and chrism used at baptism; second, the exorcism of the candidate himself.[73] The exorcism of the candidate, which appeared

---

72. Shows 4: "Renuntiasse nos diabolo et pompae eius ore nostro contestamur." Power of baptism: Apol. 27. Vanities: Shows 4, 12; Idol. 18. See J. H. Waszink, *"Pompa diaboli," Vigiliae Christianae,* 1 (1947), 13–41, esp. p. 36, and Daniélou, *Origins,* pp. 412–418. Daniélou argues that the whole secular world—the Roman state as well as pagan religion—was *pompa diaboli* for Tertullian.

73. H. A. Kelly, "The Struggle against Satan in the Liturgies of Baptism and Easter," *Chronica,* 24 (Spring 1979), 9–10. J. A. Jungmann, *The Early Liturgy: To the Time of Gregory the Great* (Notre Dame, Ind., 1959), p. 80. On baptism see also J. N. D. Kelly, *Early Christian Creeds* (London, 1958), pp. 31–38, 44, 399–409; H. A. Kelly, *The Devil,* passim. H. A. Kelly is also the author of a forthcoming study of the Devil in the baptismal rite, *The Devil at Baptism: The Demonic Dramaturgy of Christian Initiation.* See also Lukken.

The earliest known representation of the Devil or a demon in Christian art are these black figures being cast out of a pair of demoniacs. Illumination from the Rabbula Gospels, A.D. 586. The language is Syriac. Courtesy of the Bibliotheca Medicea Laurenziana, Florence.

in some early baptismal rites, possibly under the influence of Valentinian Gnosticism, gradually increased, although it carried the unacceptable theological connotation that the candidate was not only subject to Satan through original sin but was also actually and literally possessed by demons. The voluntary renunciation of Satan remained part of the tradition, symbolizing as it did the candidate's transition from the army of Satan to that of Christ. The oldest known renunciation formula is found in the early third-century "Apostolic Tradition" of Saint Hippolytus: "I renounce you, Satan, and your angels, and your vanities [*pompae*]." This renunciation was in most rites followed by the creed, making the conversion from Satan to Christ sharp and clear. In the fourth century the candidate commonly faced the west, the direction of sunset and death, to renounce Satan, and then turned to the east, toward the sunrise and light, to express his acceptance of Christ. In Greek, the renunciation was called the *apotaxis* and the submission to Christ the *syntaxis*, emphasizing the parallelism and specifically indicating the transfer of the Christian from the army (*taxis*) of the Devil to that of Christ.[74] Kelly argues that the third element, the prophylaxis against future temptation, was comparatively neglected, although it fitted the systematic demonology being developed by the fathers. The prophylaxis entailed the candidate's solemn promise to resist sin and demonic temptation in the future. The water and oil of baptism were formally exorcised in order to drive out the Devil.[75] From the time of Hippolytus and Tertullian, all baptismal liturgies in common use made the renunciation of Satan an integral part of the process of entering the Christian community, and many, especially in the East, also incorporated exorcism of the candidate. This emphasis was not nugatory. It was universally believed that the Devil holds us in his power until we are saved from him by the Passion, and that we obtain the benefits of Christ's sacrifice by baptism.[76]

The punishment of the Devil and the demons is threefold. First, they are cast out of heaven in punishment for their first sin. Second, their iron grip on the world is shattered by the Passion of Christ. But they still range the world to our harm, so a third, final punishment awaits them at the end of the world. When Christ comes again, they will burn forever in the fires of hell. Gradually a consensus arose, although usually implicit and unexpressed, that this threefold punishment occurs in three stages; in this way the fathers were able to resolve the apparent chronological contradictions in the tradition.[77]

74. The "Apostolic Tradition" of Hippolytus exists only in a later version, but the formula is so close to that reported by Tertullian that it can safely be ascribed to the time of Hippolytus.

75. Lukken, p. 24: "ipsum inimicum eradicare et explantare cum angelis suis inimicis."

76. Lukken, p. 39.

77. Marc. 2.10; Body 14; Women 2.10.

Two other fathers, Minucius Felix at the end of the second century and Cyprian in the third, both influenced by Tertullian, made minor contributions to diabology. Minucius, a rhetorician and lawyer at Rome, wrote a vivid dialogue called "Octavius," which was largely devoted to refuting the charges made against the Christians by the pagans.[78] Drawing upon Platonism, Minucius blurred the distinctions between classical demons, Christian demons, and Christian angels. The philosophers, like the Christians, recognized the existence of "unclean and wandering spirits" degraded from their heavenly status by earthly filth and lust.[79] Both demons and angels are attenuated spirits, and both may be seen as envoys or ministers of God, but while angels continue to dwell in heaven, demons dwell on earth. The demons are totally wrapped in error, being deceived as well as deceivers.[80] When the evil angels fell, they

78. Minucius was born about 150 and died about 210. For the "Octavius," see the Essay on the Sources. See also J.-P. Waltzing, "Le crime rituel reproché aux chrétiens du IIe siècle," *Bulletin de l'Académie royale des sciences, des lettres, et des beaux-arts de Belgique* (Brussels, 1925); J. B. Russell and M. W. Wyndham, "Witchcraft and the Demonization of Heresy," *Mediaevalia*, 2 (1976), 1–21.

79. Oct. 26.

80. Oct. 27: "deceived and deceivers" (nam et falluntur et fallunt). Oct. 26: angels and demons as *nuntii* and *ministri* of God. Oct. 27: Demons and angels as *spiritus tenues*. See R. Berge, "Exegetische Bemerkungen zur Dämonenauffassung des M. Minucius Felix," diss. University of Freiburg im Breisgau, 1929. Berge comments on the use of *spiritus* in Minucius and many of the fathers. For Minucius a *spiritus* is (1) air in motion, e.g., a wind, (2) breath; (3) life; (4) soul; (5) a spiritual being. The Devil is clearly a *spiritus* in this last sense. The multiple meanings this term possesses, however, make it a fuzzy-bordered concept in Latin, Greek, and modern languages as well: in Greek, the distinction between πνεῦμα and ψυχή; in Latin the constellation *anima, animus, spiritus*; in German *Geist* and *Seele*; in French *âme* and *esprit*; in English "soul," "mind," and "spirit." Humphrey Carpenter points out: "When we translate the Latin *spiritus* we have to render it either as spirit or as breath or as wind depending on the context. But early users of language would not have made any distinction between these meanings. To them a word [such as] *spiritus* meant something like spirit-breath-wind. When the wind blew, it was not merely like someone breathing: it was the breath of a god. And when an early speaker talked about his soul as *spiritus* he did not merely mean that it was like a breath: it was to him just that, the breath of life" (*The Inklings*, [Boston, 1979], p. 41.)

Efforts by philosophers and theologians to distinguish among soul, mind,

lost their simplicity of substance and took on a substance halfway between mortal and immortal.[81]

Cyprian, born about 200 into an upper-middle-class family, was educated in rhetoric and had a wide circle of worldly friends. He was converted and baptized about 245 and withdrew into ascetic seclusion, until he was summoned back to the active life to become bishop of Carthage in 248. He took a fairly hard line against those Christians who had renounced the faith during the severe persecution of Decius, but he supported Rome in opposition to Novatian, who utterly condemned the lapsed. Cyprian was martyred in 258 during the persecution of Valerian. In such painful times of danger and fear, Cyprian counseled patience, courage, and faith.[82] Though emphasizing the Devil less than his fellow Carthaginian, he followed Tertullian, whom he regarded as his "master," in arguing that the Devil works to pervert and distort God's creation. A liar and a deceiver from the beginning, Satan had been created as a great angel of majesty who then became the first of all beings to sin. He fell out of envy and jealousy of humanity and then used these and other vices to tempt us to our own original sin.[83] His

and spirit have not been very successful. Generally speaking, the Christian tradition attempted to distinguish among "soul," the immortal element in a human being, and "spirit," a spiritual being, though a "soul" could be a "spirit." It has always been unclear whether "mind" is mortal or whether it is to be equated with "soul," whether, in other words, it is to be linked with the brain-body-material world or with the spiritual world. Further, most of the fathers attributed a tenuous "body" to the spirits. Thus the definition of the Devil as a "spirit," though firmly fixed in the concept, has never conveyed a precise meaning.

81. Oct. 26–27, esp. 26.8. The pagan gods are demons; the demons cause natural and moral evils, stir up persecutions, and persuade people to believe the Christians guilty of perverse crimes such as incest, cannibalism, and infanticide.

82. For Cyprian's works, see the Essay on the Sources. They include "Letters," "The Unity of the Christian Church" (Unit.), and "Jealousy" (Jeal.). The theme of jealousy and envy—ζῆλος and φθόνος—goes back to the apostles: Daniélou, *Origins*, p. 72. An agreeable essay on Cyprian is P. Hinchliff, *Cyprian of Carthage and the Unity of the Christian Church* (London, 1974).

83. Unit. 1; Jeal. 1–4: the temptations of luxury and pleasure. Jeal. 2 presents a convincing psychological picture of the temptation offered by Satan. The Devil circles around each of us, and, like an enemy laying siege to men

chief works are persecution—the attack upon the Christian community from without—and heresy—the attack on it from within. The Devil provokes persecutions and stands against the athletes of Christ like a gladiator in the arena. The martyrs are soldiers under the generalship of Christ fighting against the hosts of Satan.[84] Schism is also the Devil's work. Heretics and schismatics believe that they are right, because the Devil has deceived them by appearing in the form of an angel of light, but in fact heretics are antichrists. The Devil does not persecute the heretics because they are already his.[85] Baptism by a heretic or schismatic is not only invalid but even creates a child of the Devil rather than a child of God.[86] The daily life of the Christian is a constant struggle against Satan, but sin ultimately is our responsibility. All evil comes from our own sin; all the good in us comes from Christ.[87]

---

enclosed in a town, he examines the walls, looking for some section that is less solid and secure than the rest, so that he can force his way in through this weak spot. He appears in seductive shapes, offering easy pleasures so as to weaken us through vice. He stirs up the tongue to insults and urges the hand to murder. He suggests possibilities of illicit gain so as to encourage the practice of fraud. Daniélou, *Origins*, p. 423.

84. Letter 10.5, 11.4, 38.1, 39.2–3, Jeal. 2–3. See E. Hummel, *The Concept of Martyrdom According to Saint Cyprian of Carthage* (Washington, 1946).

85. Letter 61.3.

86. Unit. 1, 4, 8, 15, 16; Letters 24, 51, 65 (idolatry as demonolatry), 73. Letters 58.10: the heretics as rebels and deserters from Christ's army: "miseri qui Dei desertores aut contra Deum rebelles voluntatem fecerunt diaboli."

87. Jeal. 3; Letter 1.4: the victorious Christian soldier, having defeated Satan by means of living a good life, is awarded a crown or a palm, and the martyr gains a special crimson crown of glory. See Hummel, pp. 88–90.

5 Mercy and Damnation: The Alexandrians

Why does one person sin and another not? Why does one person suffer more than another, the good often more than the corrupt? Can the inequalities in the worldly and spiritual fortunes of individuals be reconciled with the justice of God? Can they be reconciled with his mercy? Clement and Origen of Alexandria addressed themselves to these questions.

Clement (c. 150–210) was born a pagan. He studied and taught at Athens and at Alexandria. Alexandria was the cultural pole of Christianity, the center of Christian philosophy and theology, as Rome was the doctrinal pole.[1] Clement's breadth of knowledge and his open, seeking mind are apparent in his writings, which are philosophical, allegorical, gnostic in the broad sense, and characterized by ethical sensitivity and psychological understanding.

Steeped in philosophy, particularly that of the Stoics, the Middle Platonists, and the great Alexandrian Jewish scholar Philo, Clement showed an openness to pagan thought surpassing even that of Justin. Clement's mind in many respects resembled that of his Neoplatonic contemporary Plotinus. After his conversion to Christianity, Clement became a staunch opponent of pagan religion, but, like Justin, he continued to seek

1. J. Daniélou and H.-I. Marrou, *The Christian Centuries: The First Six Hundred Years* (London, 1964), p. 128.

philosophical truth, insisting that philosophy when properly understood pointed to Christ. Socrates had argued that we must examine our lives; Clement added that we must examine them in the light of divine revelation.

Clement keenly felt the contradiction of evil in God's creation and attempted to explain it within a coherent philosophical system.[2] His morality, though not nearly so extreme as Tertullian's, was a synthesis of Judeo-Christian with Stoic ethics.[3]

The Alexandrians, Jewish and Christian, introduced the use of allegory in the interpretation of Scriptures, arguing that biblical texts were to be understood in at least three discrete ways: literal, moral, and transcendent. For Clement, the Devil exists metaphysically and objectively, but he is also a metaphor for the evil activity of the human soul. One modern scholar argued that Clement "vacillates between" the two positions, but he is better understood as synthesizing them.[4] The Devil exists both inside the human mind and outside it.[5]

His Platonic philosophy caused Clement to emphasize ontology (the abstract science of being) instead of diabology, and the nonbeing of evil more than the brooding presence of evil's master. Although he was less interested in the Devil than either Tertullian or Origen, he nonetheless took him seriously, on the basis both of Christian tradition and of his concern with Gnosticism. Clement was influenced by the widespread dualism of his time, accepting that Jesus had come down to earth to reveal the hidden deity to a select few and teach them saving knowledge.[6] He adapted elements of Platonic emanationism to his own system of Christianity, but he completely rejected the

2. W. E. G. Floyd, *Clement of Alexandria's Treatment of the Problem of Evil* (New York, 1971), p. 99.

3. On Clement's work, see the Essay on the Sources. The works cited here are "The Tutor" (Tut.); the "Miscellanea" (Misc.); "The Rich Man's Salvation" (Rich); the "Protrepticon" (Pro.); fragments of the "Theodotus" (Theod.); and the *Exhortation to the Greeks* (Exhort.).

4. Floyd, p. 72.

5. See Evagrius' perceptive psychology of demonology, below, p. 178.

6. S. Lilla, *Clement of Alexandria: A Study in Christian Platonism and Gnosticism* (London, 1971).

elaborate mythological paraphernalia of Gnosticism and its exaggerated dualism. His theory of evil derives in part from his opposition to Gnostic ideas.[7]

Clement was the first Christian to attempt an explanation of evil in terms of ontology and the theology of privation. According to this theory, evil does not really exist in itself but is mere lack of being. Privation, which reflects the influence of Platonic and Gnostic emanationism, introduced a confusing, unnecessary element into Christian diabology. Clement began with God's being. God exists absolutely; his being is total and perfect, and it is totally and perfectly good. Only God is perfect; whatever else may exist is necessarily less real and good. God creates the world from nothing.[8] His motive for doing so is sheer generosity: though complete in himself, he wishes to share his goodness and extend it to other beings. Since he alone exists, he must create these other beings.[9] Because only God is perfect, the created world is necessarily imperfect. It is real, but not wholly real; good, but not fully good. This cosmos is only a poor, deficient copy of true reality.[10]

Not everything is equally deficient. A vast variety of forms

7. Floyd, p. 91.
8. It is not clear what Clement meant by "from nothing." He used the phrase ἐκ μὴ ὄντος rather than ἐξ οὐκ ὄντος. Since μὴ is a conditional negative rather than the absolute negative οὐκ, it is likely that he did not mean *ex nihilo*, but rather from unformed matter, ὕλη, which both Clement and the Neoplatonists regarded as *almost* total nonbeing. In such systems, the more real a thing is the more spiritual it is; the less real it is, the more material it is. Matter is, as Gilson once put it, tottering on the verge of unreality. This idealism is philosophically the exact opposite of the materialism prevalent in western culture today.
9. Tut. 1.9.88; Floyd, p. 13.
10. The source of this idea is Plato's cave, and its strength has been felt by all generations. Even in modern materialist society, many people respond with immediate intuitive understanding of Plato's metaphor, especially when it is translated into the obvious modern analogy: if one had spent one's entire life in a darkened cinema, seeing only what was projected on the screen, one would have but a shadowy, flickering, two-dimensional view of the world; once let outside, one would be dazzled and amazed by the rich riot of reality. This world is like the cinema screen, narrow, flat, and grossly inferior in comparison with God's world.

compose the cosmos, and the differences among these forms make it inevitable that some are more deficient than others. A chain of being can therefore be constructed. Beings lower on the scale are less real, less good, and less spiritual than beings higher on the scale; that is to say they *lack* more reality and goodness, they are more *deprived*. God, at the top, is perfect being and perfect goodness, wholly spirit. Below God range the angels, in turn divided hierarchically among themselves, the greatest angels being the most real, most good, and closest to God. Below angels come humans, then animals, plants, stones, and so on down to primal, unformed matter, *hylē*, which is least real, least good, least spiritual, most deprived of being, and consequently most evil.[11]

Since evil is the opposite of good, lack or privation is evil: here the argument confuses the moral and the ontological and

11. Clement adopted a modified version of the Platonist distinction between the κόσμος νοητός, the spiritual world of God and the angels, and the κόσμος αἰσθητός, the material world of humans and their inferiors. The *kosmos aisthētos* is but a pale copy of the *kosmos noētos*. Though Clement insists that the world was created rather than being produced by emanation, as the Platonists argued, his chain of being is really an adaptation of emanationism to Christian creationism. The two do not fit snugly, so the system, used by Augustine, Aquinas, and many other theologians, has never really worked. For matter as (almost) wholly evil in Plotinus, see Russell, *The Devil*, pp. 161–166, where, however, I blurred a distinction between Plotinus' position and that of the Christians. For Plotinus, the ultimate principle, τὸ ἕν, The One, precedes Being. Being is an attribute of The One and is engendered by The One, while for the Christians The One and Being were essentially identical. Clement's position on matter was ambiguous. For the Platonists, matter, being farthest from God, was almost wholly evil. For the Gnostics, matter was a vicious creation of an evil God. Clement sharply rejected the Gnostic position, but he leaned toward the Platonist theory that unformed matter is eternal and uncreated, and that God's creation is the imposition of form onto this preexisting matter. In this view, matter can be evil, a shadowy nothing-like thing resisting the efforts of God to form it. If God did create the universe from nothing, however, matter must at least possess some goodness and being. Clement was ambiguous, but he accepted that God either created matter or at least used it, and he insisted (Misc. 6.9) against the Gnostic Docetists that Christ had a real, material body. Clement and Origen also followed the Platonists in their division of intelligent beings into gods, humans, and demons, with the modification that they transformed the gods into angels. All the fathers rejected the Neoplatonist view that God creates the gods/angels, who in turn create humans.

begins to break down. Evil is mere privation; it is nonbeing, lack of reality. Now God chooses to create the best possible cosmos. It is not a perfect world, far from it, but it is the best world that can possibly exist. For the reason that nothing but God is wholly good, everything else must of logical necessity be to some degree less good, hence more evil. Thus evil is the inevitable by-product of creation. The cosmos is impossible without evil. One of the virtues of this argument is that it creates a spectrum from good to evil rather than a simplistic dichotomy between the two. But it fails to draw any line in the spectrum: if the best angel is less good than God, but still the best of all created beings, what sense does it make to call that being evil? And if he is not called evil, at what point in the descending spectrum are we in fact entitled to call a being evil?

The idea of the "great chain of being" was adopted by many subsequent theologians and philosophers. Ontological rather than moral, speaking to the problem of theodicy rather than to that of sin and redemption, it was better fitted for convincing philosophers than for heartening believers. The theodicy of privation is at bottom incongruent with the theology of atonement. The inconsistencies are apparent. As Frances Young put it, "God is love; God is angry. God is ultimately responsible for everything; the Devil is responsible for evil. God sent his Son to overcome evil; God has been placated by his Son's sacrifice."[12] Clement's theodicy emphasized the nonbeing of evil, while at the same time his atonement theory insisted that the reality of evil had alienated humanity from God. The overlay does not match.

Privation theory is incoherent: it may help to explain natural, physical evils, but it is irrelevant to the question of moral choice. "If evil is merely deprivation of good, why should morally free agents choose it in preference to good? If evil is the absence of good, whence comes malicious evil, deliberate rebellion?"[13] The confusion is gross. A man is ontologically higher than a cow. Then which is "better," a healthy, produc-

12. Young, "Insight or Incoherence," p. 24.
13. Young, p. 122.

tive cow, or a degenerate human sadist? A genius is ontologically higher than a retarded person. Then which is "better," a
kind retarded person or a cruel and vicious genius? The questions appear absurd because they are in fact absurd: the ontological and the moral cannot fit into the same scale.

Nowhere is the confusion more evident than in diabology. In
privation theory the Devil, being one of the angels, is ontologically very high on the scale; yet morally he is the lowest and
most debased of all beings. Ontologically, unformed matter is
the furthest from God; morally the Devil is furthest; yet any
connection between the Devil and matter is both tenuous and
illogical.

A third confusion, most basic of all, relates to the nature of
being and nonbeing. Clement said that evil does not exist. But
he was aware of rape, murder, torture, and war. When he said
that evil has no being, he really meant that evil does not share
in God's mode of being, which is absolute reality and absolute
good. Evil cannot be said to *be*, Clement thought, because it is
merely *absence* of good, like the holes in a Swiss cheese, which
are defined only by their quality of not being cheese. Yet at the
same time that he argued for the nonbeing of evil, he had to
admit that evil exercises real power, that it does act in the
world. And at this point his argument becomes virtually
meaningless: evil exists, with real, observable consequences, except that it does not share in real being and therefore does not
really exist. This irritating confusion results from the ambiguous use of "real." It is logically consistent, if not particularly
helpful, to define God's sort of being as excluding other kinds
of being; but it is neither consistent nor helpful to go on and say
that these other kinds do not have being at all; and it is hopeless
then to confuse this alleged ontological nonbeing with moral
fault. Clement's theodicy was unworkable, and though many
thinkers followed it for centuries, ultimately it was abandoned.

The Devil was created good, in Clement's view, because it is
impossible that God should hate anything that he creates.[14] The

14. Ped. 1.8: God creates only good. Since he does not will evil, he creates
nothing evil. All that is is good; God hates nothing that is. Christ, by whom
God created all things, loves all things.

Devil was a prince among angels, high in the chain of being, and turned to evil of his own free will. The first to fall, he became the chief of all evil intelligences in opposition to God.[15] Once the Devil fell, he persuaded some of the other angels to follow his banner.[16] The Devil is a thief and robber, a liar, an apostate, the accuser of sinners, a seducer, a serpent, and the scriptural "man of blood."

Following his own departure from grace, he did everything he could to alienate humans from God. Clement insisted upon the supreme importance of free will: the Devil has license to tempt, but no power to compel us to sin. He eagerly urged Adam and Eve to rebel, but the cause of their fault was neither God nor the Devil, but their own misuse of free will.[17] The

15. Misc. 5.14: τῶν δαιμονίων ἄρχοντα, "leader of demons." Misc. 1.17: ὁ δὲ διάβολος αὐτεξούσιος ὢν καὶ μετανοῆσαι οἷός τε ἦν καὶ κλέψαι, καὶ ὁ αἴτιος αὐτὸς τῆς κλοπῆς, οὐχ ὁ μὴ κωλύσας κύριος (The Devil, having free will either to renounce his theft of divine grace or else to steal it, is alone responsible for his theft; the Lord is not responsible simply because he permitted the sin to occur). Misc. 3.4: εἷς δέ τις, τῶν ὑπ' αὐτοῦ γεγονότων ἐπέσπεισεν τὰ ζιζάνια, τὴν τῶν κακῶν φύσιν γεννήσας, οἷς καὶ δὴ πάντας ἡμᾶς περιέβαλεν, ἀντιτάξας ἡμᾶς τῷ Πατρί (One among them fell and, sowing weeds in the harvest, generated evil nature; he took the rest of us with him, making us adversaries of the Father). God grows the wheat for a good harvest, but the Devil spoils it.

16. Misc. 3.7, 5.14. The fallen angels and the demons may or may not be identical. Both are sometimes identified with the pagan gods: Tut. 3.1–3.3; Prot. 1–4; Misc. 2.20, 6.3. Clement followed the old two roads metaphor of the apostolic fathers and expressed it in terms similar to those used by Valentine and the Gnostics. For Clement two kinds of angels exist—good angels of the "right hand" and evil angels of the "left hand" (δέξιοι or λαοὶ ἄγγελοι or δυνάμεις). The two types of angels struggle over human souls, especially at the particular, individual judgment that each soul must undergo immediately upon death: Rich 42.16–18; Theod. 34, 73. Clement offered no specific view of the Devil's fall, but he assumed that it was different from that of the other angels, who fell from lust. He accepted the Watcher story, but excluded the Devil from it: Tut. 3.2; Misc. 3.7, 5.1, 7.7. Like most of the fathers (Origen was the notable exception) he believed that the angels fell together and instantaneously, not by gradual degrees.

17. He is also identified with Pan and Belial. Misc. 1.17, 3.4, 5.8–9, 6.8; Exhort. 11.86. The man of blood, ἄνδρα αἱμάτων, Tut. 1.5, derives from Psalms 5:7. In Tut. 1.8 the Devil is ἀντικείμενος again (cf. p. 34 above). Misc. 4.14: ἀντίδικος, "adversary." Alienation: Misc. 2.13, 4.12. No power to compel: Misc. 4.12. Original sin: Misc. 3.12, 3.16–17, Tut. 3.2: the Devil tempted Adam and Eve through their curiosity, διὰ τῆς φιλοδοξίας.

Devil is less the agent of sin than its abettor, and "evil has taken hold of the human race because of its [own] faithlessness."[18] Original sin is an event in eternity transcending time. Though it occurred at one moment, it also occurs in every moment. Thus all humans sinned and sin together with Adam and Eve and in Adam and Eve. We are all responsible for original sin. That sin was and is our free choice to prefer our own will to God's, to choose illusion and nonbeing instead of what is true and good and real. The results of original sin were horrendous. It disturbed the entire cosmos.[19] The notion that natural ills would not have occurred without our own first fault long persisted in Christian tradition. It proceeded from the fact that Clement set the fall of humanity in the center of the cosmic stage rather than the fall of the Devil. Logically, the fall of the prince of angels, ontologically higher and chronologically prior, should have been the act that disrupted the cosmos. But for Clement, humanity, not the angels, was the focus of God's concern, for it is we who are made in his image and likeness.

18. Tut. 1.8. The Devil is always συνεργός of sin rather than ἐνεργός. Clement was close to Irenaeus in his insistence on human responsibility and free will (Tut. 1.13) and stood in a long tradition of freedom stretching from Irenaeus to Molina, as opposed to the more usual predestinarian tradition. But Floyd, p. 73, overstates the argument: "Clearly, the source of iniquity is not Satan; it is the sinful will, both angelic and human." Satan, the first being to sin, always and everywhere urges everyone else to do evil. Sin is his fault more than ours—we would sin on our own, but our sins are both more frequent and more vicious because he exists.

19. Clement's view was similar to that of Irenaeus: Adam and Eve sinned because they were childish and immature, well down on the ontological scale. This again confuses the ontological and the moral and makes it difficult to explain how such a high ontological being as the Devil also fell. See Floyd, p. 52. Original sin created in all subsequent humans a tendency to the irrational, τὸ ἄλογον (Ped. 1.13; Floyd, p. 54) and a proneness to sin that was part perversion of will and part perversion of intellect (Misc. 6.12). But the doctrine of the immaturity of humans allows for the idea of the *felix culpa*, the "fortunate fall," since humanity's sin and expulsion is a learning experience by which we gradually grow in the grace of God. Illusion: Misc. 2.19. Results of original sin: Misc. 4.14, 6.2–3, 7.11. This seems another confusion of ontological and moral, since human moral sin would not logically disrupt the physical universe.

Original sin made slaves of us; henceforth we were bound to Satan's will until the suffering of Christ liberated us.[20]

Once we had fallen into vice, the Devil and his helpers obtained God's permission to continue putting us to the test. They incite us to sin, but only our free choice admits them into our hearts.[21] The demons attempt to disrupt our reason and to lead us astray by playing upon our pleasure, they lie to us, causing us to mistake false pleasure for true joy and worldly glamour for holy beauty, and they cow us by using violence and fear. Their never-changing purpose is to lead us off the road of salvation. Every unjust person is under Satan's power whether he knows it or not, and each time a person yields to sin, the Devil's power grows within his soul. With each sin we become more alienated from Christ and confirmed in error. Among the sins that the demons promote are idolatry, heresy, atheism, evil dreams, magic, persecutions, and moral vices.[22] They sometimes take over people's bodies by possession, but most evil acts are done by people acting of their own will, not by demons acting in them.[23]

Though the Devil is the cause of pagan idolatry, Clement

20. Pro. 7, 11; Misc. 1.11, 4.14, 6.3; Tut. 1.8–9. Exhort. 1.7, 2.13, 2.20, 4.12.

21. Misc. 2.19–20.

22. Misc. 2.13, 2.20, 3.15, 5.14. Stoic influence can be seen in the idea that demons introduce false images into our minds, which we mistake for reality. Purpose: Misc. 1.17, 2.13. Devil's power in soul: Misc. 1.19, 2.20. Alienation: Tut. 1.13. We become more *alogos*, that is, more alienated from the *Logos*, Christ. Idolatry: Tut. 2.1, 2.9–10, 2.20; Exhort. passim; Pro. 2–4, 10. Paganism is an ἀπάτη, a deceit of the serpent: Pro. 2. Heresy: Misc. 1.17, 3.6, 6.8. Atheism: Exhort. 2.21: "Atheism and demonolatry are two opposite stupidities." Evil dreams: Tut. 2.9. Magic: Exhort. 4.52: magicians employ demons as their helpers. Persecutions: Rich 25. Vices: Rich 37; Exhort. 2.53; Tut. 2.1, 2.12, 3.2; Misc. 2.20, 3.12: fornication and intemperance are "diabolical passions," διαβολικὰ πάθη, and lust is the work of the Devil, τὸ τοῦ διαβόλου ἔργον.

23. Misc. 1.21, 2.20. Clement blurred the distinction between voluntary submission to the Devil through sin on the one hand, and possession, which is always involuntary, on the other. It was his emphasis on free will that caused him to associate the two: "By choosing the same things as demons, by sinning, being unstable, [the sinner] becomes a demoniac man" (Floyd, p. 71).

insisted that he is not the cause of pagan philosophy. He argued against the idea that elements of truth existed in Greek philosophy because an evil angel or angels had stolen them from God and then taught them to the philosophers. He also rejected the belief that philosophy was one of the evil arts that the Watchers taught to the daughters of men. For Clement, Greek philosophy was an illumination sent from God. Its differences with Christianity arose because the Devil fogged it with error, so that it can be only a hazy approximation of the truth. The only complete philosophy is Christian philosophy, which refines out these impurities and conveys the truth of God undistorted.[24]

As a result of original sin, we lay for ages under the dominion of death, and though we retained freedom of will, our wills were bowed heavily down toward sin.[25] For centuries we were pummeled almost to death by the savage blows of the world-rulers of darkness, who inflicted terrible wounds of lust, war, and deceit upon us. These evil powers held us in their prisons.[26] But Christ's saving act broke death's dominion, healed our wounds, strengthened our wills, and restored our freedom whole and entire to choose between God and evil.[27] God had sent Christ as his agent to conquer the powers of evil, and it struck Clement as dramatic that of all people since Eden the

24. Misc. 1.16–17, 5.1, 6.8, 6.17.

25. Pro. 1–4, 7; Misc. 1.18. For a NT root of the idea of the Passion as the defeat of evil powers, see Ephesians 2:2. Baptism represents a triumph of the Christian Trinity over the "trinity of corruption, consisting of the Devil, his Son the Antichrist, and the Evil Spirit, that is, the operation of the sinful inclination resulting from original sin." Theod. 80.3: πάσης τῆς ἐν φθορᾷ τριάδος, "of the whole trinity of corruption." See Antonio Orbe, "La trinidad maléfica (a proposito de l' 'Excerpta ex Theodoto' 80.3)," *Gregorianum*, 49 (1968), 726–761.

26. Rich 29: By the world-rulers of darkness: ὑπὸ τῶν κοσμοκρατόρων τοῦ σκότους. Misc. 1.17: Satan as a thief and robber: λῃστὴς δὲ καὶ κλέπτης ὁ διάβολος λέγεται. Here Clement draws on John 10:8.

27. Floyd, p. 91. Tut. 2.8; Misc. 1.19: liberates us from the power of Satan, τῆς ἐξουσίας τοῦ Σατανᾶ; Rich 23: I have saved you, ἐλυτροσάμην. This verb seems to imply redemption through sacrifice, λύτρον. Rich 28 uses the parable of the Good Samaritan, with Christ as the Samaritan, us humans as the beaten man, and the demons as the robbers.

Christians were the very first to be released from sin and separated from the Devil.[28]

As to the mode of the Passion's operation—whether it was sacrifice or ransom—Clement was unclear: even its effects lack definition. Resistance to the Devil still requires constant watchfulness and determination, just as it always did. The process of salvation is gradual, Clement believed. Even before Christ the Devil lacked the power to force us to sin, and Christ's Passion has only weakened, not wholly eliminated, Satan's influence. Christ reopened the road to grace, but we must choose to make the journey for ourselves.[29] The Passion's supreme effect is that it gives each human being a chance to undergo a process of transformation through participation in the divine nature.[30] Souls drained by sin can be filled with the being and goodness of God. Not everyone participates in this process. We are each free to accept or decline God's invitation. If we decline, then we remain, like our ancestors before Christ, bound in the darkness and the prison-house of sin.[31]

Clement was one of the first theologians to integrate Christ's descent into Hades as part of the act of redemption.[32] Hints of

28. Young, p. 116. Exhort. 9.69: οἱ πρῶτοι τῶν ἁμαρτιῶν ἀπεσπαυμένοι, οἱ πρῶτοι τοῦ διαβόλου κεχωρισμένοι.

29. Again, Clement stood in the Irenaean tradition as opposed to what would become the Augustinian, because he stressed free will more than predestination. "Augustine saw man as utterly helpless to win his salvation without divine grace, whereas Clement viewed man's destiny as charted on the basis of foreseen merits freely performed." (Floyd, p. 98). God in his omniscience knows from all eternity who chooses good and who rejects it, but he in no way interferes with our freedom to choose. The problem of reconciling free will with divine omniscience later became of great importance; Clement touched on it without making a concerted effort to solve it.

30. Floyd, p. 84. Floyd on pp. 84–89 speaks of Clement's atonement theory as a "theology of deification," and in fact the verb θεοποιέω—to be made divine (lit. to make god)—is actually used in Pro. 11.4 and elsewhere.

31. Pro. 12; Misc. 6.12; 7.1. The Passion was dramatic, crucial, and necessary; yet for Clement it was one stage, however important, in a long series of events leading to the final triumph of the kingdom of God.

32. Floyd, p. 81. Misc. 6.1, 6.6; Exhort. 9.69, 10.78; Pro. 8, 10. Cf. Hebrews 10:26–31. For the doctrine of the descent, see J. A. MacCulloch, *The Harrowing of Hell: A Comparative Study of an Early Christian Doctrine* (Edin-

Satan broods in the ice in the lowest circle of hell, while Dante and Vergil look down from an overhanging rock. The wings of the great angel have been changed by his sin into hideous bat wings. His frustration is total, his imprisonment eternal. An engraving by Gustave Doré for Dante's *Inferno*.

the descent appear in the New Testament, but its meaning was left ill defined.[33] By the second century the belief had already become the most widespread and popular explanation of what Christ was doing between his crucifixion on Friday afternoon

burgh, 1930); K. Gschwind, *Die Niederfahrt Christi in die Unterwelt* (Münster, 1911); J. Kroll, *Gott und Hölle: Der Mythos vom Descensuskämpfe* (Leipzig, 1932); H. Crouzel, "L'Hadès et la Géhenne selon Origène," *Gregorianum*, 59 (1978), 291–331; M. L. Peel, "The 'Descensus ad Inferos' in 'The Teachings of Silvanus,'" *Numen*, 26 (1979), 23–49; B. Reicke, *The Disobedient Spirits and Christian Baptism* (Copenhagen, 1946), S. J. Fox, "The Gehenna in Rabbinic Literature" (diss., Harvard University, 1959). Kevin Roddy is currently preparing a study of the subject.

33. Ephesians 4:8–9; Hebrews 13:20; 1 Peter 3:17–22, 4:6; Revelation 1:18.

and his resurrection on Sunday morning. That in those crucial days he somehow faced death down was universally accepted, and death's abode was thought to be in the underworld. Since the Devil was often associated with death as a chief enemy of humanity, Christ's subterranean struggle was seen as overcoming both mortal foes of the human race. The Passion consisted not only of the crucifixion but of the whole course of agony from the arrest in Gethsemane to the moment of resurrection. The descent, like the scourging and the crucifixion itself, was part of the redemptive act.[34]

Though Christ's descent into hell was an important part of the idea of redemption, no consensus existed in the first centuries as to what exactly he did in the underworld.[35] The Gnostics, with their hatred of the created, material world, argued that the descent was identical with the Incarnation. For them, in descending from heaven to earth, Christ descended into hell, since this earth itself, here and now, is the evil abode of torment and pain. Such ideas were not wholly foreign to the orthodox fathers, including Clement and Origen, who saw the kingdom of this world as a decidedly inferior copy of the kingdom of God.[36]

For the most part, however, the descent into hell became a vehicle for a theology that embraced both justice and mercy. Since God had delayed the Incarnation for centuries after original sin, millions of human beings might have been deprived of an opportunity of salvation solely because they happened to have lived and died before Christ came. The idea of such an injustice was scandalous, and the Christian community sought a way to extend salvation to both the living and the dead. If the act of salvation included the descent, and if during the descent Christ preached to those who had died previously, then the effects of redemption could be felt by all.

34. Hippolytus was the first clearly to consider the descent as integral in salvation, in his "Antichrist" (see above, p. 103). He believed that Christ redeemed the righteous Hebrews who had perished before his advent.

35. Crouzel, p. 297.

36. Origen, Beg. 4.3.10: the inhabitants of heaven fell into "this Hades," i.e., earth, εἰς τὸν ᾅδην τοῦτον καταβαίνουσι.

What was the hell that Christ visited? The Hebrews had two words for hell, Sheol and Gehenna, which the Septuagint translated respectively *Haidēs* and *Geenna*. The New Testament makes no clear distinction between Hades and Gehenna, and neither did Clement, but among the fathers as a whole a vaguely drawn difference emerged: Gehenna is a place of everlasting torment, whereas Hades is a place of purgation. After Christ's redeeming act, the just can proceed directly on the road to heaven, but before Christ the road was blocked, so that the just had to be sent to Hades to await the Savior. Those in Gehenna were vicious sinners who could not be saved, and they remained there after the Passion as they had done before. Both Hades and Gehenna were believed to be underground, and both were places of suffering. But Hades, under Greco-Roman influence, came to be conceived as a shadowy place of purgation, in contrast to the eternal flames and torments of Gehenna. Those theologians who chose to blur the distinction tended to be universalists, viewing the descent as freeing all the ancients from hell; those who felt the distinction more sharply believed that Christ descended not to Gehenna, but to Hades, and that he saved only the just, leaving sinners in hell. The distinction—never firm—was further blurred by the translations of both terms by the Latin *inferus, inferi, infernus, inferni* (cf. Fr. *enfer*, It. *inferno*, Eng. "infernal") and blurred again in English by the use of the word "hell," derived from the name of a Teutonic goddess of the underworld. Gehenna is closer to the modern concept of hell than is Hades, which somewhat resembles the Catholic purgatory. Some modern universalists have revived the milder interpretation of hell as Hades.

The central point of discussion in Clement's time was the question of whom Christ favored with his preaching in hell, and whom he released. Three general answers were possible: he preached to the people of the Covenant—that is, the Old Testament patriarchs and all devout Hebrews; he preached to all the righteous dead, both pagans and Jews; he preached to all the dead, including sinners. Ignatius, Irenaeus, and Hippolytus assumed that he preached only to the righteous Hebrews who had longed for the Messiah.[37] Marcion the Gnostic said that Christ descended to save all who believed in the true, hidden God as opposed to the evil demiurge who created the world.[38] The "Odes of Solomon" argued that together the Incarnation and descent defeated the forces of evil. Tertullian introduced the vivid image of Christ breaking the bolts and smashing down the doors of hell.[39]

As legend began to depart from theology, Hell and Death were personified. In the early third century "The Teachings of Silvanus" described a full, elaborate story: Christ descends to the underworld but finds his way barred, for Hell knows that his visit will doom its power. Christ smashes the iron bars and bronze bolts of hell's gate. When he enters, Hell tries to catch and bind him, but he bursts the chains. Finding Hell and Death arrayed with the Devil against him, he humbles them all and "breaks Hell's bow" to show that its power is forever vanquished.[40] By the fourth century the myth was frequently expressed in a dramatic dialogue between Christ and the powers of darkness.[41] From the sixth century that form was established. For example, in the "Gospel of Nicodemus," Satan or Beelzebub, the "heir of darkness," informs Hell that he has in-

37. Reicke, p. 15, but 1 Peter 3:17–22, a difficult passage, seems to imply something more, that Christ preached even to sinners, the "disobedient spirits in prison": ἐν ᾧ καὶ τοῖς ἐν φυλακῇ πνεύμασι πορευθεὶς ἐκήρυξεν. See Reicke, p. 26. For the early fathers on the descent, see Tertullian, Soul 55; Justin, Dial. 72.4; Irenaeus, Her. 3.20, 4.22, 4.27, 4.33, 5.31; Odes of Solomon 22.3; 42.15–20; Hippolytus, Antichrist, 26. Augustine and most later Christian writers denied that 1 Peter referred to the descent and hesitated as to whether it released all or only some of the dead: Reicke, p. 38.

38. MacCulloch, p. 86.

39. Tertullian, Res. 44: quae portas adamantinas mortis et aeneas seras inferorum infregit.

40. Peel, pp. 39–40. Rather inconsistently, the "Teachings of Silvanus" link this active destruction of Satan by Christ with the passive notion that Christ was offered as a ransom for the souls held hostage in hell: "Teachings" 104.12–13; Peel, pp. 47–49.

41. Two dramatizations are found in Ephraim the Syrian (see MacCulloch, p. 111) and the "Gospel of Nicodemus." On Nicodemus, see Hennecke, 1:445–481, and G. C. O'Ceallaigh, "Dating the Commentaries of Nicodemus," *Harvard Theological Review*, 56 (1963), 21–58. Four versions of Nicodemus exist—Coptic, Syriac, Armenian, and Latin—but none appears to be

stigated the crucifixion. Christ is dead, the Devil exults to his ally, and now let us make sure that we keep him in our power, for he will do everything he can in order to foil our plans. Hell expresses skepticism of Satan's ability to hold Christ in his power, but Satan upbraids him for cowardice. Hell is frightened: if Christ could with a word loose Lazarus from the shadows, then he may have the power to free everyone. Please, Hell begs Satan, don't bring him down here, for he may rob me of my prisoners. But Satan insists, and Hell, as it were, shrugs his shoulders and tells him to go out and stop Christ if he can. Hell bars all his doors, but in a moment of triumphal glory Christ speaks but a word and they crumble, letting light flood in. Christ seizes Satan, orders the angels of light to bind him, and turns him over to Hell to hold him until the second coming. Hell, once Satan's ally, now becomes his jailer, and he reproaches his former friend for his folly. You are defeated, he says, and the King of Glory has taken all of my dead away from me. "Not one dead man is left in me." The cross has broken both of us. This passage hints that Christ freed all whom death and the Devil had held in bondage from the beginning of the world until the Incarnation, yet the rest of the "descent" passage, while specifying that Adam, the prophets, and "the saints" are liberated, is vague as to whether the "just" Hebrews were freed, all Hebrews were freed, both good Hebrews and good pagans were freed, or everyone was freed. Tradition never resolved these points, but Clement, with his wide sympathy and learning, opted for the salvation of all the just, Hebrews and Gentiles alike.

Indeed, Clement suspected that in time Satan himself might be saved. He admitted that the Devil had sinned in the beginning and persisted in his sin ever since.[42] But a number of considerations prompted Clement toward universalism, the idea that the fullness of time will bring universal salvation. First, the

---

earlier than about 555 A.D. See the detailed account of the descent in the "Apocryphal Gospel of Bartholomew" (fifth to seventh century) in James, *The Apocryphal New Testament*, pp. 166–186.

42. *Frag. adumbratio in epistolam primam Johannis* (MPG 9, 738).

limitless nature of God's mercy seemed to call for the ultimate salvation of all free and intelligent beings. Second, the indelibility of free will suggested that the Devil might continue to retain the capability of repentance at any time. Third, Clement's ontology called for the ultimate fulfillment of potential goodness on the part of every created thing. Fourth, Christ at his second coming would wish to extend his goodness to all.[43] But Clement was quite unclear on these points and left it to his pupil Origen to develop the idea of apocatastasis, the ultimate return of all beings, including Satan, to the God from which they sprang.[44]

Origen, the most inventive diabologist of the entire Christian tradition, was born in Alexandria in 185.[45] His family was both affluent and Christian, and his father, Leonidas, taught his son the faith. The martyrdom of Leonidas during the persecution of 197–204 made a terrible impression on the young man and prepared him for a similar end. Origen's world was a frightening one whose apparent securities could dissolve in a moment into unprotected terror and whose threats could be fended off effectively only by God's mercy. Studying arts and philosophy, Origen came under the influence of Middle Platonism and Gnosticism, and for a while he taught grammar at his own academy in Alexandria. Clement helped him understand Christianity on a sophisticated level. Undergoing an intense religious experience, he sold his books and began to practice an ascetic life of poverty and chastity that he eventually took to the extreme of self-castration. His fame grew as he traveled about the Mediterranean teaching philosophy and the Scriptures, and he was widely sought for discussion and debate. Frequently he spoke on the problem of evil, and in debating the pagan Celsus he declared that "no one will be able to know the origin of evils

43. Misc. 1.17, 4.8, 4.14, 6.6.
44. A possible, though forced, reading of Misc. 1.17 would be that Satan could have repented after the theft of divine secrets by the fallen angels.
45. On Origen see especially B. Nautin, *Origène: Sa vie et son oeuvre* (Paris, 1977); H. Crouzel, *Bibliographie critique d'Origène* (The Hague, 1971); and J. Daniélou, *Origen* (New York, 1955), esp. pp. 220–245.

who has not grasped the truth about the so-called Devil and his angels, and who he was [before] he became the Devil, and how he became" the Devil.[46]

Against Celsus, Origen explained how a benevolent God could create a world in which inequalities existed among spiritual beings. Later, in a debate with the Gnostic Candidus, he firmly rejected Gnostic dualism. The two debates helped Origen define his monist position that all things come from God.

The period from 220 to 225 was the richest and most productive for Origen's thought about evil, and it was then that he wrote his most powerful work, "The Beginnings."[47] Growing opposition to him by those in the church of Alexandria who disliked his brilliance as much as they deplored his extreme asceticism generated charges of heresy. Origen left Alexandria for Palestine in 230, and sought ordination there but was denied the priesthood owing to his castration. When in 231 at Antioch he met and impressed the empress Julia Mamaea, his future seemed assured. Traveling widely, he was at last ordained in Caesarea in Palestine in 232, and a quiet, happy period followed during which he wrote his work against the ideas of Celsus. The latter years of his life were disturbed by a growing quarrel with the bishop of Alexandria, who attempted to secure his condemnation as a heretic, and finally by the persecution launched by the emperor Decius in 250–251. Like his father, Origen went to prison when he refused to renounce his faith. Unlike his father, he was eventually released, but his health was broken, and he died a few months after regaining freedom in 251. Origen did much to fix traditional views of the Devil. He is said to have written hundreds of works, but, partly because of his reputation as a heretic, many are lost, and the rest

46. "Against Celsus," written between 245 and 250 (Cels.). 4.65. Quotations are from the Chadwick translation (see the Essay on the Sources).

47. *De principiis*, or Περὶ ἀρχῶν. Origen wrote in Greek, but the original has been lost except for fragments, so that the earliest extant version of the work is a Latin translation by Rufinus.

exist mostly in Latin translations more or less doctored by the translators.[48]

Like Clement's, Origen's view of the world emphasized freedom. God created the cosmos for the purpose of adding to the sum total of goodness, and he wishes an optimum world in which all can be saved. Since moral goodness requires freedom of choice, God created the cosmos such that created beings with true freedom exist. Without them the world would be incapable of good and therefore pointless. Such freedom entails the ability to do evil.[49] If any free being were consistently compelled to do good, its freedom, and therefore its nature and the purpose of its existence, would be destroyed. Robots or puppets, no matter how skillfully designed, cannot be morally good or evil.[50] Therefore evil is necessarily entailed in creation.

God first created a number of intelligent beings, a number that remains forever fixed. These intelligences were all created equal. They were also created free. Using their freedom, they all chose to depart from the divine unity. God permitted this in order to fill up the universe with a diversity of forms. All the intelligences thus departed from perfection, but in great differences of degree, so that each sank as far away from God as he chose. Those who departed least remained in the ethereal realms near heaven and possessed merely ethereal bodies; those who departed further fell into the lower air and had thicker material bodies. These beings remained fine intelligences, more spiritual and generally better than humans. The custom of call-

48. The most relevant of Origen's works in addition to "Against Celsus" and "The Beginnings" (Beg.) are the "Homilies on Numbers" (HNum); "Commentary on Saint Luke" (CLuke); "Homilies on Genesis" (HGen.); "Homilies on the Song of Songs" (HSong); "Homilies on Exodus" (HExod.) "Commentary on Matthew" (CMatt.); "Exhortation to Martyrdom" (Exhort.); "Commentary on John" (CJohn); "Commentary on Romans" (CRom.); "Homilies on Judges" (HJud.); "Homilies on 1 Kings" (H1Kings); "Homilies on Jeremiah" (HJer.); "Homilies on Leviticus" (HLev.); "Homilies on Ezechiel" (HEzech.); "Homilies on Joshua" (HJos.); "Prayer" (Pray.). See the Essay on the Sources.

49. Beg. 3.1.1.

50. Beg. 3.1.2–5.

ing the higher intelligences "angels" blurs the concept, but it was already so common in Origen's time that neither he nor his contemporaries were able to overcome it.

Other intelligences fell yet further, even down to the earth, where they took on gross material bodies and became human. Still others fell all the way into the underworld, becoming demons. For Origen the fall was a fall, not of angels who sank into a human or demonic state, bur rather of pre-angelic intelligences. He was misinterpreted on this point, even by those, such as Evagrius of Pontus, who agreed with him. Rather, the original intelligences fell into two (or three) categories, angels, humans, and demons. This fall was an ontological diversification, not a moral lapse.[51]

Many difficulties exist with this theory, and it is no wonder that Origen was misinterpreted. He had to supplement ontological diversification with a truly moral fall. Some of the intelligences who became "angels" later sinned and were ontologically demoted, some to the status of humans, some to that of demons. But not all angels who became humans were sinners. Elijah, John the Baptist, and, *par excellence*, Christ, took on human bodies for good purposes rather than because of sin. The intelligences who became human also sinned, confirming their earthly grossness or sinking further into the realm of the demons. Since all the intelligences were originally equal, all have the potential for rising or falling. One's position in the cosmos is one's own choice, and one can choose either to mount upward or to sink further.[52] All who respond to Christ and accept

51. Beg. 1.8.3, 2.1, 2.3, 2.9. Intelligent beings: νόες or *rationabiles creaturae*. J. N. D. Kelly, *Early Christian Doctrines*, pp. 180–181; J. Daniélou, *Gospel Message and Hellenistic Culture* (Philadelphia, 1973), pp. 418–419. The angels fell and had "to roam about the grosser bodies on earth which are unclean": Cels. 4.92. The best study of the fall of the intelligent beings is J. Laporte, "La Chute chez Philon et Origène," *Kyriakon: Festschrift Johannes Quasten*, 1 (1970), 320–355. I follow Laporte's interpretation of the fall of the intelligences. Matter is not eternal but created: Beg. 1.3.3, 2.2.

52. Beg. 1.5.3–5, 1.6.2, 1.8.4, 2.2–3; Cels. 4.92. Jerome, Comm. John 16: "Origenes . . . dixit cunctas rationabiles creaturas incorporales et invisibiles, si neglegentiores fuerint, paulatim ad inferiora labi et iuxta qualitates locorum, ad quae defluunt, adsumere sibi corpora, verbi gratia primum aethera, deinde

God's help will rise in the chain of being. Since intelligences remain free to change at any time, a human can become an angel or a demon, and part of God's plan of salvation is to fill up the gaps that the fallen "angels" have left in the angelic ranks with the purified souls of humans. The angels too may change: an archangel may become a demon, and the Devil may rise again to be an archangel.[53] The essential problem with this scheme is that in spite of Origen's efforts to maintain the distinction between the ontological and the moral, the two become muddled in his idea that one can rise or fall ontologically depending on one's moral choice.

The purpose of the world is to train us to love God, Origen said, and any action not aimed at the love of God is without real purpose. Purposelessness is the hallmark of sin, which is foolish action leading us further and further away from reality. Some people pile sin on sin until, swollen with putrescence, the abscess bursts, and their salvation begins with their revulsion from the surfeit of evil. "The history of salvation . . .," Daniélou wrote of Origen's view, "is to be the progressive restoration of the spiritual creation to its primal state."[54] Sin points us away from God's being toward the nonbeing of evil.

God created everything good, including the Devil, but the Devil freely chose to prefer nonbeing and purposelessness to real being and true purpose. Satan was created a good angel,

---

aerea, cumque ad vicinam terrae pervenerunt, crassioribus corporibus circumdari, novissime humanis carnibus alligari" (Origen said that all intelligent, incorporeal, and invisible creatures, if they were negligent in their duty to God, quickly fell to lower parts of the cosmos, and took on the bodies appropriate to their station; some, by God's grace, ethereal bodies, others aerial ones, and others, who fell as far as the vicinity of the earth, gross corporeal ones, and those who fell even farther were bound to human bodies). Beg. 1.6.2: at the end, "restituetur in illam unitatem," everything will be restored to its pristine unity.

53. Again I follow Laporte. One logical conclusion was the transmigration of souls with its corollary, reincarnation. Beg. 1.5.3, 1.6.2, 1.8.4. Another was apocatastasis, the eventual return of all creatures to their proper state of perfect being and goodness in God: Beg. 2.3.3. For apocatastasis, see below, p. 144.

54. Daniélou, *Origen*, pp. 220–221; 422.

but that angel made himself into the Devil. So it is with all who follow him: "those who have given up their part in the Being, by depriving themselves of Being, have become Non-Being." Demons were created by God as rational beings, but their free will transformed them into demons.[55] The Devil exists, because his being was made by God. But insofar as he has given himself over to evil, he lacks being. Since he is almost wholly given over to evil, he is almost wholly nonbeing. Yet he is the most powerful force of evil in the cosmos. Here again Origen, like Clement, muddled the ontological with the moral. Though in the ontological sense evil is nonbeing, evil exists as the very real result of the free-will choice to do the wrong thing.

Origen made valiant attempts to find a rational basis for packing the ontological and the moral into one hamper. Unlike most of the fathers, he was at least aware of the problem. His belief in the potential perfection of every being is a coherent answer to the disproof of God's existence on the grounds that the amount of evil in the cosmos is greater than is needed to preserve free choice. Taking the entire course of existence as a whole, we each, in spite of temporary miseries, enjoy perfect happiness. However much we may suffer on earth, or even in hell, in the course of time God will grant us such happiness as will answer his justice and his mercy. However much we may sin on earth, in the course of time God will grant us such desire for repentance that we will eventually choose the good. This is also powerful salvation theory, because it accepts the infinity of God's mercy and enhances the idea that Christ died for all. But Origen seems to have thought of recurrent cycles of sin and salvation, and that possibility undermines the unique necessity for Christ's Passion. For this reason (as well as their dislike of its author) Origen's contemporaries rejected his theory, and his successors generally ignored it, in spite of the fact that their own theories were at least as inconsistent as his.

Origen's theodicy had no inherent logical requirement for the

55. CJohn. 2.7. Demons created good: Cels: 4.65. Free will of intelligent beings: Beg. 1.5.4–5, 1.8; Cels. 7.69.

existence of the Devil. First, his emphasis upon the responsibility of human free will led him to argue that human sin would occur without demonic temptation. Second, he believed that evil is nonbeing. Third, he knew that in one sense evil is relative: we are inclined to define good and evil in terms of what we personally do not like, as when we call a clear autumn day good and a destructive windstorm evil, though both events are natural and both were designed for a purpose, however obscure it may seem to us. God knows how to turn even the consequences of moral evil to a providential end. Nothing that he creates is evil.[56] Yet Origen insisted upon the reality of the Devil in his debate against Celsus, and his theology gave a greater place to Satan than Clement's, for though his theodicy did not require a Devil, his salvation theory demanded one.

The pagan Celsus argued that Christian diabology was absurdly dualistic. It is both silly and blasphemous, he stated, to imagine that God's will can be impeded. God wishes the good, and no opposing power can possibly frustrate him; if it could, he would not be God. That the Devil should have been able to inflict pain upon God himself in the person of the suffering Christ is simple nonsense. Origen's reply relied upon Old Testament texts that presumably were meaningless to Celsus. He defended the Christian idea of the Devil as more reasonable than Celsus' pagan myths and fitted it into a scheme of cosmic degeneration. God, Origen reiterated, created everything good. Satan was "the first of all beings that were in peace and lived in blessedness who lost his wings and fell from the blessed state." Satan's fall, his own fault, was no part of God's plan. The Devil had sung among the cherubim, but he chose to debase himself, thus subtracting almost all being and goodness from himself and becoming almost pure nonbeing.[57]

56. Cels. 6.44. Nothing created evil: Beg. 1.4.3; 1.8.3, 2.3, 2.9.6. Matter is neither evil nor the cause of evil: Cels. 4.66. God does not create evil, but evil exists as the "shavings and sawdust" left over by a carpenter, or as the debris left behind in a lot when the builder has finished his work: Cels. 6.55. God's providence: HNum. 13–14.

57. Cels. 6.42–43. Satan's fall: Cels. 43–44. Beg. 1.5.4, 1.8.3; Cels. 6.43, 7.69; CJohn. 2; HNum. 13. Devil as nonbeing: Origen had to say that the

The sin of the Devil and of the angels who followed him occurred before the creation of the material world. In fact, God created the material universe in order to compensate for the loss of goodness resulting from their sin. Since the angels' fall preceded the creation of Adam and Eve, they could scarcely have fallen out of lust for, or envy of, humanity. Rather, their motive was pride, willingness to substitute their own will for that of God.[58] Later, Augustine would argue that the Devil's envy arose from his pride, but he believed that the Devil envied God, not humans. Origen's argument was convincing, and from his time onward it was believed that the Devil had sinned through pride and that his fall had taken place before the creation of Adam and Eve.

This ordering of events allowed Origen to make a new connection between Satan and Lucifer.[59] Bringing together a num-

---

Devil became *almost* totally nonbeing; his nature, since it was created by God, remains good, though he distorts it as much as he can. Devil among the cherubim: Beg. 1.5.4, 1.8.3; this derives from Origen's use of Ezechiel 28: see below, p. 131.

58. Beg. 1.5.5, 1.8.3; HNum. 12; HEzech. 9.2; Pray. 26.5; CLuke. 30.2.

59. Exhort. 18: Devil as Lucifer. I was probably wrong in *The Devil*, pp. 195–197, to date the amalgamation of Satan and Lucifer back to the apocalyptic period. I owe sincere thanks to H. A. Kelly for a number of helpful suggestions on this point. Kelly is the first and only scholar to discuss the relevance for demonology of the redating of *The Secrets of Enoch*, which links Lucifer and Satan. See Kelly, "The Devil in the Desert," esp. pp. 203–204. If the *Secrets* was in fact written in the first century, including the Lucifer passage, then the view I took in my earlier volume is correct. If the *Secrets* is later than the third century—and the best opinion now seems to place it as late as the seventh—then Origen is probably the inventor of the identification of Lucifer with Satan, as Kelly argued. R. Van den Broeck, *The Myth of the Phoenix According to Classical and Early Christian Traditions* (Leiden, 1972), gives a resume of the dating problem of 2 Enoch (pp. 287–293), and says that the *Secrets* cannot be earlier than the seventh century at least in its present form. In any event, Origen is the first writer known certainly to have made the connection. See J. C. Greenfield and M. E. Stone, "The Books of Enoch and the Tradition of Enoch," *Numen*, 26 (1979), 98–99, on the date. The date is unsure, but in this volume I follow the more probable interpretation that it is late. Charlesworth postulates an original Greek version of the *Secrets* dating from before the fall of the temple in 70 A.D., but even if this is true, such an original version would not necessarily contain the Lucifer/Satan identification of the later manuscripts. See J. H. Charlesworth, *The Pseudepigrapha and Mod-*

ber of diverse Old Testament traditions from Job, Ezechiel, and Isaiah, he argued that Lucifer, the Prince of Tyre, and the Dragon were all identical with the Devil. He used the scriptural texts to underline Satan's pride and his headlong fall from heaven. Lucifer is Satan:

How art thou fallen from heaven, o Lucifer, son of the morning! . . . For thou hast said in thine heart, I will ascend into heaven, I will exalt my throne above the stars of God. . . . I will ascend above the heights of the clouds; I will be like the most High. Yet thou shalt be brought down to hell. [Isaiah 14:12]

The Prince of Tyre is Satan:

Thou sealest up the sum, full of wisdom, and perfect in beauty. Thou hast been in Eden the garden of God. . . . Thou art the anointed cherub . . . and I have set thee so. . . . Thou wast perfect in thy ways from the day that thou wast created, till iniquity was found in thee . . . . Thine heart was lifted up because of thy beauty, thou hast corrupted thy wisdom by reason of thy brightness: I will cast thee to the ground. . . . I will bring forth a fire from the midst of thee, [and] it shall devour thee. [Ezechiel 28:12–19]

The Dragon Leviathan is Satan:

Canst thou draw out Leviathan with an hook? . . . Canst thou put an hook into his nose? [Job 41:1–2][60]

---

ern *Research* (Missoula, Mont., 1976), pp. 103–106, for comment and bibliography. Professor Kelly informs me that Francis Anderson is preparing a new edition of the *Secrets* with a full bibliography, forthcoming in J. H. Charlesworth, ed., *Pseudepigrapha*.

60. Job's image of the dragon caught with a hook and the imagery of Revelation 12:9, where the Devil is both serpent and dragon, inspired Gregory of Nyssa's angling metaphor for salvation. Mythologically the serpent had legs before it was cursed for tempting Eve. Iconographically the serpent gradually regained its legs in the Middle Ages and Renaissance, so that the dragon in art and legend is usually legged. See H. A. Kelly, "The Metamorphoses of the Eden Serpent during the Middle Ages and Renaissance," *Viator*, 2 (1971), 301–328.

These colorful passages firmly established the tradition that the
Devil had been among the greatest of the angels, beautiful and
perfect, that his pride had at the beginning of the world led him
to rebel against God, and that he had been expelled from
heaven and awaited punishment in fire. A great deal of the
vivid elaboration of legend and literature on the Devil's nature
arises from Origen's initiative in using these texts.[61]

The angels fell in the beginning along with Satan, and for the
same reason, pride. Satan was their prince. Origen was sometimes inclined to conceive of the Devil's office as elective: the
fallen angels, cast down from heaven, chose one among them as
a leader.[62] By eliminating the Watchers and their lust, Origen
did away with the distinction between demons and fallen
angels.[63] Differences among the demons were ontological, dis-

61. Names assigned to Satan by Origen: The Devil, or Zabulus (from *di-
abolos*): Cels. 6.43, HJer. 20.1, HiKings. 1.14–15; Satan: Beg. 1.5.1, 3.2.1,
CMatt. 12.40, 13.8–9; Cels. 2.49, 6.44; dragon: Beg. 1.5.5, 3.2.1; Lucifer:
Beg. 1.5.5; the wicked one: Beg. 1.5.1, Pray. 29–30; the strong man: HExod.
4; the enemy of God: Beg. 1.5.1; the accuser: HiKings. 1.15; the adversary:
Cels. 6.44, CLuke 35.5; robber: HLuke 34, Cels. 7.70; Belial: Cels. 6.43;
serpent: Cels. 6.43; Beelzebub: Cels. 8.25; tyrant: Cels. 1.1, Pray. 25; Azazel:
Cels. 6.43; the spoiler (*exterminator*): Beg. 3.2.1, Cels. 6.43; the prince of this
world: CMatt. 13.9, Beg. 1.5.2, Cels. 8.4, 8.13, HJos. 14.2, HLuke 35.5,
HNum. 12, HGen. 9.3, Pray. 25. Origen maintained that the Devil is called
prince of this world not because he created it, as the Gnostics said, but rather
because this world is full of sins and sinners who follow him. The Devil is
like a roaring lion: HJos. 8.4; HGen. 9.3.
62. Cels. 4.65, 5.54–55, 7.69–70, 8.4, 8.25; CMatt. 13.8, 13.22; Beg. 1.
pref. 6, 1.5.2; Pray. 26. The angels' choice of a leader looks back to Jewish
apocalpytic and ahead to *Paradise Lost*. When they fell, the angels lost their
angelic nature: Cels. 4.65. The amalgamation of the Devil with the other
fallen angels both as to motive and chronology was a logical necessity in Origen's overall theology, and it accompanied an emphatic rejection of the canonicity of Enoch. This was the end of the Watcher story in eastern theology
(except Methodius), and it soon died out in the West as well.
63. Origen sometimes showed a residual belief in the existence of some
natural demons in addition to the fallen angels, but this distinction had no
function since for Origen all intelligent creatures had fallen from perfection in
one or another degree, and the idea withered away: Cels. 4.92, 5.2, 7.5,
7.67–69. Origen's demons existed objectively, not simply as allegories of
human psychological traits: see E. Bettencourt, *Doctrina ascetica Origenis seu quid
docuit de ratione animae humanae cum daemonibus* (Rome, 1945), pp. xiii, 1, and
passim. In Cels. 4.92 Origen spoke of the Titans and giants but equated
them with the other demons.

tinctions that may actually have been produced by a difference of degree of moral sin. The same is true of humans. Humans who strive against Satan rise ontologically and become more spiritual; those who yield to him sink and become more and more fleshly (*sarkes*).[64] Origen's idea of a spectrum between bodies that were least material and those that were most material ran counter to the growing tendency in his time to reject the idea of spiritual bodies altogether. Overall, his effort to unite ontology and morality by making moral choice responsible for ontological status failed. Whatever its potential value, he could not find a way to defend it with consistency.[65]

Demons influence both the natural and the human worlds.[66] That natural catastrophes were in part caused by demons figured in Origen's general notion that God shared the governance of the cosmos with the angels, whom he put in charge of the elements of earth, air, fire, and water, and who regulate the movements of all natural bodies, including stars, animals, and plants. They are "virtues who preside over the earth and the seeding of trees, who see to it that springs and rivers do not run dry, who look after the rains and winds, the animals that live on land, those that live in the sea, and all that is of earth."[67] The lower ranks of spirits are in charge of the natural functions of the universe, and the higher ranks rule human affairs. These angels usually work for our good, but they may work against us in two ways. First, some natural disasters and diseases are necessary parts of God's plan, and God gives license to evil angels to cause such ills for his own providential purposes. The

64. Beg. 1.5.4–5, 1.8.3, 3.4.2.
65. Origen was also unclear as to whether the demons lived in the air, on earth, or underground. Consistency dictated that they should dwell in the grossest, most material part of the universe, which logically was the center of the earth, the place farthest from heaven, while those spirits dwelling in the air should be superior to humans. In fact Origen usually followed the earlier fathers in placing the abode of the demons in the air. They nourish themselves on the smoke and odor of pagan sacrifice. Cels. 4.32, 7.5–6, 7.35, 7.56, 7.64, 8.30–33, 8.60–61; Mart. 45. Curiously the idea that humans may become angels at death was revived by eighteenth-century German pietism and remains in the popular imagination today.
66. Cels. Bk. 8 treats the powers that demons exercise in this world.
67. HJer. 10.6–7; Cels. 4.92–93. See Daniélou, *Origen*, pp. 224–225.

demons would like to be allowed to cause even more evils, but God restrains them, limiting them to what is needful, and whatever harm they do he turns to ultimate good. Thus even in their malice they are mocked. Demons cause droughts, famines, barrenness, plagues, and similar calamities. "Like public executioners, they have received power by a divine appointment to bring about these catastrophes, . . . either for the conversion of men, . . . or with the object of training [them]." Through such trials both the just and the unjust are made to reveal their true natures.[68] The entire natural order, alienated from God, is penetrated by the work of demons, and the Devil controls the ultimate natural evil, death.[69]

Human society is a battleground between angels and demons. After the human race was divided at the Tower of Babel, God gave each people over to the charge of angels. Each nation, province, and region is controlled by two powerful angels, one good and the other evil.[70] The evil angels of the nations are responsible for causing persecutions and unjust wars. The pagans are right to venerate the angels of the nations, whom they mistakenly call gods, but they make the terrible error of worshiping not the good but the evil angels, thus making the demons their gods. Christ's Incarnation, which reunited the human race in one Christian community, rendered the power of the angels null and void.[71] Individuals not associating themselves with the Christian community are left unprotected by any national angel. Origen was inconsistent on one point here: Christ has destroyed the power of the angels of the nations, yet

68. Cels. 8.31–32; 1.31, 5.30–31, 7.70: "wicked demons are appointed for certain tasks by the divine Logos who administers the whole world."

69. CMatt. 13.9. Possession is a mode of demonic attack similar to illness: Beg. 3.3–4. Each species of animal has a variety of demon attached to it, and demons are especially active in cruel and rapacious beasts: Cels. 4.92–93.

70. CLuke: 12.4, 35.3–4; Beg. 1.5.2, 1.8, 3.3–4; Cels. 5.30; Exhort. 18; HNum. 12. Origen sought scriptural basis for this idea in Deuteronomy 32:8 and in current Jewish traditions. See J. Daniélou, "Les sources juives de la doctrine des anges des nations chez Origène," *Recherches de science religieuse*, 38 (1951), 132–137.

71. Cels. 4.32, 8.33–42; HNum. 12. The demons of the nations will end the persecutions when they realize that martyrdom is building up the church: Cels. 8.44. Angelic power nullified: Cels. 1.31.

they continue to cause persecutions, wars, and other evils. At least this inconsistency is consistent with another, that is, the effects of Christ upon the human situation in general. Christians have always been in the difficult position of having to argue that the Passion of Christ was totally effective, sufficient unto itself for the salvation of the world, yet the world will not be wholly changed until the second coming.

God cares for individuals as well as nations, and he places the direction of individuals under the responsibility of less powerful angels. Everyone has two angels, a guardian angel of justice and a corrupting demon of iniquity.[72] In each person a psychomachia or internal moral struggle rages between the good and evil angels, the good angels drawing us ever upward toward the spiritual, in the direction of God, the evil angels pulling us down, away from God, toward matter and nothingness. The Christian life is a daily struggle of conscience, aided by the good angel, against the temptations of the evil angel. After the sin of Adam and Eve, the balance was tipped in favor of the evil angels, and the human race henceforth was bent in the direction of sin.[73] God's covenant with Israel, the Old Law, was only partly successful in freeing us from that sin, and it required Christ's suffering to break the power of the evil angels and restore order to the cosmos.[74] Now the good angels have the upper hand, at least for those who follow Christ. Even though God permits the Devil to continue to tempt us, we always retain our freedom to resist. "Each person's mind is responsible for the evil which exists in him, and this is what evil is. Evil is the actions that result from it."[75]

72. CLuke 12.4: Per singulos homines bini sunt angeli. CLuke 23.6–8; Pray. 6.4, 11.5, 31.5; Beg. 1.8, 3.2–4. The idea goes back to Barnabas and beyond.

73. Cels. 4.40, 5.31. Compare the demons of vice, note 85 below.

74. CRom. 2.13.

75. Cels. 4.66. Origen was certain that every human being was under the charge of a spirit or spirits, but he was unclear whether Christ's suffering (1) left Christians with both good and evil spirits, though weakening the evil; (2) left Christians with only good spirits; (3) left pagans with both good and evil spirits; (4) left pagans with neither spirit; (5) left pagans with only the evil spirit. See Bettencourt, p. 24. Temptation continues even after the Passion: Cels. 8.33–34, 8.64.

A burly pair of demons lead a disconsolate soul toward the gates of hell; inside the damned are already being tortured. A ninth-century illumination from the Stuttgart Gospels. Courtesy of the Württembergische Landesbibliothek.

Ironically, the Devil, having urged us to vice, also appears as our prosecutor both at the last day and at our individual judgments. The idea of the individual, "particular" judgment had not existed in the primitive church, but as the Parousia delayed, people wondered what happens to human souls in the years, decades, and centuries elapsing between death and the last judgment, and the idea of a particular judgment spread rapidly in the third and fourth centuries.[76] At the particular judgment, our guardian angel stands as our advocate, while our personal demon is charged with prosecuting us. If the angel is successful in showing that our lives basically have been lived in the faith of Christ, we mount upward; if the demon is successful we sink lower into the material depths, even unto the flames of hell.[77] The last judgment will confirm the decisions of the individual judgment.

The demon or demons dwelling in our souls under the lead-

76. Jean Rivière, "Rôle du démon au jugement particulier chez les pères," *Revue de sciences religieuses*, 4 (1924), 43–64, esp. pp. 43–47. The iconography became very popular in the Middle Ages: quantities of representations exist showing the soul of the deceased being weighed on the scales of judgment, a good angel and a demon standing eagerly by awaiting the result. Often the demon is shown cheating by interfering with the scales.

77. CLuke 23.1.

ership of Satan constantly tempt us to sin, using whatever "instruments" will work.[78] But they have no power to compel us, and whatever sin we commit is our own responsibility. Even original sin could have occurred without the Devil's intervention, and we would now continue to sin even if the Devil did not exist.[79]

The constant tension between our guardian angel and his opposite demon requires us to develop "the discernment of spirits," the ability to distinguish between them before making any judgment or decision. The Devil is a liar, always disguising good as evil and attempting to persuade us that what he proposes is right and good. But even if he should propose something that is right in itself, we should never do it under his suggestion, for inevitably he will strive to turn the deed to evil and use it to our ruin. A wise discerner of spirits will know, for example, that an action leading to peace and lack of strife is usually prompted by the good spirit.[80] But the Devil knows how to disguise evil as good and play upon the evil inclination within us. The evil inclination is the tendency to sin as a result of the fall of Adam and Eve. The Devil or evil demon uses the evil inclination to excite our minds and play upon our base desires.[81]

78. CMatt. 13.22.

79. Exhort. 42.48. The good angel is always there to help us: Beg. 3.2.4. Though the Devil tempted Adam and Eve, their sin was their own responsibility. Since sin would exist without the Devil, Origen had no logical need for him: Beg. 3.2.2–5, 3.3.40; Cels. 6.43. The Devil's part in original sin is that he urges the serpent to tempt Eve: Beg. 3.2.1. Presumably more sin exists than would be true if the Devil were not constantly tempting us, but the Devil has no power to infringe upon human free will: Beg. 3.2.2. Free will: Cels. 8.34–35. The Devil as accuser as well as tempter: CIKings. 1.15.

80. HJer. 20.4. Discernment: Beg. 3.3–4: the discernment of spirits, διάκρισις. Temptations: Beg. 3.2.2; HEzech. 6.11.

81. The evil inclination, which Origen called the πονηρὸς διαλογισμός, derived from the rabbinic *yetser ha-ra* and the evil spirit described by Barnabas. A λογισμός is a rational function that can be turned to good or evil; there are good and evil *logismoi*. See HNum. 6. The psychological description is very apt: as soon as we open our minds to the evil spirit, vicious thoughts flood in and the Holy Spirit is pushed out. Evagrius of Pontus would call the *dialogismos* the *poneros logismos*; see below, p. 181. The evil judgment is associated with the πνεῦμα ἄλογον, the irrational, destructive spirit, which struggles against the πνεῦμα λογικόν, the faculty of reasonable moral judgment.

He employs two approaches, tempting us from outside with the sensual blandishments of this world and from inside with our private lusts and longings. Christ erased the evil tendency from the minds of the baptized, but when a baptized person sins he revives the ancient tendency and reopens the door to the Devil.[82]

Origen's theory of redemption emphasized the Devil. He contrived to wed a belief in the efficacy of the redemption with a realistic psychology based upon a world in which temptations are seen to exist. It should have been clear to everyone that the act of redemption had not markedly changed human behavior, however much it may have affected essential human nature. Though Christians are more protected than non-Christians from the evil inclination and the demon who works with it, they remain vulnerable.[83]

Each time your soul chooses right, it advances a step in its spiritual course, approaching closer to God, and at each step upward the powers the demons have against you are weakened.[84] But as you rise spiritually, the temptations that the Devil uses against you become more and more sophisticated and clever.[85] Whenever you choose wrongly, your soul sinks further away from spirit, and if you continue to make evil

---

Temptations arise even without diabolical activity: Beg. 3.2.1–2. Again, the demon and the Devil do not cause sin, but rather, as it were, weigh in on the side of sin, encouraging evil tendencies already present in the soul. The quantity of evil is greater and its quality more horrible than if the Devil did not exist.

82. Bettencourt, pp. 73–76. Sins of the baptized: HExod. 6.9; Beg. 3.3.3; HEzech. 8.3, 13.2; HLev. 12.7.

83. Cels. 8.27, 8.36.

84. Rising with virtue and sinking with sin: HExod. 4.9, 6; 9; HNum. 27.12.

85. A different demon rules each vice, the more sophisticated vices being the domain of the more sophisticated demons: HJos. 15.5–6; HEzech. 6.11. There is a demon of fornication, one of wrath, one of avarice, and so on. There is also a sub-demon of each vice operating in each of our souls, so that arrayed against us is a vast bureaucracy of evil resembling the Gnostic demonocracy. Origen's CLuke 23 refers to the demons as publicans to which the soul must pay spiritual taxes on its progess upward, a concept similar to Clement's idea of demons acting as customs officers.

choices, you will become a small Satan. In this way, "over against the body of the church with Christ at its head, a body of sin is formed, the head of which is the Devil."[86] Magicians, idolaters, heretics, and those who live immoral lives are all part of the bristling array striking at the Christian community.[87] With the help of this army, a mystical body of evil, Satan rules the kingdom of this world.

Before the Incarnation, the kingdom of this world, the old eon, dominated the earth. Christ's whole mission was a struggle against the Devil, demons, and death. From the very moment of his birth, Christ's "great power" began to undermine the power of Satan, preparing it for its final ruin.[88]

Christ's Passion is the crucial event in this long struggle. Origen's view of the Passion was eclectic, embracing a number of ideas. First, Christ's death reconciled us to God after we had alienated ourselves from him by original sin. Christ took us and our sins upon himself and offered us up to the Father in the sacrifice of his own death. The Father found this sacrifice fitting and acceptable and so forgave humanity for its transgressions. Second, the Passion is the first shattering blow to the Devil's power over us, the second being the Parousia. Third, Christ was a ransom paid by God to the Devil. The ransom

---

86. Cels. 6.44. Mystical body of sin: CRom. 5.9: "Corpus peccati . . . cuius corporis caput sit diabolus, sicut Christus caput est corporis ecclesiae." Christ and the Devil as two extremes diametrically opposed: Cels. 6.45. Some angels are of God and some of the Devil: Cels. 8.25.

87. Magicians: Cels. 1.6, 1.22, 1.60, 1.69, 2.49, 2.51, 6.39, 7.5, 7.69, 8.59, Beg. 3.3.3–5; idolaters: Cels. 3.28–29, 3.35–37, 5.5, 7.35, 7.64–69, 8 passim, Exhort. 45–46, HExod. 6.5; In Ccls. 5.5, 7.69, 8.25, 8.57, Origen and Celsus disagree on the use of the term "demon," Celsus maintaining as a pagan that demons were capable of doing good and Origen as a Christian that they were not. For Clement both gods and demons could be either good or bad; for Origen gods were demons and were always bad, as opposed to angels, who were always good. Heresy: Cels. 2.49, 5.63, HNum. 12, 13; CMatt. 10.1: the Devil sows tares (heresy) into the wheat (orthodoxy).

88. HJos. 14.1; HNum. 20. Christ's mission: Origen sometimes identified death with the Devil (e.g. HNum. 9; HJos. 8.4; CMatt. 13.8–9); in any event they are closely related, and the Devil is responsible for having brought death into the world. Christ's career as a struggle against the Devil: Cels. 1.60, 6.45. Undermine Satan: CMatt. 12.4.

theory differs radically from the sacrifice theory in that Christ delivers himself up not to God, but to the Devil. Origen attempted to reconcile the two through allegory. God was not really angry with us, he argued: his anger was a metaphor of his desire to lead us to wisdom through suffering and experience. God did not demand Christ's sacrifice; he did permit it, as a means of overthrowing the powers of evil.[89]

The attempted reconciliation of sacrifice and ransom was neither clear nor compelling, however, and ordinarily Origen simply relied on the theory of the ransom and trick.[90] In order to rescue us from Satan's power without violating justice, God was obliged to pay the Devil a ransom. The only ransom the Devil would accept was a perfect man, so when God offered him Christ, he seized him eagerly, and in turn handed him over to vicious humans to torment and kill him. Death and the Devil exulted in their triumph, but only for the flicker of a moment, for the ransom was a trick.[91] Since Christ was God, the Devil could not hold him, and since Christ was without sin, it was a violation of justice to try to hold him, a violation that annulled Satan's claim to keep the rest of us in bondage. The slate, wiped clean, meant that we were free. Satan had been duped, gulled, cheated, and made a fool of. This idea of Origen's that God is a master cheater is not only undignified but illogical, for it hinges upon Satan's ignorance of Christ's sinlessness and divinity. Had Satan really been thus ignorant, he would not have been willing to accept Christ as sufficient payment to begin with.

Whether sacrifice or ransom, the crucifixion had a double

89. J. N. D. Kelly, pp. 185–186. Ransom and sacrifice: CMatt. 16.8. Origen's attempt to reconcile: Young, pp. 117–118. God permits Christ's sacrifice: CJohn 6.35–36; CRom. 4.11.

90. Young, p. 118. Origen's ransom theory: CRom. 2.13, 3.7, 4.11; CJohn 6.32–33; CMatt: 13.8–9, 16.8; CLuke 6.6. The ransom theory found biblical support in Isaiah 53:3–6 and Matthew 20:28. Origen developed it well past the position taken by Irenaeus (see above, p. 83, and J. Pelikan, *The Christian Tradition*, 3 vols. [Chicago, 1971–1978], 1:148–151).

91. CMatt. 13.8–9, 16.8. Origen was one of the earliest proponents of the trick refinement of the ransom theory; though further developed by Gregory of Nyssa, it was rejected by most theologians and faded from the tradition.

meaning, according to Origen. In the eyes of the world it meant the defeat of Jesus, but in the real world of God it meant the destruction of the Devil.[92] By his death and resurrection Christ shattered the power of the demons and cast down the kingdom of the Devil, sending Satan sprawling. He broke the power of idolatry, giving us dominion over the evil spirits who had long deluded us into thinking that they were gods. He eliminated the authority of the angels of the nations, both good and evil, because the disunity of the nations was now replaced by the unity of the Christian community in the Body of Christ.[93]

Though Christ "removed the evil spirits" and destroyed "a great demon, the ruler of demons," the Passion did not immediately pull down Satan's proud tower, but rather set in motion a process that was to culminate in the second coming.[94] The Passion was the crucial moment, for at that point the Devil recognized the folly of his effort to seize Christ and the inevitability of his ultimate defeat. Such an impression did this revelation make upon the powers of evil that some of the demons may even have converted. After the Passion, the good angels join Christ in open warfare against Satan in a battle that will rage until the second coming.[95] The Devil meanwhile continues to tempt and assault the human race and holds particular power over sinners, infidels, Jews, and heretics, who form part of the mystical body of Satan. Such a view ran the risk of representing the Passion as a stage in the process of salvation rather than

92. HJos. 8.3.

93. Power of demons: Cels. 1.3, 1.60, 3.29, 8 passim. Defeat of the kingdom of the Devil: Cels. 1.60, 8.54, 8.64. Broke idolatry: Cels. 3.36, 8 passim. Angels of nations: CJohn 13.59; CLuke 35.

94. "Removal of evil spirits": Cels. 1.31; "great demon": Cels. 1.31. The Passion included the harrowing of hell: "Jesus died in order to become the lord of the dead": Cels. 2.65; CRom. 5.10. Cf. Romans 14.9. Cels. 7.17: Christ's death is the ἀρχὴν καὶ προκοπήν, the "beginning and an advance," of the καταλύσεως τοῦ πονηροῦ διαβόλου, "the overthrow of the evil Devil," who had subjected the whole earth. Cf. HJos. 8.4. An alternative view is to see three steps in the process of salvation: incarnation, passion, and second coming. But for Origen as for the whole Christian tradition, the Passion overshadows the Incarnation.

95. CJohn 13.58–59. Warfare: HNum. 14.2; Cels. 8.47.

as the act of salvation itself, thus devaluing Christ's sacrifice, but it did speak to the demonstrable fact that sin and evil continue.

Origen followed Clement in his emphasis upon freedom of choice, an emphasis markedly different from Augustine's later predestinarian views. Christ died for the whole human race, and in Origen's view he may have died for the angels as well, for he wished everyone to profit from his saving act.[96] But only those who willingly join themselves to him in faith benefit from salvation. Though Christ invites everyone to be baptized and to share in his happiness, not everyone accepts his invitation. Only those who choose to receive baptism can participate in his saving act, and only those who persist in their faith after baptism are saved; those who sin subsequently open the door to the Devil again. Yet the will of Christ that we be saved is so strong, and his mercy so great, that in the end it may be that all will by his grace come at last into heaven.

The Devil's realization that the Passion had undone him drove him despairing to new and more frenzied assaults upon humanity. God permits these assaults in order to provide those who associate themselves with Christ the opportunity of achieving higher virtue by opposing them.[97] Each time a Christian successfully resists a demon's temptations, that demon's power is reduced.[98] In this way the Devil and his minions gradually

96. Modern theologians have thought about the possible relationship of Christ to people who may exist on other planets. The existence of intelligent populations on other planets would have excited, not confounded, Origen. God created the world populated by a number of intelligences, and there is no reason why other intelligent beings should not exist beside humans, angels, and demons. The question would then be whether the Passion of Christ affected these other beings. Origen might have been inclined to think that it did; if it affected the angels, its virtue extended beyond the human race. Christian tradition as a whole, however, restricted its effect to humanity.

97. HJos. 14.1: "Isti omnes daemones, ante adventum Domini et Salvatoris nostri, quieti et securi humanas animas possidentes, in earum mentibus corporibusque regnabant" (these demons, quietly and securely possessing human souls before the coming of our Lord and Saviour, ruled both their minds and their bodies). But after the Passion, "ab illis iniquis veteribus possessoribus . . . pugnae exoriuntur proelia" (battles are joined against these ancient and vicious usurpers). Opportunity for virtue: HNum. 13.7.

98. HJos. 15.

decline until the second coming annihilates their evil once and for all.

Until a person is baptized, the Devil retains his power over him, so he always attempts to delay conversion and baptism as long as he can.[99] When baptized, the new Christian passes out of the hands of evil demons and into the hands of his guardian angel. Whereas hitherto he has inclined to sin, he is now fortified in virtue.[100]

The Devil never gives up trying to lure the converted Christian away from grace; accordingly, Christian life is a constant struggle against the powers of darkness.[101] So long as one is fully bound to Christ by faith one is immune to the attacks of demons. Faith, a moral life, prayer—these are the defenses that make successful "athletes of piety."[102] None of these detracts from the necessity of the Passion, but each partakes of it, for without Christ all efforts against the forces of evil would be impotent.[103] To use later language, works were effective not in themselves but only so far as they proceeded from grace.

The second coming of Christ will be preceded by a final assault upon the Christian community led by Antichrist, "the son of the evil demon, who is Satan and the Devil."[104] Christ will then come to lead the church in final triumph over evil, and at that time the Devil and his followers will be condemned to hell.[105] Various conceptions of the punishment of the powers

99. HExod. 5.4.
100. HNum. 12.4; HEzech. 1.7; Cels. 8.36.
101. HGen. 9.3. Using allegory, Origen explained that the continued need for resistance was metaphorically equivalent to the fact that after Pharaoh was drowned in the waters of the Red Sea while the Hebrews safely crossed (baptism), the Jews were still obliged to fight Amalek. Cf. HNum. 19.1; HExod. 6. Devil and vices: HExod. 3; 6. Devil causes persecutions: HExod. 6, where the demons are perceived as warriors on horseback riding down the saints.
102. Cels. 8.34–36. Defense against Devil: Cels. 8.55.
103. Bettencourt, pp. 62–67, 124.
104. Cels. 6.45–46. Cf. CLuke 30.1.
105. Beg. 2.5.2, 2.10; Cels. 6.24–26; Exhort. 18; HExod. 13; HNum. 19.4; HJos. 8.4; CMatt. 13.9. On Origen's ideas of hell, see Crouzel, "L'Hadès," and H.-J. Horn, "Die'Hölle' als Krankheit der Seele in einer Deutung des Origenes," *Jahrbuch für Antike und Christentum*, 11/12 (1968–1969), 55–64. Origen's view of Hades is consistent with his concept of the nonbeing of evil, for Hades is a place of formlessness and shadow (Crouzel, p. 309). This of course

of evil became current in later patristic thought: (1) Satan and the demons were imprisoned in hell at the time of the Passion and would be confined there until allowed to emerge and support the Antichrist in the last battle. (2) Some demons are even now in hell, while others are allowed under God's permission to roam the world seeking the ruin and destruction of souls. (3) The demons go in shifts to and from hell, sometimes being punished and sometimes tempting. (4) The demons in hell are jailers of the damned as well as prisoners themselves.[106] Origen inclined to the view that punishment was reserved till the end of the world.

The most striking aspect of Origen's diabology was the potential salvation of Satan. Influenced by Clement and by Neoplatonism, drawn by the logic of his doctrine of the non-being of evil, and especially urged by his personal conviction that God in his mercy wishes the happiness of everything that he has created, Origen argued for apocatastasis, the idea that all things will eventually return to the God who has made them. In the fullness of time, God will be all in all.[107]

---

is also close to the classical conception. Gehenna on the other hand is a place of undying fire—πῦρ ἄσβεστον, αἰώνιον—and of eternal, unending punishment (Crouzel, p. 313; HJer. 18.15). For Origen, free-will choice of sin placed one in Gehenna. He attacked the Valentinian schema dividing the human race into three groups, the ὑλικοί, σαρκικοί, χοϊκοί, those damned by their nature; the ψυχικοί, who could choose, and the πνευματικοί, who were saved by their nature. Rather, he argued, we are each free to choose whether to be children of God or children of the Devil, and our choice determines our place in the universe (Crouzel, p. 314; CJohn 20.13). One's motives may be mixed. Fear of punishment may save one from hell, though desire for the good is nobler (Crouzel, p. 315). The saved become angels of God; the damned angels of the Devil (Crouzel, p. 316). Origen seems to have believed that hell was not eternal. His apocatastatic views called for the termination of hell when all things come back to God, but his insistence on free will restrained him, for as long as freedom exists, intelligent beings will sometimes choose evil, and hell will be needed. On the whole, he seems to have preferred the idea of purification of individuals through fire to that of a common place of punishment for all.

106. H. A. Kelly, *Devil, Demonology, and Witchcraft*, p. 37.

107. Beg. 1.6.1–4, 2.3.5, 2.10.8, 3.5.7, 3.6.5–6, 3.6.8; CJohn 1.16; CMatt. 15.31; HJos. 8.4. Origen found scriptural basis for his position in 1 Corinthians 15:26–28; Romans 5:17, 11:36; Philippians 2; 1 John 4:8; and Acts 3:21: χρόνων ἀποκαταστάσεως πάντων, "during the times when all things

Origin developed this view in the period between 220 and 225 when he was debating Candidus the Gnostic. "The destruction of the last enemy may be understood in this way," he wrote, "not that its substance which was made by God shall perish, but that the hostile purpose and will which proceeded not from God but from itself will come to an end. It will be destroyed, therefore, not in the sense of ceasing to be, but of being no longer an enemy and no longer death."[108] Everything that God created will in the end be reunited with him. The Devil will be destroyed at the end of the world in the sense that the lack in him that constitutes his evil will be destroyed, so that he will cease to be the Devil, but his angelic nature, being good, will be redeemed, reconciled, and reunited with the Lord.[109] Origen may have meant that in the divine plan the Devil must inevitably be saved, or he may have meant only that the Devil may possibly be saved. The former inclination pro-

---

are restored." On apocatastasis in general, see G. Müller, "Origenes und die Apokatastasis," *Theologische Zeitschrift*, 14 (1958), 174–190. The passage of Acts on which Origen relied refers to the eschatological end of the old eon and contains no hint of the doctrine of universal return. Even Origen's translator Rufinus rejected Origen's views: J. N. D. Kelly, *Jerome* (London, 1975), p. 248. Müller notes (p. 176) that the closest parallel to Origen's idea is the Frashkart of Mazdaism whose dualist doctrines resembled those of Origen's Gnostic antagonists. Müller also finds some similarities in Pythagoreanism, Stoicism, and Judaism (p. 177). He argues (pp. 188–190) that it was Origen's cyclical doctrine of *repeated* creation, fall, and restitution (like the system of Empedocles) that earned him condemnation, rather than apocatastasis itself. Not the return, but "the myth of the eternal return," with its roots in eastern religions, seemed impermissible to the Christian community. Gregory of Nyssa was not condemned for teaching apocatastasis *without* cycles. See J. Daniélou, "L'apocatastase chez Saint Grégoire de Nysse," *Recherches de science religieuse*, 30 (1940), 328–347.

108. Beg. 3.6.5. C. A. Patrides, "The Salvation of Satan," *Journal of the History of Ideas*, 28 (1967), 468. This translation is from the Latin version that Rufinus adapted from the original Greek and bears the marks of his tempering: "Non ut substantia eius quae a deo facta est pereat, set ut propositum et voluntas inimica, quae non a deo sed ab ipso processit, intereat." Though the word "death" appears rather than "the Devil," both are to be understood. Origen often identified the Devil with death, and other early summaries of his position specify the Devil.

109. Nautin, p. 422.

ceeded from Origen's view of the limitlessness of God's mercy, the latter from his view that the essential being (*ousia*) of all that exists proceeds from God, as opposed to the essential nonbeing of evil.[110]

In Origen's debate with Candidus, the dualist Gnostic asserted the absolute and unredeemable evil of Satan. According to Candidus, the Devil's evil really exists. It is real, it is absolutely and unchangeably evil, and it can in no way be redeemed. In reply Origen argued that the existence of the Devil logically demands that some aspect of his being, if only his mere existence, must derive from God and will be drawn back to God in the apocatastasis.[111]

In Origen's universalist doctrine, the punishments of hell may be "curative, not penal," because God's mercy and goodness are "all-inclusive and irresistible."[112] This irresistibility poses an important problem. Apocatastasis appears inconsistent with Origen's emphasis upon free will. If rational creatures retain real freedom until the end of the world, that freedom entails the possibility of choosing evil, so that it is improbable that any point will be reached at which everyone will have chosen the good and be ready to return to God at the same moment in time; if God impelled them irresistibly, he would abridge their freedom. Possibly Origen meant that every creature will return to God in its own time, so that apocatastasis is a gradual process. Because of these inconsistencies, he seems to have vacillated as to whether the Devil must be saved or whether he merely had the potential to be saved.[113] But it appears that

110. Nautin, p. 169, cites Jerome's resumé of the debate: "Asserit Candidus diabolum pessimae esse naturae et quae salvari numquam possit" (Candidus asserts that the Devil's nature is totally evil and incapable of ever being saved), a natural Gnostic position. "Contra hoc recte Origenes respondit non eum periturae esse substantiae, sed voluntate propria corruisse et posse salvari" (against this Origen correctly replies that the Devil's substance is not perishable, that he was corrupted by his own free will, and that he therefore can be saved).
111. Nautin, p. 422.
112. Patrides, p. 469.
113. Crouzel, "L'Hadès," p. 325.

Origen was willing to reconcile the two in an even more radical way, by postulating a cyclical pattern of creation, fall, and restoration. And this idea in turn could not be reconciled with the basic Christian doctrine that Christ needed to die only once to save the world. Christianity could not permit the idea of repeated Passions.

Origen's apparent affirmation of the Devil's salvation in his book, "The Beginnings," is offset by a more specific denial in a letter written to friends in Alexandria.[114] In the letter he accused his enemies of distorting his position and added that only a fool could assert that Satan certainly would be saved. On balance Origen seems to have maintained an open mind, posing possibilities rather than making assertions. The mercy of God might save the Devil: uninhibited freedom of will might eventually bring him to repentance; or else his evil choice may have been so reinforced over eons as to make him permanently unredeemable. For Origen these were all possible options.[115]

Origen's views were generous but difficult to reconcile with Christian tradition. Whereas the New Testament had spoken of apocatastasis in terms of the moral union of believers with Christ, Origen spoke of a physical return. The idea that the Devil will be saved was often viewed as shocking and blasphemous; and the inevitability of God's drawing all unto himself seemed to remove ultimate responsibility for sin from the individual and to blur a distinction between the just and the unjust. Origen's opponents lost sight of his more moderate argument that the Devil might possibly be saved, and his abrasive personality made it easy for them to take his surmises as assertions. So apocatastasis passed out of the tradition.[116] Origen did not

114. Ibid., p. 326; Crouzel, "A Letter from Origen to 'Friends in Alexandria,'" *The Heritage of the Early Church: Essays in Honor of G. V. Florovsky,* Orientalia Christiana Analecta, 195 (Rome, 1973), 135–150.

115. HJos. 8.5; HJer. 18.1: here Origen seems willing to admit eternal damnation for the Devil and his demons.

116. Following Origen were Gregory Nazianzenus, Rufinus, and Eriugena, and to some extent Gregory of Nyssa and John Chrysostom. But Gregory of Nyssa's view of apocatastasis was quite different from Origen's: see note 107 above. Jerome's opposition appears in his Letter 84.7, and Augustine's in

deserve the insensitive severity with which he was treated, however, and apocatastasis has sometimes been proposed again in modern form as a plausible solution to the problem of pain. Even though the tradition rejected it, Origen's diabology remains one of the most thoughtful in the history of the concept.

"The City of God" 21.17. Apocatastasis was formally condemned as heretical by Justinian in 543 and by the Second Council of Constantinople in 553. In the "nine anthemas" of Justinian against Origen, the ninth condemned the idea of the ἀποκατάστασιν . . .δαιμόνων ἤ ἀθεῶν ἀνθρώπων, "the return [to God] of demons and godless men." The condemnation of 553 also included the idea that souls can change from angelic to human to demonic or back again (item five).

6 Dualism and the Desert

In the third and fourth centuries the power of the Devil seemed to grow as the security of life in the Roman Empire waned. Increased insecurity and fear abetted a revival of dualism, which found new expression in the church father Lactantius, in a powerful new heresy, Manicheism, and in monasticism's psychological penetration of sin and evil.[1]

Lactantius (c. 245–325) was born and brought up in Africa as a pagan. A professional rhetorician and an effective classical stylist, he taught Latin at Nicomedia. He may have studied with Arnobius; he converted to Christianity about 300 and after his conversion wrote a number of influential books.[2] Designed to defend Christianity against the pagans, his works explain evil less by privation than by the active power of the Devil. Lactantius demanded to know why the just suffer as much as, or more than, the unjust.[3] His answer was that it was the work of the Adversary. Lactantius was a dualist in several senses. He was an ethical dualist, emphasizing the opposition

1. Other third-century writers—Julius Africanus, Commodian, Victorinus, Methodius, Arnobius, and Eusebius of Caesarea—gave due attention to the Devil but did little to advance the development of the concept. For their works, see the Essay on the Sources.

2. The relevant works of Lactantius are the "Divine Institutes" (DI); their shortened version, the "Epitome" (Epit.); "The Anger of God" (Anger); "The Death of the Persecutors" (Death); and "The Work of God" (Work).

3. DI 2.3, 5.7–8, 5.21; Anger 20.

between the two ways, the road of justice and the road of sin;
he was an anthropological dualist, observing the tension in human beings between soul and body, spirit and matter; he was a
cosmological dualist, saving the goodness of God by ascribing
evil to God's adversary. But though pronounced, Lactantius'
dualism was not extreme or Gnostic; it was mixed with both
monist and traditional Christian elements.[4] His thought is characterized by recurrent references to duality—earth vs. heaven,
hell vs. heaven, darkness and shadow vs. light, death vs. life,
night vs. day, down vs. up, cold vs. warm, left vs. right, west
vs. east.[5]

Lactantius, perceiving such dualities, asked why God provided for them, especially the duality of evil and good. "Why,"
he asked, "does the true God permit these things to exist instead of removing or deleting the evil? Why did he in the very

4. F. W. Bussell, "The Purpose of the World-Process and the Problem of
Evil as Explained in the Clementine and Lactantian Writings in a System of
Subordinate Dualism," *Studia Biblica et Ecclesiastica*, 4 (1896), 133–188. Bussell, p. 184, sees three incompatible ideas in Lactantius: (1) the Platonic idea
that matter is coeternal with God and is a refractory substance that God is
trying with difficulty to make conform to his divine plan; (2) the monist position that evil exists as a necessary part of a cosmos in which God expresses
himself in opposites; (3) the more traditional Christian position that the world
is created good but has been perverted by the free will of angels and humans.
5. Some of the most strongly dualistic passages of "The Divine Institutes"
have been questioned, but recent writers accept the passages as being probably genuine and agree that if they are not from the pen of Lactantius himself
they were written during his lifetime by someone who shared his views. No
inconsistency exists between the disputed passages and the rest of Lactantius'
work. See Bussell; V. Loi, "Problema del male e dualismo negli scritti di
Lattanzio," *Annali delle facoltà di lettere filosofia e magistero dell'Università di
Cagliari*, 29 (1961–1965), 37–96; E. Heck, *Die dualistischen Zusätze und die
Kaiseranreden bei Lactantius* (Heidelberg, 1972). Heck, pp. 201–202, sum-
marizes the conclusion: Lactantius is probably the author of the disputed
passages (DI 2.8, 7.5); the dualistic texts are probably anterior to the later
version, where they do not appear (Heck opposes Brandt's deletion of the
dualistic passages as later additions to the text); the texts were composed during Lactantius' lifetime; if not by him, they at least represent his line of
thought. No doubt has ever been raised about the strength of Lactantius'
ethical and anthropological dualism. See DI 2.9 for west vs. east: east is good
because the dawn comes from the east; south is better than north because it
has more light, and so on.

beginning make a prince of demons who would corrupt and destroy everything?"[6] And "what is the cause and principle of evils?"[7] His answers are original. First, evil is logically necessary. "Good cannot be understood without evil, nor evil without good."[8] It is a logical inevitability that good be defined by distinguishing it from evil and vice versa. Second, it is positively desirable that evil exist. "I tell you in short that God wishes it to be so."[9] God wishes it because we could not comprehend virtue unless we understood the alternative of vice. If God had created a world without evil, he would have created a world without the alternatives that make freedom possible. "We could not perceive virtue unless the opposite vice existed also, nor could we accomplish virtue unless we were tempted to its opposite; God willed this distinction and distance between good and evil so that we might be able to grasp the nature of good by contrasting it with the nature of evil."[10] "To exclude evil is to eliminate virtue."[11]

These arguments constitute a powerful theodicy. The contrary view grants the necessity for evil but observes that the quantity and refinement of evil in the world far exceeds that which is necessary for freedom of will. Yet Lactantius' argument swallows even that objection, for evil must not only exist, it must exist powerfully and compellingly, so as to define by contrast God's power and glory. If only petty vices existed, only petty virtues would exist. If no vast and terrifying power of evil impressed itself upon our minds, we would have no conception of the vast and awesome goodness of God. Only this

6. Epit. 29: "Cur ergo verus ille Deus patitur haec fieri ac non potius malos vel summovet vel extinguit? Cur vero ipse daemoniarchen a principio fecit, ut esset qui cuncta corrumperet, cuncta disperderet?" Note the *verus ille Deus*, the true, as opposed to the false god, who is the lord of this world. Gnostic, dualist influence is obvious.

7. The "caput horum et causa malorum," DI 2.8.

8. DI 2.8. See also 6.2–4, 3.29, 5.7; Epit. 29.

9. Epit. 29.

10. DI 5.7: "Virtutem aut cerni non posse, nisi habeat vitia contraria, aut non esse perfectam, nisi exerceatur adversia. Hanc enim Deus bonorum ac malorum voluit esse distantiam, ut qualitatem boni ex malo sciamus."

11. Epit. 29.

contrast permits us to grasp the nature of good and to be aware of the great opportunity that we have to serve against evil in the army of the Lord. "Throughout our whole life, God reserves an adversary for us, so that we may be able to win virtue. . . . God willed this opposition because he wanted us to take on the responsibility for combat and to stand prepared in the line of battle."[12] Wisdom as well as virtue is the prize. Lactantius argued a variation of the *felix culpa* theme, the idea that original sin was a "fortunate fall." If evil did not exist, we would be simpletons, bland puppets; it is the experience of temptation and the struggle to overcome it that enable us to become wise.[13]

The third part of his answer is that the evil that God creates is a real, malevolent personality, the Devil.[14] "Before he made anything else, God made two sources of things, each source opposed to the other and each struggling against the other. These two sources are the two spirits, the just spirit and the corrupt spirit, and one of them is like the right hand of God while the other is like his left."[15] Because it is not fitting that evil should proceed from God, God created the Devil such that a corrupt will and total injustice inhered in him. All good derives from one source and all evil from the other.[16]

12. DI 6.4: "Sic in omni hac vita, quia nobis adversarium Deus reservavit, ut possemus capere virtutem. . . . Voluit enim deus, qui homines ad hanc militiam genuit, expeditos in acie stare." Cf. DI 7.5: "Nulla enim virtus esse poterat, nisi diversa fecisset, nec omnino apparere vis boni potest nisi ex mali comparatione."

13. Anger 13: "si malum nullum sit, nullum periculum . . . tollitur omnis materia sapientiae" (if no evil existed, no danger would exist, and there would be no basis for wisdom).

14. DI 2.8: "In the beginning, God made good and evil. The good cannot be understood without the evil, nor the evil without good. . . . This evil is a spirit which the Greeks call the Devil" (*diabolon*). This and other English passages quoted from the DI are from M. F. McDonald's translation.

15. DI 2.8: God "fecitque ante omnia duos fontes rerum sibi adversarium inter seque pugnantium, illos scilicet duos spiritus, rectum atque pravum, quorum alter est deo tamquam dextera, alter tamquam sinistra."

16. DI 6.6: "Fons autem bonorum deus est, malorum vero ille scilicet divini nominis semper inimicus, de quo saepe diximus: ab his duobus principiis bona malaque oriuntur" (God is the source of the good; the source of evil is that eternal enemy of the divine name, about which we have often written: from these two principles all goods and evils derive).

This effort to shift responsibility from God to his adversary does not work. God is responsible for the existence of the power who creates evil; thus God is responsible for the existence of evil. Given his previous argument that evil was a logical and moral necessity, Lactantius need not have tried to evade God's responsibility. And perhaps he did not: he may simply have been insisting that it was improper for evil to proceed *directly* from God and that God therefore fastidiously chose to appoint an intermediary to keep himself clean. But the explanation encounters further difficulties. Was Lactantius opting for monism or dualism? He often officially used the term "two principles," which has a distinctly dualist ring if the term "principle" is taken precisely and the two principles considered coeternal. But Lactantius did not intend that meaning. He insisted that God stands behind both principles, good and evil—a view that sounds a great deal like primitive monism. Lactantius was certainly no absolute dualist. The entire first book of his "Divine Institutes" is devoted to defending the unity of God not only against popular polytheism but also against the philosophical idea of the eternity of matter. Neither matter nor the Devil can really be a principle coeternal with God.[17]

God arranged and contrived the cosmos in such a way that the two principles of evil and good, though not themselves eternal, would be locked in endless battle one against the other. But what is the good principle, and what is its relationship to the Devil? Here Lactantius sounds ambivalent. Sometimes the good principle is God himself, sometimes God's Son. When Lactantius argues that it is the Son, he makes Christ and Satan appear as twin angels, one beloved, the other rejected, heavenly counterparts of Cain and Abel. But this brotherhood of Christ and Satan is metaphor. They in some ways resemble twins, but Lactantius did not posit this as a literal relationship. Of the two

17. DI 1.passim, esp. 1.3. DI 2.8 also denies the eternity of matter. E. Schneweis, *Angels and Demons According to Lactantius* (Washington, 1944), pp. 118–119, insists that Lactantius was no cosmological dualist, since he denied the eternity of matter and since he argued that Satan "is a finite created principle."

principles God loved one like a good son; the other he loathed like an evil son.[18] After establishing the two principles and observing them set in their eternal strife, God created the angels. Some of the angels chose to follow the evil principle and were cast out of heaven on account of their bent will. Others chose the good and remained in heaven. Consequently two distinct groups of angels exist, one having at its head the good principle and the other the evil.[19] The evil principle, of course, is the Devil.

Lactantius was a strong subordinationist, believing that the Son was inferior to the Father. Indeed, he sometimes perceived Christ as an angel, though greater than all other angels. This impression is reinforced by his use of the word "spirit." Christ is a breath (*spiritus*) of God; God makes him by breathing and then goes on to create the other angels also by breathing, so both Christ and the angels are spirits or breaths of God.[20] Lactantius was quite inconsistent, elsewhere making a sharp distinction: "God begot the Son and only later created the angels."[21] Though God "breathes" both the Word and the angels, his "breathing" of the Word is a special kind of breathing in which the divine breath utters that which is God himself. The Word is truly divine, while the angels are a part of creation. The language making Satan Christ's brother was figurative, but Lactantius' writings are not consistent as to what degree it was figurative. To the extent that Christ appears as an angel, his nature is parallel to Satan's (no matter how opposite his function); to the degree that he is perceived as a part of the

18. DI 2.8: "Ita duos ad certamen composuit et instruxit, sed eorum alterum dilexit ut bonum filium, alterum abdicavit ut malum." Lactantius has a number of doublets in mind, especially Cain and Abel. It is clear that *filium* is to be understood after *malum*, "the bad son" as opposed to "the good son." But it is also virtually certain that Lactantius did not mean that God generated Christ and the Devil as two sons. The word *ut* is crucial: "like" or "as" is intended. The principles are *like* two sons.

19. DI 2.8: The angels fall *perversa voluntate*. The two princes: "Angeli omnes, quorum principes erant illi duo."

20. DI 2.8, 4.8. See Schneweis, pp. 30–37, 68.

21. DI 4.6.

divine, both his nature and his function are different. In any event, Lactantius' use of image and language nudged the concept in the direction of dualism again.

Lactantius observed from experience that the evil principle was active in the world as an "anti-God," the "enemy of good and the foe of justice who wills the opposite of what God wills."[22] This perverted power rejoices in human error; it is his sole and perpetual occupation to blind human souls to the light, in order that they may give up hope of heaven and serve him instead.[23] God has placed him in charge of the material world, but the Devil perverts these legitimate responsibilities. He chooses to envy God and to direct the malevolence proceeding from his envy against God, against God's Word, the Christ, and against humanity.[24] Yet God needs him. God needs a principle of evil by which the good can be known and uses his providence to turn Satan's envy to ultimate good. God "forbade the evil angels to do what he knew that they would do, so that they might have no hope of pardon." This again is a remnant of the original Hebrew monism that held that Yahweh hardened Pharaoh's heart so that he might not repent.[25]

These ideas are not necessarily as inconsistent as Lactantius left them. The tension between free will and providence has never been resolved, but it was better addressed by later writers, such as Augustine, who saw the issues more clearly.

Satan's envy, said Lactantius, is the root of all evil.[26] Satan is

22. "Anti-God": *antitheus*: DI 2.9. This is not so powerfully dualistic a term as it seems, since it was used by other fathers and is one of Lactantius' many dual antipathies. DI 3.29: "inimicus bonis hostisque iustitiae, qui contraria faciat quam Deus." For the necessity of the evil power through observation, see DI 5.7, 4.30, 4.38, 6.4; Anger 13; Epit. 29.

23. DI 2.1: "aliquam perversam potestatem, quae veritati sit semper inimica, quae humanis erroribus gaudeat, cui unum ac perpetuum sit opus, offundere tenebras et hominum caecare mentem, ne lucem videant, ne denique in caelum aspiciant, ac naturam corporis sui servant."

24. DI 2.14; Epit. 27. Envy: DI 2.8, 2.14; Epit. 27. DI 2.8: envy of the Logos, his elder brother (?): "invidit enim antecessori suo."

25. DI 2.14; Epit. 27. Cf. Russell, *The Devil*, ch. 5.

26. DI 2.8; 2.17; 3.29; 6.6; Epit. 29. The Devil's names include pravus antitheus (corrupt anti-god), adversarius (adversary), subdolus spiritus (cheat-

the leader of evil angels, who are his "satellites and ministers," and whose fall from heaven, which caused them to lose their pure forms and to sink with gross bodies down into the lower air, was their "first death." In this first death they lost their purely spiritual being and their immortality, a loss that prepared them for the second death to come.

Retaining the Watchers story, Lactantius maintained that there were two classes of demons, heavenly demons (*daemones caelestes*), including Satan and the fallen angels, and earthly demons (*daemones terreni*), consisting of the giant progeny of the Watchers and women. The knowledge of both angels and demons is greater than that of humans but much inferior to that of God. Satan was not created evil but fell "in the beginning" through envy of Christ, his "antecessor." The fall of the other angels occurred sometime before the flood. Satan fell from envy, the Watchers from lust for women. The chronology is: (1) creation of the spiritual world; (2) fall of Satan; (3) creation of the material world, including human beings; (4) fall of humans; (5) fall of other angels. With Methodius, Lactantius was one of the last fathers to retell the outmoded Watchers story, but he shared Origen's emphasis upon free will. The angels are not fixed in their choice. Even the good angels are not fixed in good, and they retain their freedom to sin until the last judgment.[27]

Lactantius' views of the two deaths of the evil angels are inconsistent. By angelic "death" he meant not corporeal death but rather the loss of that spiritual nature which they had originally shared with God. Three stages actually exist in the ruin of Satan and his followers: their initial fall from heaven, their ruin through Christ's death and resurrection, and their final punish-

---

ing spirit), inimicus (enemy), hostis (enemy), perversa potestas (perverted power), dux praevaricator ac subdolus (lying and cheating leader), criminator (accuser), serpens (serpent), dominator ille terrae fallacissimus (most treacherous lord of the world), conlucator noster (our oppressor): DI 2.1, 2.8, 2.9, 2.14, 2.16, 3.29, 6.2, 6.6, 6.7; Epit. 27; Work 1.7. Chief of all evils, "fons . . . malorum vero ille scilicet divini nominis semper inimicus," DI 6.6. "Machinator omnium malorum," DI 7.24. "Dux damnatus qui vitiis praesit et malis," DI 6.2.

27. DI 2.14–15, 7.24; Epit. 27.

ment. By the two deaths Lactantius seems to have meant something different: that the fallen angels first lost their true immortality and later will suffer a second death by eternal punishment in the flames of hell.[28] Like other Christians, Lactantius had to face the fact that the first coming had not destroyed Satan and that the second coming was being delayed. God's reason for the delay, he believed, is to give the Devil ample time to test Christians and so prove their faith. The Devil tempted us to original sin and continues to tempt us through frauds and deceits, but whatever he does he does with God's permission, and he has no power to subjugate us so long as we arm ourselves with faith in Christ. The demons feign great power, but all that they seem to accomplish is illusion.[29]

The Devil's success in tempting us comes from the inherent dualism in our own character. Lactantius was an anthropological dualist, perceiving a deep split between the human soul and body. God creates the universe such that two antagonistic principles struggle within each person. "We"—that is, our true personalities—are quite different from the bodies in which we are "draped."[30] Though Lactantius was obliged to grant that the

28. DI 2.9, 2.12, 2.14–17, 4.27, 5.18, 7.26; Epit. 28, 51.

29. Delay of Parousia to test Christians: DI 3.29; eternal punishment of humans who yield to the Devil: DI 2.17. Fraud and essential weakness of Devil: DI 2.14–16, 3.29, 4.13, 6.7. "Some he gets through laziness, some from overzealousness; he has one approach to fools, another to philosophers": DI 6.7, 7.18; Epit. 27–28. Demons cause illness and possession: DI 4.27, 5.21. They pretend to heal: DI 2.14–15. They are the cause of some dreams: DI 2.7. "They spread darkness and cover the truth with a cloud of smoke, so that men may not know the Lord, may not know their Father": DI 2.16. They cause idolatry: DI bks. 1–2 passim, 3.29, 5.20; Epit. 7–28. They tell us that Zeus rules many gods in order to mock their knowledge that God in fact rules many angels. They cause heresy (DI 4.30), persecutions (DI 5.21–22), death (passim), and sensual temptations (DI 6.4, 6.22–23). The Devil led Adam and Eve to original sin (DI 2.12) and Cain to fratricide (Epit. 27).

30. Work 19: "hoc corpusculum quo induti sumus" (this contemptible little body in which we are draped); cf. Anger 15. Dualism: DI 2.12, 6.3; see Loi, p. 36, and Bussell, p. 177. Lactantius' two ways go back to Barnabas, while his continued emphasis upon ethical pairs resembles that of the strongly dualist Clementine Recognitions of the third century. For humans the two deaths are different from the two deaths of the angels. For humans, the first death is physical death, the separation of soul from body, and the second is the ruin of the souls who have chosen the darkward path.

body is created by God, he nonetheless perceived it as belonging to the Devil, something that God permits to exist as a foil for the soul. God wishes us to follow our soul's urges to generosity and love; Satan wishes us to follow the desire of our bodies for drink, sex, wealth, power, and prestige. Each man and woman stands at a crossroad where one path leads to heaven and another to hell. Once we start on the downward road, the shadows of material pleasures envelop us more and more, progressively blotting out harmony, repose, and joy in a growing clatter of commotion, noise, indecision, complaint, and purposelessness. We have the choice. We can set foot confidently on the right road, turning our faces joyously toward the light, or we can slip miserably down and down into a mire from which it is difficult ever to emerge. As we stand at the crossroad, faith in Christ will guide us to take the right turning. Only those who lack faith, fear demons, and are weakened by sin will take the wrong road and slip into the pit.[31]

The time will come when all these problems will be forever resolved. Of all the early fathers, Lactantius was the most inclined to apocalyptic speculation.[32] The Devil has been cast down by Christ's Passion, but he is regathering his forces, and when the time is ripe Antichrist will appear, and the evil spirits will rise up and help him lead a final assault on the Christian community. For a short while they will triumph, and then Christ will come again to earth and thrust them down forever into eternal fire, bringing the rest of the cosmos back into eternal harmony with God. Lactantius' rather literalist rendering of the Book of Revelation was in sharp contrast to Origen's allegorical reading. For one thing, allegory allowed Origen to make the cosmic harmony complete, while Lactantius conceded only partial harmonization, and only at the expense of the destruction of part of the cosmos. More important, Lactantius' strong

31. DI 2.15, 6.22. With the help of Christ the believer has a number of weapons against the Devil, including martyrdom, patient forebearance, exorcism with the name of Christ and the sign of the cross, and the practice of a virtuous life: DI 4.27, 5.21–22, 7.27.

32. B. McGinn, *Visions of the End* (New York, 1979), p. 23.

millenarian stand precipitated a split of opinion throughout the Christian community that has persisted down to the present. Some theologians, following Lactantius, emphasized millenarian apocalypticism, including the Antichrist, the Last Battle (Armageddon), and the thousand-year reign of the saints while Satan is bound in hell. The majority followed Origen in reading Revelation allegorically and rejecting millenarism as incoherent and functionless. Millenarism was on the whole extruded from the Christian concept of evil, but it remained tugging at the edges, like an outer planet exerting gravitational pull on the inner circles of the system. That Christ would come again and put a final end to the Devil and his works was generally agreed, but the complex chronological calculations of Lactantius and other millenarians were generally rejected.[33]

Given the dualist tendencies in patristic thought, it is not surprising that new dualist heresies appeared. Christianity cannot be flatly defined as a nondualist religion, for several reasons. (1) The differentiation between monism and dualism is seldom clear in any religious tradition. Monist religions are often polytheist and often allow for manifestations of both good and evil in their gods. Sometimes this moral ambivalence is ex-

---

33. DI 24–27. Among the numerous difficulties of millenarism is its chronology. Millenarians have an endless variety of chronologies, each of which fits the extremely vague sense of the Book of Revelation. In one version, for example, the Antichrist comes aided by evil spirits; Christ comes down and defeats him, binding Satan in hell for a thousand years; then the evil spirits are loosed again for a short time; at last they are defeated and destroyed. Some argued that it was the first coming of Christ that bound Satan for a thousand years, so that he is now (i.e., in the fourth century A.D.) bound and will burst loose in A.D. 1000 (it was, by the way, as yet undecided how to date the Christian era). Virtually infinite modifications exist. A few fathers such as Cyril of Jerusalem followed Lactantius, but most interpreted Revelation allegorically and rejected millenarism. McGinn, pp. 25–26, writes that Eusebius of Caesarea was one of the leaders in the rejection of apocalyptic ideas, and that Jerome and Augustine also reacted against overt apocalypticism. "Augustine is the fountainhead of all anti-apocalyptic eschatology in the Middle Ages." The weight of opinion was heavily against millenarism, and from the fifth century onward pronounced millenarism was generally considered heresy. But the attraction of apocalypticism peripherally remained. Even Augustine incorporated "many themes of earlier patrisitic apocalyptic speculation" (McGinn, p. 27).

pressed in a struggle between "good" and "evil" gods, both of which proceed from the one divine principle; sometimes it is expressed in the two natures of one deity, such as the Hindu Kali, who is both destroyer and creator. At the opposite end of the spectrum, even an extreme dualist religion such as Mazda-ism has some monist elements; the Mazdaists always assumed a predetermined victory of the good spirit over the evil one, and they frequently postulated behind the two principles of good and evil a single ambivalent principle that generated both. Few if any religions are purely monist or purely dualist. (2) Even when terms are redefined so that "dualism" means a modified, mitigated dualism, Christianity is not simply a monist religion. Though Christianity has insisted historically upon the unity and omnipotence of God, it has granted great power to the Dev-il, God's opponent, a power not enormously less in degree than that granted by the Mazdaists to the evil Ahriman; it has held beliefs very similar to the Mazdaist idea that the cosmos was wracked by a struggle between a good spirit and an evil spirit. (3) Anthropological dualism has to be distinguished from cosmic dualism. Anthropological dualism is largely Greek in origin and was most sharply expressed in the Orphic belief in a tension between soul and body. Christianity drew upon this belief. (4) The struggle between Gnostic and less dualist fac-tions in the first two-and-a-half centuries of Christianity cannot be read historically as a struggle between heresy and ortho-doxy, since orthodoxy had not yet been defined. To imagine a struggle between church and antichurch at that time is to im-pose later theological ideas upon the period—and to take the polemics of some early writers too seriously. Both sides—or, to be more accurate, the variety of sides—viewed themselves as Christian. Only gradually did one set of opinions win out over the others and become the accepted, orthodox, "Catholic" posi-tion. Early Christianity thus understood included views that were strongly dualist, and many early Christians who were not Gnostic showed strong dualist tendencies. Thus the perennial appearance of dualist views and dualist "heresies" throughout the history of Christianity was not the intrusion of strange, external ideas, but rather the upwelling of dualist views inherent in Christianity from the beginning.

Of the dualist heresies arising at the end of the third century, Donatism was relatively mild and of limited importance for diabology. The Donatist schism arose from a dispute as to the degree to which Christians must resist persecution. The Donatists argued that those who had yielded to fear of persecution and had sacrificed to the pagan gods or otherwise betrayed the church could not be forgiven and restored to membership in the Christian community, and that any sacrament performed or ordination conferred by a sinful priest or bishop, especially those who had yielded in time of persecution, was invalid. Just as the orthodox accused the Devil of being behind heresies, so the Donatists claimed that Satan stirred up the persecutions and backed the Catholic party's preaching forgiveness of those who had yielded to them. When in Numidia their cause was linked through political circumstances with that of the landless poor, the Donatists came to argue that Satan was supporting the wealthy landholders as well. They were gradually isolated, and with isolation they increasingly felt that the entire world, except their own sect, was in the Devil's hands. One Donatist leader, Lucifer of Cagliari, argued that the "Church has become a brothel" and that "the entire universe belongs to the Devil," but the Donatist position differed from the Catholic only in degree. The dualism of both sprang from the same source and origin.[34]

The Donatist schism raised some essential questions. The Donatists took the logical position that God extends his grace and the human being responds with faith. The external sign of that grace and faith is the baptism by which the Christian is received into the community. For a Christian to sin mortally, as

34. On the Donatists see Frend, *Martyrdom and Persecution in the Early Church*, pp. 409–413; Frend, *The Donatist Church: A Movement of Protest in Roman North Africa* (Oxford, 1952). The followers of Lucifer of Cagliari were called "Luciferans," but their name derives from the bishop, not from the Devil. "Lucifer" means "bearer of the light." The Luciferans were staunch, even violent, antidiabolical Christians and are not to be confused with the later medieval "Luciferans" accused of worshipping Satan.

in betraying his religion for fear of persecution, signifies that he is not a true member of the Christian community. The Catholic position was doubtless more charitable, and it had the additional merit of seeming to respond to the lived psychological experience of most baptized Christians, who find themselves sinning and repenting more than once.

But the Catholic position, which prevailed, did not fully face the logic of Donatism. Instead it left ambiguities, one of which has to do with one's personal relationship to Satan. The fathers implied a struggle of the mystical body of Christ against the mystical body of Satan. It was never clear, however, whether membership in one body or the other was fixed. Might a person, through sin and repentance, change his allegiance more than once? Or was the person's membership assigned on the basis of his life taken as a whole? Or considering the state of his soul at the moment of his death? Or might souls even repent after death, as Origen thought? And the first ambiguity leads to the second, whether even Satan and the angels are fixed in their choice, and if they are, why. Later theologians would argue that angels—and human souls after their separation from the body—must be fixed in their choice because mutability is a function of matter, so that spirits are by definition immutable. But this explanation was not offered by the early fathers, and it has in any case a glaring flaw, for everyone agreed that the spirits had in fact changed already at least once, that is, at the moment of their fall. Further, many of the fathers assigned tenuous bodies to the angels. Origen's view that the fallen angels were not fixed in evil was not accepted. Origen was not certain whether the good angels were fixed in their goodness. On the one hand he insisted on preserving free will, but on the other hand he argued that all would eventually return to God and that once one dwelt in God's presence it would be difficult, if not impossible, to tear oneself away. Yet, again, the angels had done so originally. Augustine later would try to make sense of these ambiguities, fixing both the good and the evil angels in their choice as part of his doctrine of predestination.

Manicheism was far more pronounced in its dualism than

Donatism, yet its distance from orthodox Christianity was also a matter of degree. Scholars have debated whether to define Manicheism as a separate religion or as a Christian heresy. The argument is partly semantic. The relevant points for diabology are that the Manichean position was close to Christian Gnosticism; that it was the source of many later Christian heresies; and that it even influenced orthodox thought as well.[35]

The founder of Manicheism was a Mesopotamian Persian named Mani, who was born into a princely family near Babylon on April 14, 216. He may have been brought up as a Gnostic Mandaean; in any event, Mesopotamia, being a Persian province near the Roman border and a trading center, was influenced by Judaism, Christianity, Mazdaism, and even Buddhism. At the age of twelve, Mani had a revelation that he was a twin of the Holy Spirit and the last of a series of prophets whom he identified as Adam, Seth, Enoch, Noah, Buddha, Zoroaster, and Jesus. Traveling and preaching extensively, Mani attracted a great following. But he ran afoul of the severely orthodox Mazdaist high priest Kartēr, and his family connections could not save him from arrest, execution, and flaying. He died on February 26, 277. The influence of his ideas was felt for a thousand years, and from medieval France to Ming China.

Manicheism was an eclectic doctrine, but its closest affinities were to Gnosticism. Mani taught that two uncreated eternal

35. On dualism in general, see P. Siwek, "The Problem of Evil in the Theory of Dualism," *Laval théologique et philosophique* (1955), 67–80 (caution: this is an antidualist polemic). On the Manicheans see especially H.-C. Puech, *Le manichéisme* (Paris, 1949); R. Manselli, *L'eresia del male* (Naples, 1963); G. Widengren, *Mani and Manichaeism* (London, 1965); F. de Capitani, "Studi recenti sul manicheismo," *Rivista di filosofia neo-scolastica*, 65 (1973), 97–118; G. Quispel, "Mani the Apostle of Jesus Christ," in *Epektasis: Mélanges patristiques offerts au cardinal Jean Daniélou* (Paris, 1972), pp. 667–672; L. J. R. Ort, *Mani: A Religio-historical Description of His Personality* (Leiden, 1967). I incline to the view that Manicheism is better seen as a heresy than as a separate religion. The ease with which Manichean-Gnostic views were incorporated by indigenous Christian heresies in twelfth-century Europe is an indication that the points of view are not so different as to characterize two separate religions. The fathers, e.g. Hegemonius and Augustine, regarded Manicheism as a heresy.

elements existed in the cosmos, the principle of light and truth; and the principle of matter, darkness, and falsehood. These two elements are personified as God and the Prince of Darkness, and although they are both eternal, only the principle of light is divine. The kingdom of God has three aspects, light, force, and wisdom, which exist in serene harmony, but the kingdom of darkness is chaotic, noisy, and confused. Mani's doctrine took on a series of Gnostic complications. God creates the Mother of Life, and she in turn creates Primeval Man; the three exist in a Father/Mother/Son Trinity. The Prince of Darkness attacks and defeats Primeval Man, who in his fear prays to his Father and Mother. So powerful is his prayer that it itself is a divine being; and so powerful is the divine parents' response that it too is divine. The Father sends a Redeemer, the Spirit of Light, to rescue Primeval Man. But even after his redemption, his soul remains trapped in the commotion of darkness, and a new redeemer, the Living Spirit, is sent down to attack the archons or demons of darkness. Defeating them, he rescues the soul of Primeval Man and cleanses and purifies the light, making the sun and the moon. Still some particles of light were left entrapped in the darkness, so the Father sent a Third Messenger. The Third Messenger presents himself as a beautiful virgin to the male archons, who, lusting for her, ejaculate the light that they had been holding trapped inside them as sperm, and this sperm/light falls upon the earth, causing vegetables to grow. Thus vegetables are very high in light content and are to be eaten by believers in preference to meat, whose corporeality and sheer fleshiness reveal it as a product of darkness.

Meanwhile the female demons have perceived the Third Messenger as a handsome youth; though they are already pregnant, their lust for him causes them to produce their children more rapidly. These children come to earth as monsters and eat the young plants, recapturing light inside themselves. The archons now plot further against the light, engendering Adam and Eve. Az, the personification of darkness, produces two demons, one male, the other female. The male demon devours the monsters who have consumed the light-bearing plants so as to assimilate their souls; afterward he mates with the she-demon. The children of this union are the first humans. Thus men and women are the product of a diabolical plot consisting of a filthy combination of cannibalism and lust. But the Father of light again replied, undeterred by all this, and sent down the Third Messenger again, this time in the aspect of Ohrmazd or Jesus, whom the Manicheans called Yisho Ziwa, "Jesus the Shiner, or Light-bearer."

Jesus goes to Adam and tells him the truth: that his body is an evil imposture invented by demons, and that he must try to rescue his soul for the world of light. Thus the function of men and women in the world is to grasp the saving gnosis, the message of Jesus, and to work at freeing the soul from the body. That freedom is what is meant by salvation. Thus three ages of the cosmos exist: the age prior to the diabolical mixture of spirit and matter; the present age of mixture; and the third age, that of salvation, when after a great final war spirit will be liberated from matter, Jesus will rule the cosmos for a while, and then all matter will finally be destroyed. While the saved mount to heaven, those who have not recognized the truth and so have pursued the paths of darkness will be rolled together with matter into a dense, dark mass and buried in an eternal pit.

This mixture of mitigated cosmic dualism with extreme anthropological and moral dualism was similar to Gnosticism in its effort to remove responsibility for evil from the true God by interposing a complex series of mythological figures between him and the actual world of human existence, and it fails for the same reasons that Gnosticism failed. The mythological complexities, which far exceed the bare outline presented here, serve no function and in the end only confuse. Nonetheless Mani's idea that the cosmic struggle between two opposed principles is working itself out in each person as a struggle between body and soul attracted many converts, including Augustine himself at an early stage of his life. The presence of such dualism at the edge of the tradition sharpened the tension between soul and body and enhanced the view of the Devil as lord of matter, using the human body as the vehicle for his temptations.[36]

The combat between body and soul was a dominant theme in early Christian monastic thought. Monasticism, whose purpose was to provide a life of solitude and reflection in which an individual might devote his entire time to the contemplation of God undisturbed by the distractions of life in society, had a remarkable significance for diabology. The first known monk, Saint Anthony (251–356 are the dates traditionally assigned him), withdrew from his village into the desert to lead the life of a hermit, and in a similar setting Saint Pachomius (286–346) later founded cenobitic (community) monasticism. In one respect monasticism was a surrogate for martyrdom. With the accommodation of Constantine to Christianity after 312, the persecutions ceased, and the Christian community began to focus more on dangers from within, especially preoccupation with the things of this world. The desert replaced the arena as the place where the Christian was most severely tested. By withdrawing from society, the monks undertook to struggle against worldly pleasures and desires and their prince. To withdraw from society in Egypt was to move up out of the fertile valley of the Nile and live in the desert, a region that for millennia had been thought of as spiritually as well as physically threatening. The Christians also believed that the prayers of the communities in the increasingly Christianized empire were driving the demons out of the cities and that they were now congregating in the desert instead.

When a monk withdrew into the desert, he expected to struggle both physically and morally against hordes of demons, his defense being an ascetic life under the protection of Christ. The desert took on a dual meaning for the monks: it was a place of refuge from the temptations of society, but it was also a place where temptations came directly from the Devil. In the desert one could get away from petty distractions, from small vices and small virtues, and take part directly in the cosmic struggle

36. This brief sketch primarily follows Widengren, *Mani*, pp. 43–68 and Puech, pp. 74–82.

between Christ and Satan. And the monks were quite right. Whether one interprets demons as external beings or as internal psychological forces, no doubt exists that the monks felt themselves under almost incessant attacks from the powers of evil. Their experiences, and the interest engendered in the wider Christian community by accounts of their experiences, brought about a marked growth in fear of the Devil. The deeds of the monks against the demons were known even to unbelievers, who mocked at them. Julian the Apostate wrote that "these two things are the quintessence of [Christian] theology, to hiss at demons and make the sign of the cross on their [own] forehead."[37] The demons attacked hermits more than cenobites, because the higher one rose in the spiritual life the more impressive the attacks of the enemy on one became. The monks replaced the martyrs as the "athletes of God."

Through the lives of the monks written in the fourth century run numerous topoi, stock stories told first about one monk and then about others. These stories were not intended to be historical. The writers had in mind the ideal, archetypal monk, and each individual was seen as a representation or copy of the ideal, the result being that a story about one monk can justly be applied to another. To the modern eye it sometimes appears that the hagiographers—the composers of saints' lives—stole one another's ideas and falsified evidence. To see them thus is to misunderstand their aims. The hagiographers did not intend to write biography or history. They were writing instead about eternal principles. Because hagiography is so packed with topoi and so little concerned with distinguishing individuals, the lives of the monks of the fourth and early fifth centuries are best considered in terms of an archetype. It indicates what the church expected of its holy men and women.

The function of "holy men" in the Christian community at that time was extraordinary. The concept of the "holy man," perhaps finding its social model in the secular leadership of cities and towns in the eastern Mediterranean, came to have an

37. Pelikan, *The Christian Tradition*, 1:136.

importance almost as great as that of the hierarchy of bishops and priests. People who set themselves apart from society by withdrawing into the desert and practicing an ascetic life were believed to have great wisdom. Many left the cities to follow them and to become monks themselves—hence the rapid growth of monasticism in this period—and many more who did not become monks took the monks as their models for the conduct of a good life. As the Roman Empire deteriorated, there was almost a rush to shift allegiance from the secular world to the transcendent world. Among the powerful images that monasticism broadcast through the Christian community was the idea of the monk as a warrior against the Devil.[38]

The model of monasticism was Christ himself. As Christ had withdrawn into the desert to be tempted by Satan, so the monks went likewise, prayed and fasted, and, under the protection of their Master, struggled against the powers of darkness. As the monks imitated Christ, so the community endeavored to imitate them, and the tales told of their battles with the Devil were accepted and incorporated into the popular view of the world. The monastic hagiographies added detail and color to the person of Satan.

One of the most influential works of monastic diabology was written by Athanasius. Athanasius, born in 295, worked as a deacon and secretary for Bishop Alexander of Alexandria and became bishop himself in 328. He led the fight against the Arians and was the most influential voice in the first ecumenical council at Nicea in 325. Among his works was the short and immensely influential "Life of Saint Anthony," written about 360, which paints the hermit's existence as a constant struggle against the Devil and his powers.[39]

Athanasius assumed, like the Alexandrian fathers, that evil

38. On monastic literature and demonology see A. C. Guillaumont, "Démon dans la littérature monastique," *Dictionnaire de spiritualité ascétique et mystique*, vol. 3, and the Essay on the Sources.

39. For Athanasius' works, see the Essay on the Sources. The most significant are: "The Incarnation of the Word" (Inc.); "To the Bishops of Egypt" (Bish.); "Orations against the Arians" (Ar.); "Against the Heathen" (Heath.); "On Virginity," (Virg.); and the "Life of Anthony" (Ant.).

In this unusual representation of the temptation of Christ, Jesus appears to preside at the top of the temple while Satan, at his left, vainly tries to persuade him to cast himself down. Angels hover above, and a multitude watch. Illumination from the Book of Kells, c. A.D. 790. Courtesy of the Board of Trinity College, Dublin.

was basically nonbeing, but he also believed that an active and malevolent power ruled over that nothingness. The Devil was a great angel who fell from heaven. He led other angels into sin and became "the great demon," their leader. With this fall the Devil and his demons separated themselves from the rest of the cosmos, condemning themselves to a life of nothingness, darkness, monstrosity, and nonbeing.[40] Inherently only negatives such as tumult, trouble, and disorder, the demons can take visible forms and thereby create images and fantasies in the minds of their victims. They eagerly rely on this power to vanquish the monks.[41] The Devil can change his shape at will. Often Athanasius thought of him as a huge giant living in the air and using his terrible form and might to prevent us from rising up to heaven. Or he might appear as a black boy, a sign of the emptiness and darkness of his soul and also of his inherent weakness against the power of Christ. He and his demons often take the form of beasts, in symbol of their brutish stupidity, or monsters—"a beast like a man to the thighs but having legs and feet like those of an ass"—to symbolize the fact that they have no true being and no true place in the cosmos. Athanasius drew from Job a description that remained fixed in iconography: the Devil's "eyes are as the morning star. From his mouth proceed burning lamps, and hearths of fire are cast forth. The smoke of a furnace blazing with the fire of coals proceeds from his nostrils. His breath is coals and from his mouth issues flame." The Devil can take the form of an angel of light, and the demons can delude us by singing beautifully, quoting Scripture, echoing words of prayer, and even assuming the appearance of monks. But feigning good is too great an effort for them, and they slip back toward their own reality, manifesting ugliness and emitting stench. In their truest form they are heavy, invisible substances drawn down toward darkness and ruin.[42] Before the

40. Inc. 4; Heath. 6; Virg. 5; Bish. 1–2; Ant. 22.

41. Ant. 22, 31: Visible forms, σχήματα, producing fantasies, φαντασίαι. Names of the Devil: Behemoth, the Evil One, the enemy, the dragon, a liar, the great demon (Ant. 5, 6, 11, 24).

42. Translations from *Nicene and Post-Nicene Fathers*. Forms of Devil and demons: Ant. 6, 9, 23–25, 40–41, 53, 66; Bish. 1–2. The most common beasts

demons sinned, they lived in heaven. Owing to their fault, they were cast down into the lower air, where they are buffeted about in a roiling, cacophonous commotion. Darting swiftly through the air, they occupy the earth, fixing their chief abode in the desert.[43]

Before the Incarnation, the demons had shut the road to salvation completely, but Christ's sacrifice opened it up again. Yet the demons still lurk around us in the air as we try to climb that road, and they use everything in their power to stop us. Whatever sins we commit during our lives are debts we owe to the demons, and as we rise toward heaven they demand payment before they let us through. On earth they use a variety of techniques against us, including internal temptation (for example, lust), external assault (terror), and treachery (feigning goodness or defeat).[44]

The Devil, said Athanasius, was worried by the desert monks. For one thing, he had sought the desert as his refuge after the prayers of the Christians had lessened his hold upon the cities. For another, he knew that the monks' imitation of

---

whom the demons choose to resemble are dragons, serpents, scorpions, lions, bears, leopards, bulls, wolves, hyenas, and roosters: cf. Guillaumont, col. 192. Cf. Job 41:18–20, the description of Leviathan. Athanasius followed his compatriot Origen in amalgamating Satan with Leviathan, the Prince of Tyre, and Lucifer, and in defining pride as Satan's first sin. Pachomius saw the Devil appear as a young black girl who tried to seduce him (*Historia Lausiaca*, 23.76–77). Pachomius drove the girl off with a blow of his hand; afterward the stench lingered on his hand for two years. Macarius was also bothered by a mob of small black demons (Rufinus, *Historia monachorum* 29).

43. Ant. 8, 13, 21–22, 28, 65; Inc. 25; see Daniélou, "Démons." Daniélou's observation that the air does not appear as the dwelling place of demons in either the Old Testament or in the apocalyptic literature is rejected by H. A. Kelly, *The Devil, Demonology, and Witchcraft*, pp. 25, n. 1 and 26. Paul's "principalities" are mediators of the Mosaic law and therefore not demons. Found in the New Testament, rabbinic literature, and most of the fathers, the idea seems to derive from the Platonic tradition. Philo, Plutarch, and Porphyry all followed Plato in holding that the *daimones* (who were for them not necessarily evil) dwelt in the air.

44. Ant. 11, 23, 65; see Daniélou, "Démons," pp. 142–144; Kelly, *The Devil, Demonology, and Witchcraft*, pp. 105ff. Athanasius followed Clement and Origen in imagining the demons as customs officers barring our way until we pay for our sins.

Christ is a leaven of salvation impeding his own efforts to make the world sink in a leaden mass down to hell. Accordingly, the higher the monks rise in their quest for God, the more hatefully the Devil attacks them. Since solitude is a great virtue, each time Anthony decided to withdraw deeper into solitude, he exposed himself to an especially sharp incidence of attacks: first when he withdrew to a tomb near his village, then when he went off to live in a ruined fort in the desert near the river, and finally when he went deep into the deadly desert near the Red Sea. Pachomius too was molested more fiercely when he was a hermit than later when he had assembled a monastic community around him, and Hilarion also suffered the most when first he sought desert seclusion.[45]

Demonic assaults are usually managed by subsidiary demons, but the Devil himself takes over if the monk's resistance is great enough. The demons' techniques are varied and resourceful. When Anthony decided to go out to the abandoned tomb, the Devil, hating his youthful goodness and fearing his spiritual potential, first whispered in his mind temptations good in themselves. Anthony should think of the good that he could do with his money, the Devil suggested, and of the responsibility that he had for his young sister: the Devil particularly likes to lower a monk's defenses by using as a temptation something that is good in itself. Later, when Anthony was more advanced in the spiritual life, the Devil tried to tempt him to extreme measures of asceticism so that he would necessarily fail and come to regard his monastic vocation as a burden. The demons use other practices to deceive. They appear in the form of good angels, monks, or even the Lord himself. They pretend to honor and revere the monk in order to catch him off guard. They sing psalms and recite verses from Scripture, or they tell a small truth in order to inspire confidence before uttering a big lie. They pretend to foretell the future by using their great speed to report distant events. For example, if they see a man setting out to visit his brother, they will rush to the brother to "predict"

45. Ant. 5, 8, 11–12, 23.

the visit. They pretend to cringe and grovel; Anthony was able to penetrate this ruse on the part of "the little black boy" and thus succeed in casting him out.[46]

Temptations can be cruder. When the young Anthony failed to yield to thoughts of his estate and his sister, the Devil put into his mind images of wealth, banquets, and glory. He caused him to consider the great dangers and discomfort in what he was planning to do, thus raising in him a great cloud of doubt. Then, when that too at length failed, he suggested lewd thoughts, even going so far as to take the form of a sexy young woman. The demons often used the temptation of lust against younger monks, turning to the quieter comforts when dealing with older men.[47]

One evening a demon took the shape of a pretty woman traveling in the desert. She came to the door of a monk's cave, pretending to be tired and exhausted from her journey. She fell at the monk's knees as if to beg him for mercy. "Night overtook me," she said, "while I was still wandering in the desert, and now I am frightened. Just let me rest in a corner of your cell so that I don't fall prey to the wild animals." The monk, feeling pity, received her inside the cave, asking her why she was traveling alone in the desert. She began to converse normally enough but bit by bit sweetened her words and played upon his sympathies. The sweetness of her speech gradually took possession of his mind until she had turned it entirely to thoughts of lust. She began to mix jokes and laughter with her speech, reaching up to touch his chin and beard as if in reverence, and then stroking his throat and neck. The monk began to burn with desire, but just as he was about to consummate his passion, the demon let out a terrible shriek in a hoarse voice, slipped away from his embrace, and departed, laughing filthily at his shame.[48]

After temptation, the Devil's next step is to awaken fear. The border between internal and external demonic assaults is

46. Ant. 5, 23–28, 31–40.
47. Ant. 5; Hilarion 7. The demons also tempt to idolatry and heresy: Inc. 11; Ant. 78–80, 94.
48. Rufinus, *Historia monachorum*, 1.

porous. The demons sometimes send dreams and hallucinations to frighten the monks, but sometimes the demons are actually externally present, exhibiting the sight, sound, and smell of various beings. Taking on the appearance of holy men, they tell lies; taking on the forms of giants, wild beasts, and creeping things, they frighten and disgust. They exude disgusting odors, and frequently they will set up a nerve-shattering racket and din. Sometimes they confuse these effects. Anthony was once awakened by horrible shrieking noises and the wall of his hut shaking; then the demons irrupted in numerous terrifying shapes as "lions, bears, leopards, bulls, serpents, asps, scorpions, and wolves," all threatening him with grating, guttural, howling noises. Saint Hilarion heard babies crying, cattle lowing, women weeping, lions roaring, and the muffled sounds of ignorant armies clashing by night; he witnessed a terrible struggle of gladiators before his very eyes, one falling dead at his feet before he realized that all was the dumb-show of demons. The demons are not proud; they will descend from the horrible to the silly in order to distract the monk from his contemplation. They dance, laugh, whistle, caper, fart, and prance; sometimes they stage comedies: Pachomius watched tiny demons carefully attach a rope to a leaf and then pretend to strain in a vain effort to budge it. Ordinarily it was assumed that demons, however much they threaten and frighten, did not have the power actually to harm the monk, but sometimes physical assaults were recorded. The Devil leaped on Hilarion's back and whipped him; once the Devil and a pack of demons waylaid Anthony, beating him and whipping him and leaving him unconscious on the ground. In his old age Anthony used to recount to his younger brothers that he had often fended off the Devil with physical blows.[49]

How is the historian to take such stories? It is difficult to judge what the authors intended as a literal account, what they

49. Hilarion 6–8; Ant. 8–9, 23, 26–27, 35, 39–40, 51–52, 63. C. S. Lewis' description of the physical combat between Satan and Ransom in his space novel *Perelandra* is not a schoolboy fantasy, as some critics maintained, but a tradition well rooted in diabology.

intended as dream or hallucination on the part of the monk, and what they intended simply as a moral and archetypal tale. If it is hard to judge the intention, it is impossible to say what really may have happened. One is properly skeptical of the historicity of such stories, but the sophisticated historian does not reject alleged events merely because they do not fit our contemporary world view, which, like all world views, is precarious. What we do know is that these stories were widely—almost universally— taken as accurate descriptions of demonic behavior.

To combat these diabolical assaults, the monks had the same weapons as other Christians: faith in Christ and the practical use of the sign of the cross and the name of Jesus. The demons fear these particularly; they are burned painfully by them in token of their future punishment in hell. To these the monks could add their spiritual acumen and experience, always aided by the grace of God. Anthony's ascetic life, fasting, and vigils blunted the enemy's attacks. Other monastic weapons were exorcism, showing contempt by ignoring the demons or blowing on them (possibly in imitation of the saving breath or Word of God; this is what Julian the Apostate meant when he jeered at the monks for hissing at demons), and simple fearlessness. When a spirit approaches, one should boldly confront it and ask it what it is. If an angel, it will reveal itself; if a demon, it will flee such courage in gibbering fear.

Of all defenses, the discernment of spirits is the most important. One receives discernment as a gift from God; by using it wisely one can become a great monk. The doctrine of discernment became the vehicle for a sophisticated psychology. We are all aware of our shifting urges and changing moods, and we know that what seems right one day may seem wrong the next. We can make serious mistakes because we are misled by passing impulses. By the exercise of discernment, then, monks could tell whether a given impulse came ultimately from God or from the Devil, whether it was helpful or harmful. They learned to do this both for themselves and for others, so that they were frequently visited by people in ordinary life seeking advice. The discernment of spirits gave the monks skill in interpreting dreams and in what Freud would call, centuries later, the psychopathology of everyday life.[50]

All successful resistance to the Devil is rooted in the grace of Christ, without which nothing would be effective. "The Devil, the enemy of humanity, has fallen from heaven and wanders in the lower regions of the air . . . but the Saviour has come to defeat the Devil, purify the air, and open the road to heaven."[51] The cross that raised Christ up into the air was the sign of his destruction of the demonic powers of the air; his descent into hell was the sign of his defeat of the demons under the earth, and his resurrection was the final seal of his triumph. Ephraim the Syrian constructed a dramatic dialogue in which Death, Gehenna, Sheol, and Satan all lament the death of Jesus, which they had hoped to use against God and humanity but which he cleverly turned against them.[52]

Athanasius had to face the fact that in spite of Christ's sacrifice the demons still range the world. He explained it by saying that Christ mortally wounded the demons and rendered them powerless over humankind save insofar as he gave them permission to tempt or to accuse. Christ has put the hook into Leviathan's nose and leads him about. But it is now up to us to associate ourselves with Christ's mission. By relying on his grace and practicing virtuous lives we associate ourselves with his sacrifice and help move the cosmic process toward the Devil's final ruin. The light that the demons feign actually proceeds from the flames of hell. The Devil and his minions will burn without hope of repentance in eternal fire. When that nothingness is cauterized, all again will be whole, and all things will be with God.

Athanasius puts this story into Anthony's mouth:

Once some one knocked at the door of my cell, and going forth I saw one who seemed of great size and tall. Then when I enquired, "Who art thou?" he said, "I am Satan." Then when I said, "Why art thou here?" he answered, "Why do the monks and all other Christians

50. Ant. 5, 7, 13, 21–25, 35–41, 62–64, 71; Hilarion 6, 16.
51. Inc. 25.
52. For Ephraim's work, see the Essay on the Sources.

blame me undeservedly? Why do they curse me hourly?" Then I answered, "Wherefore dost thou trouble them?" He said, "I am not he who troubles them, but they trouble themselves, for I am become weak. Have they not read, 'The swords of the enemy have come to an end, and thou hast destroyed the cities'? I have no longer a place, a weapon, a city. The Christians are spread everywhere, and at length even the desert is filled with monks. Let them take heed to themselves, and let them not curse me undeservedly." Then I marvelled at the grace of the Lord, and said to him: "Thou who art ever a liar and never speakest the truth, this at length, even against thy will, thou hast truly spoken. For the coming of Christ hath made thee weak, and He hath cast thee down and stripped thee." But he having heard the Saviour's name, and not being able to bear the burning from it, vanished.[53]

Evagrius of Pontus was born in that city in 345, the son of a bishop. Influenced by Basil the Great and Gregory Nazianzenus, he was ordained deacon by the latter in 379. With many wealthy and powerful connections, he preached in Constantinople and moved in high circles. But by 383 the life of luxury and fame had begun to pall, and he withdrew into the Nitrian desert in Egypt with a group of monks influenced by Origen. A close friend of Rufinus and of Melania, both of whom were devoted Origenists, Evagrius adopted Origen's ideas as the basis of his own theology. In the desert he became a disciple of the great spiritual leader Macarius the elder, and, writes a modern student of his work, he "led a most austere life, living on small amounts of bread and oil. He underwent the most severe trials against chastity and met them with heroic efforts, such as passing the night exposed to the winter cold standing in a well."[54] Evagrius gained the reputation of possessing discre-

53. Inc. 30, 46–48; Ant. 23–24, 28, 42; Virg. 5; Ar. 3.40. See Young, "Insight or Incoherence," pp. 124–125; Daniélou, "Démons," p. 146. The long quotation is Ant. 41, trans. *Nicene and Post-Nicene Fathers*, 4:207.

54. J. E. Bamberger, *Evagrius Ponticus: The Praktikos; Chapters on Prayer* (Kalamazoo, Mich. 1972), p. xliii. Quotations from Bamberger are with the kind permission of the Institute of Cistercian Studies at Western Michigan University and its director Rozanne Elder. On Evagrius' life, see Bamberger's excellent summary, pp. xxxv–xlviii; the Guillaumonts; and S. Wenzel, *The Sin of Sloth* (Chapel Hill, 1960), pp. 3–22.

tion—the discernment of spirits—to an extraordinary degree, and stories recounting his triumphs over demons were famous. An eloquent, personal, colorful writer, Evagrius was "a much better analyst of the human psyche than a theoretical [theologian]." He remained in the desert until his death in 399.

Displaying a combination of psychological acumen and an acquaintance with every level of society from the highest circles in Constantinople to the simple Coptic monks of the Nitrian desert, Evagrius' works were widely circulated until 553, when the third ecumenical council at Constantinople included them in its condemnation of Origen's views. After 553, Evagrius sank into increasing obscurity. Some of his works continued to circulate without his name; in an effort to make them respectable, scribes attributed them to the orthodox monk Saint Nilus. Only in the twentieth century has a grasp of his ideas and influence been renewed. He had a vast effect upon Byzantine and Syrian spirituality and a scarcely less profound influence on the monasticism of the West through Palladius, Maximus Confessor, and Cassian, who in turn influenced the monasticism of Gaul and of Ireland.[55]

Evagrius' theory of the fall is a variant of Origen's with further Neoplatonic flavoring. God, the "Primitive Henad," creates the Henad, which is pure intelligence; the pure intelligence (*nous*) multiplies into a number of equal intelligences (*noes*). But some of the intelligences "fall" in a "movement" (*kinēsis*) away from God. The only nous that does not fall is the Lord, the Son of God, who proceeds to make the second creation, which is the material world. The degree to which the spirits fall depends on the degree of their sin. The good angels, made of fire, remain in heaven. Some fallen spirits become human, made of earth. The most sinful become demons, who are made of air. Each step downward is darker, thicker, grosser, more material. The demons are heavy and ice-cold, made of air that is devoid of light.

---

55. On Evagrius' works, see the Essay on the Sources. They include the "Practical Advice" (Pract.); the "Kephalaia gnostica" (Keph.); "Prayer"; the "Antirrhetikos" (Antir.); the "Eight Spirits of Malice," actually part of the "Antirrhetikos"; "On Evil Thoughts" (Evil); "Gnostics."

The *noes* who fall become *psychai*, souls. The *psychē* is the seat of passions; among humans the dominant passion is sensuality; among demons it is wrath. With the help of God, one may through asceticism and prayer climb the ontological scale until one rejoins God. This will gradually happen with all the intelligences. On the "seventh day," the intelligences will be sentenced in the last judgment either to rise to heaven or to sink into hell. On the "eighth day," however, all the intelligences will be brought back to God, and evil will cease to be.[56]

Influenced by the "Life of Anthony," Evagrius gave demons an important role in the monastic life. Out of the hundred chapters of his "Practical Advice," demons play an important part in sixty-seven. The demons are not evil in essence. They fall through free will, and since the degree of their fall depends upon the degree of their sin, ranks of demons exist, the lower being the more evil.[57] The angels, dwelling close to God, have great knowledge and power, but the demons lost these qualities when they fell. They have no true knowledge and lack all understanding that truth points to God. They can no longer see God or even the good angels. They are able to observe humans and derive specious knowledge from what they perceive. They are unable to penetrate into our souls, for our souls are marked by a trace of desire for God that only he and his good angels can plumb. Thus the demons rely upon their observation of our actions, our words, our bodies, even our "body language," to interpret the state of our souls. They are clever in this, they have mastered human languages and human sciences, and they constantly use their skills to trick and delude us.[58]

The demons dwell in the air, where they travel by flying with wings. They can become tiny, and so enter our bodies in the air we draw through the nose (hence the superstition of saying "bless you" to someone who sneezes). They have thin,

56. Bamberger's study of Evagrius' doctrines, pp. lxxv–lxxvii, is generally good but unclear on a number of points; the Guillaumonts' is better, in *Traité*, pp. 38–112.
57. Pract. 45, 59.
58. Antir.8.56; Pract. 44, 47.

whistling, windy voices. They have size, color, and form appropriate to their low cosmic status, but though they can see us, we can never see them, unless they take on false shapes (*schēmata*) in order to delude us; they may appear as angels of light, pretty women, warriors, or whatever they wish; in these forms they grind their teeth and emit groans and stenches.[59]

As each demon occupies a different place in the hierarchy of hell, so each has his own purpose and personality. Some demons are more vicious, some more persistent, some quicker, some more cowardly than others. The monk used his discernment not only to distinguish a good from an evil spirit but also to determine what sort of evil spirit he was dealing with.[60] The purpose of demons is to attack the human soul so as to destroy God's image and likeness within us. They attempt to abort every virtue, and they attack us most viciously when they suspect us of contemplating any good action. For this reason they assault monks more than ordinary people, hermits more than cenobites, and those illuminated by divine knowledge or gnosis more than the ignorant. Evagrius' thought, like that of Origen and Athanasius, contained an underlying, implicit assumption that martyrs, monks, and the enlightened form a spiritual elite among human beings, a lightning rod attracting the hostile attention of the demons away from the rest of the community, an elite armed by God with special grace and fortitude to fend off these savage attacks. Evagrius' special class of the enlightened is close to the Gnostic *pneumatikoi* or spirituals, the difference being that the Gnostics believed that people are born into a spiritual category, while for Evagrius the individual can through free cooperation with grace rise in the spiritual scheme.[61]

The demons attack us through both mind and body.

---

59. Antir. 4.47, 8.17, 4.13, 2.15, 2.32, 4.23, 4.34, 8.24. The coldness of the demons became a cliché of the early modern witch-craze, when women who believed that they had had sexual intercourse with the Devil claimed that his body and semen were cold.

60. Pract. 43.

61. Pract. 5, 43, 45; Prayer, 46, 50, 97, 148.

Although they cannot enter into our souls, they can by working on our brains suggest images, fantasies, fears, and temptations. Again, the demons discriminate. Most men they tempt to gross deeds; with monks they have a subtler chore: "The greater the progress the soul makes, the more fearful the adversaries that take over the war against him."[62] Sophisticated demons subtly divert sophisticated monks from their contemplation of God, introducing illusions and obsessions of such delicacy that only the discerning monk specially protected by God's grace can readily find the means to resist. The demons can attack anywhere on the spectrum from a refined temptation to do something apparently good, through coarser temptations of lust and greed, all the way to brutal physical assaults. They take on fiery forms and cause fearsome apparitions; they meddle with our bodies, tickling our noses, scratching our ears, tightening our stomachs, making us drowsy during prayer, swelling us with flatulence, causing serious disease or injury, or even leaping onto us to beat and maul us, all in order to divert us from our divine purpose.[63]

Evagrius' psychology of temptation was precise. Our souls, having fallen from heaven and being now embedded in the body, are bent, their vision of God blurred. They are dominated by emotion (*pathē*) that they cannot shake off. The emotional turmoil of our souls is endemic in our fallen state. It is *pathē* that we must transcend through the grace of Christ if we are to ascend again into heaven. From *pathē* arise emotional thoughts, inclinations, or desires (*empatheis logismoi*). Not all "thoughts" are evil, of course, but Evagrius uses the term almost always in a negative sense. These *logismoi* are the "raw

62. Pract. 59, trans. Bamberger.

63. Prayer 46, 50, 72–73, 94–99, 111; Pract. 54; Antir. 1.44, 2.25, 2.34, 2.50, 2.52–55, 4.14–62, 8.62. Pract. 48: attack monks through their thoughts, διὰ τῶν λογισμῶν. In his introduction to Bamberger's translation, Jean Leclercq observes that Evagrius' description of the demons' activities in the Antirrhetikos make "the temptations of St Anthony seem as the dreams of a mere infant. . . . That which is called today 'depth psychology' does not in actual fact reach the deepest part of man where the image of God resides in him"; the psychology of Evagrius does (p. xii).

material" that the monk must master if he is to rise above them; they are open gates for the demons attacking us. Watching us carefully, the Devil sees when we are weakened by a particular *logismos*, and then he sends in demonic troops specifically trained to exploit it. "The *logismoi*," writes Siegfried Wenzel, "are the tools or 'weapons' used by the demons as instruments of temptation: 'the demons war against the soul by means of the *logismoi*.' . . . Temptation and moral evil [are] thus the result of a combination of an external agent and a disposition in human nature."[64] Without demonic temptation we could still sin through the logismoi that arise in our own souls, but the demons use the logismoi in two ways: they bolster and reinforce them, making them more difficult to resist, and they rush through them as through holes in the moral dike. Everyone has had the experience of yielding to a small sin, or of yielding in a small way to sin, only to have that small beachhead rapidly expanded and fortified by much more powerful temptations of the same genre. The logismos of lust, for example, may cause a man to desire a woman; if he chooses to dwell upon the thought, his mind may be flooded with lewd images until his soul is finally confused, obsessed, and enslaved. The logismos of avarice may cause a woman first to dwell too carefully upon the investments she plans for her security; if she begins to attend too much to money, she may find her mind obsessed by financial schemes, until need has turned to greed and she is a slave to her wealth. In every such case, the demons take the small opening created by the logismos and rush through it in a great flood that can be stemmed only with the help of grace.[65]

Both the logismoi and the demons are specialized. Evagrius conceived of eight powerful demons presiding over various aspects of practical morality, each set at the head of a host of demons prepared to exploit a particular kind of sin. The eight

---

64. Quotations from Wenzel, p. 14. Passionate desires or inclinations: ἐμπαθεῖς λογισμούς. The term λογισμός, also used by Origen in the form διαλογισμός, derives from the διαλογισμός or "evil thought" of Matthew 15:19. Behind the logismoi is the doctrine of the *yetserim*.

65. Pract. 37–39, 43, 48; Prayer 46.

divisions of demons correspond to eight logismoi, namely gluttony, pride, lust, avarice, despair, anger, acedia (spiritual sloth), and vanity. The demons do not attack all at once, for they see that the soul is more deeply corrupted by wallowing in one or two vices at a time, and some vices are mutually contradictory in psychological practice: for example, it is difficult to practice gluttony and spiritual pride at one and the same time.[66] Each vice is watched carefully by the demon in charge so that it may be exploited to the utmost. Of the eight vices, acedia is the most subtle and the most to be feared by monks, since they have risen relatively high in their spiritual progress:

The demon of *acedia*—also called the noonday demon—is the one that causes that most serious trouble of all. He presses his attack upon the monk [during the four midday hours]. First of all he makes it seem that the sun barely moves, if at all, and that the day is fifty hours long. Then he constrains the monk to look constantly out of the windows, to walk outside the cell, to gaze carefully at the sun to determine how far it stands from the [dinner] hour, to look now this way and now that to see if perhaps [one of the brethren appears from his cell]. Then too he instills in the heart of the monk a hatred for the place, a hatred for his very life itself, a hatred for manual labor. He leads him to reflect that charity has departed from among the brethren, that there is no one to give encouragement. Should there be someone at this period who happens to offend him in some way or other, this too the demon uses to contribute further to his hatred. This demon drives him along to desire other sites where he can more easily procure life's necessities, more readily find work and make a real success of himself. He goes on to suggest that, after all, it is not the place that is the basis of pleasing the Lord. . . . He joins to these reflections the memory of his dear ones and of his former way of life. He depicts life stretching out for a long period of time, [inducing the monk] to forsake his cell and drop out of the fight.[67]

66. Pract. 31, 58–59. For the eight demons of vice and their logismoi, Pract. 6–14.

67. Pract. 12, trans. Bamberger, pp. 18–19. On the noonday demon see R. Arbesmann, "The 'Demonium Meridianum' and Greek and Latin Patristic Exegesis," *Traditio*, 14 (1958), 17–31, and R. Caillois, "Les démons de midi," *Revue de l'histoire des religions*, 115 (1937), 142–173; 116 (1937), 54–83, 143–186.

The chief remedy against such assaults is with the help of grace to practice discernment, distinguishing between good and evil spirits and among the varieties of evil spirits, so that one may judge what weapons to turn back against the demons. Evagrius also prescribed the conventional good life, prayer, asceticism, and the name of Jesus. He advised active and angry resistance. One should not be passive when tempted by demons, but rather thrust them angrily out of the mind and then

---

The logismos of acedia, ἀκηδία, is watched by the demon or spirit of acedia, τὸ τῆς ἀκηδίας δαίμων or a τὸ τῆς ἀκηδίας πνεῦμα, who exploits the logismos against the monk to the best of his ability. Noon, like midnight, was in many cultures a time of intense activity by spiritual powers. The Christians, with their hostility to such powers, defined them as evil. The monastic writers tended to identify the noonday demon with the spirit of acedia, but later it was identified with Satan himself. See below, Ch. seven, n. 14. It is not my intention in this book to investigate the history of the seven (or eight) cardinal sins, which has already been skillfully examined by other scholars. The roots of the doctrine have been found in Jewish thought (e.g., The Testaments of the Twelve Patriarchs) and in Greco-Roman thought (e.g., Horace). Among Christian writers, versions of the doctrine appear in Cyprian, Origen, Cyril of Alexandria, Macarius, and the early eremitical and monastic writers in general. The ultimate origin may lie in the ancient astronomical theory of seven heavens plus the one unmoving sphere above them; it was this combination that made the number eight sacred among the Gnostics. Evagrius, though influenced by earlier writers, was the first to establish a precise list of eight specific sins, an idea that had great influence. The adoption of the modified scheme of seven cardinal sins by Gregory the Great (pope from 590 to 604) fixed the idea firmly in Christian tradition. Evagrius listed the eight sins as γαστριμαργία (*gula*, gluttony); πορνεία (*luxuria*, lust); ὀργή (*ira*, anger); ἀκηδία (*accidia* or *acedia*, spiritual sloth); λύπη (*tristitia*, despair); φιλαργυρία (*avaritia*, avarice); κενοδοξία (*vana gloria* or *vanitas*, vainglory or vanity); ὑπερηφανία (*superbia*, pride). Later lists of seven often dropped despair. On the seven (or eight) deadly sins, see especially M. W. Bloomfield, *The Seven Deadly Sins* (East Lansing, Mich., 1952) and Bloomfield, "The Origin of the Concept of the Seven Cardinal Sins," *Harvard Theological Review*, 34 (1941), 121–128; Wenzel, *Sin of Sloth*; Wenzel, "The Seven Deadly Sins: Some Problems of Research," *Speculum*, 43 (1968), 1–22. See also A. Vögtle, "Achtlasterlehre," *Reallexikon für Antike und Christentum*, 1 (1941), 74–79; I. Hausherr, "L'origine de la théorie occidentale des huit péchés capitaux," *Orientalia christiana*, 30 (1964), 164–175 (a somewhat different view of their origins); L. K. Little, "Pride Goes before Avarice: Social Change and the Vices in Latin Christendom," *American Historical Review*, 76 (1971), 16–49. Note the distinction between the cardinal sins and the deadly sins, as explained by Bloomfield, *Seven Deadly Sins*, p. 43.

go on to take diversionary counteractions. A monk tossing awake at night with lustful thoughts, for example, should quickly rise and go to the sick-room to perform an act of kindness for someone who is ill, thus flouting the Devil by making one of his temptations the occasion for a positive act of virtue.

The goal of the Christian in defeating the demons is, of course, to rise to God, and the state of the soul requisite to this rising is *apatheia*. Apatheia is quite different from the modern "apathy," though both mean "lack of feeling." For Evagrius, apatheia was freedom from pathē, the confused emotional state into which we were plunged as a result of the fall, from the logismoi produced by pathē, and from the demons summoned by the logismoi. Apatheia is "the freedom from disturbing passions, obtained through rational control over one's senses, desires, feelings, and memory." Apatheia brings *hēsychia*, the quiet, calm centering of the soul that is natural to a spirit in the company of God; in regard to our earthly existence it brings *agapē*, that noblest state of soul described by Saint Paul, in which we desire only that which is truly good for ourselves and for others.[68]

Evagrius, Athanasius, and the others who described the monastic struggle against the demons in the arena of the desert lent the concept of the Devil color, particularity, and immediate sensual reality. The Devil is present every moment, ready and eager to attack us with every weapon from false intellectual sophistication to lewd thoughts to physical assaults to petty distractions. Behind these manifestations lurks an emerging sense of a cold, heavy, monstrous presence, clever, yet idiotic, weighing down the world toward darkness.

68. Pract. intro., 2, 81. Pract. 2: "The kingdom of heaven is *apatheia* of the soul along with true knowledge of existing things." Trans. Bamberger, p. 15. See Wenzel, *Sin of Sloth*, pp. 13–14.

7 Satan and Saint Augustine

Christian tradition in the fourth and fifth centuries began to be divided between Greek East and Latin West. The division did not become pronounced until the eighth century or formal until the eleventh, and the Council of Chalcedon, which in 451 had summarized the basic doctrines of the Trinity and the nature of Christ, remained the cement of a united Christendom. Nonetheless, theological traditions were beginning to diverge. Basil the Great and John Chrysostom had much influence among the Greeks and little among the Latins; Jerome and Augustine, the greatest of the Latin fathers, had little influence in the East, and Augustine knew virtually no Greek. Yet diabology, eclipsed in this period by the monumental debates on the Trinity and Christ, was largely a summary and refinement of the already established main lines of the concept. With the exception of Augustine, who broke significant new ground, the theologians of the period both eastern and western can still therefore be treated as a community.[1]

Evil was still widely perceived in Platonic terms as privation, but it was seen as limited nonbeing rather than as absolute

1. These theologians include Cyril of Jerusalem, Basil of Caesarea, Gregory of Nyssa, Gregory Nazianzenus, John Chrysostom, Cyril of Alexandria, Theodoret, Jerome, Ambrose, and Hilary of Poitiers. A summary of these writers with representative works and passages relevant to the Devil is found in the Essay on the Sources.

nothing. Saint Jerome argued that evil could not be absolute negation, because truly absolute negation would be a principle in itself and concurrent with God. Evil lacks being in the sense that it is deprived of God's true reality, but it is not literally nothing, not wholly nonexistent.[2] The Devil, the leader of the forces of evil, is not a principle of evil, as the Manicheans would have it. His evil derives from his free will, which he misused through pride compounded by envy of God. The root of this pride, according to Gregory of Nyssa, was love of power. The Devil's fall preceded the creation of the human race. The Devil envied humans as well as God, but his envy of humanity came after his fall. Where his envy of God caused *him* to sin, his envy of humanity caused him to tempt *us* to sin. The other sinful angels also fell from pride, and at the same time as their dark master.[3]

The Devil and his followers, both angelic and human, constitute a kingdom in opposition to the kingdom of God, just as they are the root of evil and death opposite to the way of truth and life, a city of darkness opposed to the city of light, and the mystical body of Satan against the mystical body of Christ. But the kingdom of Satan is not a legitimate kingdom. The idea that demons rule this world is a false, pagan notion. Though they are called "world-rulers" (*kosmokratores*), the cosmos that they rule is not God's created universe, but rather the mass of sinful humanity. *Kosmos* here has retained most of its New Testament

2. J. Huhn, *Ursprung und Wesen des Bösen und der Sünde, nach der Lehre des Kirchenvaters Ambrosiens* (Paderborn, 1933), p. 45. For limited as opposed to absolute non-being, see ch. 5, n. 8.

3. The Devil's pride, τύφος, *vana gloria*. Satan's pride and his envy of God as the cause of his fall: Ambrose, *Explanatio super Psalmos*, 3.34, 16.15, 35.11; *Expositio de psalmo 118*, 7.8; *De Paradiso* 2.9, 12.54; Jerome, Letter 12, 22, 108. Ambrose and Jerome were somewhat ambivalent on the subject of the Watchers, allowing hints of the old idea of the lustful angels to persist. Theodoret, *Haereticarum fabularum compendium*, 5.8; Basil, *Homilia de invidia* 11.4; Basil preferred envy to pride as the motive of Satan's fall: ὁ καταπεσὼν διὰ τοῦ φθόνου. Basil, *Adversus Eunomium* 1.13; Gregory of Nyssa, *Oratio catechetica magna* 21–24; Gregory Nazianzenus, *Carmen* 1.1.7; "Discourse" 36.5; *Oratio* 39.7. Chryosotom's rejection of the Watcher story was decisive for the eastern church: *Homila in Johannem* 16.4; *Homilia in Genesin* 22.2.

flavor: it is the community of sinners, of the mundane. Satan's kingdom is of this world in the sense that "this world" means the tendency of humans and angels to look away from the reality that is God to the less real: the selfish and transitory. "This world" is our sinful state.[4] God permits the Devil to exercise power in this world so that we will be obliged to exercise our spiritual powers and so that the saints may confound Satan by their miracles. The saint (the holy man or woman) succeeds the monk and the martyr as the type of the athlete of Christ struggling in the arena against the Devil. The imagery gradually changes too. Whereas the martyr was the athlete in the arena, the saint becomes a soldier on the battlefield. The shift reflects the end of the persecutions and the fact that military service was now deemed proper for Roman Christians. And, in the last analysis, God always takes the results of sin and turns them to his own providential ends.[5]

The pagan persecutions are past, but "you are mistaken," warned Saint Jerome, "if you suppose that there is ever a time when the Christian does not suffer persecution." The Devil, the true enemy, never ceases to persecute us by tempting us.[6]

4. Jerome, *Commentarium in Abacuc* 2.3.14–16; Ambrose, *Expositio in Psalmum 118*, 1.13; Chrysostom, *Diabolus* (*Sermon against Those Who Say that Demons Govern the World*) 1.6; *Homilia in Epistolam ad Ephesios* 22.3; *De incomprehensibili Dei natura* 4.2. Here Chrysostom mentions a variety of types of angels: angels, archangels, thrones, dominations, rulers, and powers: Εἰσὶ μὲν γὰρ ἄγγελοι, καὶ ἀρχάγγελοι, καὶ θρόνοι, καὶ κυριότητες, καὶ ἀρχαὶ, καὶ ἐξουσίαι.

5. Chrysostom, *Adversus Judaeos* 1.7; Theodoret, *Graecorum affectionum curatio* 3.102; Basil, *Homilia quod Deus non est auctor malorum* 9.9; Jerome, *Commentarium in Isaiam* 12.41, 21–24; Ambrose, *Expositio super Psalmum 32*; *Expositio evangelii secundum Lucam* 7.115; *Parad.* 2.9. Of course many hermits and monks were considered saints, but the concept of sainthood, of "holy men and women," was now gradually extended beyond martyrs and monks to anyone demonstrably living a life devoted to Christ. For "soldiers of Christ," *milites Christi*, see M. P. McHugh, "Satan and Saint Ambrose," *Classical Folia*, 26 (1972), 97. In the Middle Ages, when *miles* came to mean "knight" rather than "soldier," the Christian warrior was perceived as a knight of Christ. The chief duty of the Christian warrior is to enter into combat with Satan (McHugh, p. 100).

6. Jerome, Letter 14.4. Jerome argued against Jovinian, who claimed that "Christians who have received baptism with full adhesion of faith cannot

With the hand of the Father stretching down from heaven in approval, Christ, armored like a knight, destroys the dragon and the lion, symbols of demonic power. A ninth-century illumination from the Stuttgart Gospels. Courtesy of the Württembergische Landesbibliothek.

Ambrose argued that "evil has not been established by God the creator, but rather arises from us," in our free-will assent to the temptations of Satan." The greater danger lies not in attacks from outside but from within ourselves. Inside us is the adversary, inside us the author of error, inside us, I say, closed up within our very selves. . . . This evil within us is not natural. . . . Not God, but we, are the cause; it proceeds not from nature but from our own will."[7] God permits possession as well as temptation, and though possession may wrack a body God never allows it to corrupt a soul.[8]

----

henceforth fall under the dominion of the Devil." See J. N. D. Kelly, *Jerome* pp. 181–184.

7. Huhn, pp. 21–40: "Intus est adversarius, intus auctor erroris, intus, inquam, clausus in nobismetipsis." Evil is not "quasi naturalis iniquitas . . . non per naturam deliquit, sed per voluntatem. . . . Non substantialis sed accidens est malitia." Cf. *Expositio in Psalmum 118*, 4.22.

8. Chrysostom, *Ad Stagyrium* 1.1, 2.1; *Diabolus* 1.6. The victim does not knowingly will possession, but he can unknowingly encourage it by dabbling in magic, for example, or by allowing himself to sink into depression, ἀθυμία: Cyril of Jerusalem, *Catechesis de spiritu sancto* 1.16.

The image of the Devil grew more sinister in these years, perhaps in response to the growing dislocation of Roman society. He frequently appears in literature as a serpent, lion, dragon, dog, or wolf. Among the Copts (Egyptian Christians), ancient Egyptian religion retained some influence, for they described demons as having the "heads of wild animals, with tongues of fire sticking out of their mouths, with teeth of iron," and they frequently saw the demons as their ancestors had seen the old deities, with human bodies but the heads or faces of ibises, crocodiles, scorpions, asses, dogs, or lions.[9] Elsewhere the Devil might appear as a fisherman with attendant demons wielding nets and hooks, a reference to Leviathan—and, possibly, to the weapons once wielded by the gladiators in the arena. The Devil might be a giant, as in the fifth-century "Gospel of Bartholomew," where he is 1,600 cubits long and 40 cubits broad, with wings each 80 cubits long. In this form he has a "face like lightning, eyes of darkness," and stinking smoke escaping from his nostrils. "His mouth was as the gulf of a precipice."[10] Jerome compared him with Behemoth, a huge being with "strength in his loins, force in his navel," and inordinate sexual powers.[11] The Devil is usually black in token of his lack of goodness and light. Theodoret, for example, relates that a black demon once prevented a bishop from burning down the temple of Jupiter. The Devil wears black clothing or black armor, and he has black eyes, hair, and skin. This swarthy hue was originally not meant as a racial slur, for his features were not stereotypically African: for example, he is often specified as having sharp features, a thick beard, and fine hair. Initially, the blackness of the Devil signified one thing: his emptiness.

The Devil was sometimes portrayed as good-looking, but

9. J. Zandee, *Death as an Enemy According to Ancient Egyptian Concepts* (Leiden, 1960), p. 329.

10. "Gospel of Bartholomew," in James, *The Apocryphal New Testament*, p. 174. The fisherman: "Coptic Narrative of the Ministry and Passion of Jesus," James, p. 149; "Arabic Gospel of the Infancy," James, p. 82.

11. Jerome, Letter 22.11, following Job 40:11. Jerome also says that he is black and white and like a roaring lion. See also Letter 130.10.

with time he grew increasingly ugly.[12] The trident he sometimes wields may symbolize, as it seems to have done for
Poseidon, lordship over sea, earth, and underworld, or else its
origin may be an instrument of torture, which has certainly
been its chief connotation through the ages. He brandishes an
ax against the doors of the soul. He is a usurer, imprisoning the
soul and demanding huge interest payments before liberating it.
He is associated with salt water through his connection with
Leviathan and ultimately with the ancient principle of chaos,
but on the other hand salt was also a positive symbol of a nutri-
tional staff of life and was administered at baptism in order to
ward off evil. Fresh water, a symbol of renewal, is also an element hostile to evil and the most important element in baptism.
In later legends, demons—and witches—were thought to be incapable of crossing rivers or other bodies of fresh water. Yet the
Devil was sometimes portrayed with the characteristics of an
ancient river god. He was most often associated with fire,
which, particularly in the western church, symbolized torment
and destruction.[13] Jerome offered a new interpretation of the
"noonday demon," hitherto identified as the spirit of sloth, equating it instead with Satan himself and with the heretics who are
"the arrow that flieth by day." The heretics, like Satan, disguise themselves with light in order to deceive us with their
doctrines of darkness.[14] All the shapes taken by the Devil are, of
course, feigned, disguising his true form or his complete lack of
form. The notion that he in fact had no proper shape of his own
was growing common. Whereas earlier it was often believed
that demons possessed gross material bodies, it became usual to
regard them as pure—though purely corrupt—spirit.[15]

12. C. Naselli, "Diavoli bianchi e diavoli neri nei leggendari medievali,"
Volkstum und Kultur der Romanen, 15 (1941–1943), 233–254, esp. p. 251;
Zandee, p. 329; Jerome, Letter 22.

13. W. H. C. Frend, *The Rise of the Monophysite Movement* (Cambridge,
1972), p. 97. In the eastern church, fire often signified purification instead.
See Zandee, p. 339. For axes and for usury, see McHugh, pp. 97–100.

14. Arbesmann, "The 'daemonium meridianum,'" esp. 25–26.

15. Gregory of Nyssa, *De pauperibus amandis*, 1; Cyril of Jerusalem, *Catechesis de spiritu sancto*, 1.16.

Christ's mission was to save the world from the power of the Devil into which it had fallen as a result of humanity's original sin. Like the earlier fathers, those of the fourth and fifth centuries inconsistently affirmed a theodicy arguing that God permits evil in order to train us and punish us, at the same time teaching a salvation theory attributing evil to a source alien to God. Gregory Nazianzenus, prefiguring the abbé Paneloux in Camus' *Plague*, once explained to his congregation that a hailstorm which had destroyed their crops was a sign of divine displeasure with their sins; yet on other occasions he stressed the need for our redemption from radical evil. Saint Basil argued that a distinction between natural and moral ills was necessary: God permits all evils in order to discipline us, but moral evils, unlike natural ones, are our own fault.

These theologians also alternated the sacrifice theory of salvation with the ransom theory. This inconsistency came out into the open with Gregory of Nyssa and Gregory Nazianzenus, who debated the issue sharply. The former defended the ransom theory on the grounds that because of original sin we justly deserved to be in Satan's power. The Gospels report that Christ called himself a ransom for many, and Gregory of Nyssa took the New Testament view that after the sin of Adam and Eve Satan exercised great power in the world, so that God, he thought, "had to defeat Satan on his own ground." But Gregory Nazianzenus insisted that the idea of God's paying ransom to Satan was both irrational and revolting. Christ's death, said Nazianzenus, was a sacrifice to God. God neither demanded nor required such a sacrifice, but he accepted it as a means of cleansing human nature so that we might be fit to be reconciled with him. The Devil is a robber, Nazianzenus declared, and has no just claim to a ransom at all. Basil, Gregory of Nyssa's brother, explained that justice demanded ransom and that no ordinary man could be a suitable ransom; what was needed was a human who transcended human nature.[16]

16. The idea of ransom, λύτρον, is derived from Matthew 20:28 and Mark 10:45. See Young, "Insight or Incoherence," esp. 119–125; A. J. Philippou, "The Doctrine of Evil in Saint Gregory of Nyssa," *Studia patristica*, 9 (1966),

The most bitterly controversial aspect of the ransom theory was Origen's variation that the Passion was a trick that God practiced upon Satan. Gregory of Nyssa defended this variation dramatically, drawing upon the story of Leviathan for the image of the baited hook. The sinless Jesus was the bait that Satan snapped up, only to find himself caught on the hidden hook of Jesus' divinity. As Gregory of Nyssa explained it, Satan watched Christ's miracles and realized that this was a man of extraordinary power. He thought that it would be a good bargain to accept this wonder worker in exchange for the human race, which Satan had justly been holding in prison. Later he was amazed to find that Jesus was God. Having transgressed justice and overstepped his powers, he lost both Jesus and the entire human race. The western theologian Ambrose agreed with this account, adding that when Satan tempted Christ he was trying to find out who he really was; the effort failed, but Satan stupidly proceeded with the bargain. In the East, Nazianzenus indignantly rejected the whole idea, and even Gregory of Nyssa's brother Basil was dubious.[17] The idea of the trick faded, decisively rejected in the West by Augustine and in the East by Chrysostom. Chrysostom dismissed both trick and ransom, arguing that the Devil's overturning justice in claiming Christ automatically stripped him of his power over us: no ransom was needed. According to Chrysostom, the scenario was as follows: (1) humanity sinned, putting ourselves in the Devil's power; (2) the Devil henceforth had jurisdiction over us; (3) the Devil reached out to seize the Son of Man, exceeding his jurisdiction; (4) thus he lost his rights over us. At the moment that the Devil

---

251–256, esp. 255; J. N. D. Kelly, *Early Christian Doctrines*, p. 382; Gregory Nazianzenus, *Oratio* 45.22; Basil, *Adversus Eunomium* 2.27; *In Ps.* 48.3; Chrysostom, *Expositio in Psalmum 134*, 7; *In Epistolam ad Colossenses* 6.3; Theodoret, *Haer.* 1.pref; Cyril of Alexandria, *Commentarium in Isaiam* 5; *De Incarnatione Domini* 13; Hilary of Poitiers, *Tractatus super Psalmos* 64.9–10, 67.2, 68.14, 139.11, 143.11; Ambrose, *Commentarium in Lucam*, 7.92, 10.106–109.

17. Gregory of Nyssa, *Orat. cat.* 21–26; Gregory Nazianzenus, *Orat.* 45.22; Ambrose, *In Luc.* 2.3, 4.12, 4.16; Cyril of Alexandria, *De incarnatione Domini* 11; *Ad reginas de recta fide oratio altera* 31; Theodoret, *De providentia orationes* 10. Cyril and Theodoret rejected both the ransom and the trick.

seized Christ, Chrysostom said, "all the world was acquitted through him."[18]

In just punishment for their radical evil, Satan and his minions are consigned to torment and spiritual death. According to Jerome, Michael the archangel has "slain" Satan. Acting as God's agent to punish Satan's original sin of pride, Michael cast him out of heaven and deprived him of his spiritual dignity and life.[19] The question whether Satan might eventually be saved was still alive. Gregory of Nyssa, with his penchant for lost causes, defended Origen's doctrine of apocatastasis. The eastern church, eager to preserve Gregory's reputation, carefully excised the offending passages from his *Life of Moses*, but recent scholarship has restored them. In any event, Gregory's view was less radical than Origen's. Gregory had grasped the most radical weakness of the original theory: that if in fact all intelligences are eventually restored to their pristine state in union with God, just as they had been in the beginning, then we would revert to a state in which we could sin again. The process would be cyclical and meaningless. The saving mission of Christ would have only a temporary effect and would have to

18. Chrysostom, *In Johannem* 67.2; *In Hebraeos* 5.2, 16.1, 17.1. See Kelly, *Early Christian Doctrines*, p. 384.

19. Michael was an angel frequently considered by the Hebrews as a special protector, and this function was transferred from Israel to the Christian community. In the New Testament, Jude 9 and Revelation 12:7–9 refer to a struggle between Michael and Satan. Gradually the idea grew that Michael was God's agent in the destruction of the Devil. Devotion to Michael existed in the very early church; by the fifth century it was growing rapidly, particularly in Constantinople and the East, and it then entered Italy and became important in the reign of Pope Gregory the Great (590–604), when Mount Gargan became a center of devotion to Michael. In the eighth century the cult of Michael spread widely in France, with Mont Saint-Michel established as a cult center similar to Gargan. It was generally accepted that Michael fought a great battle with Satan and defeated him, but when this battle was supposed to have taken place was not clear. Jerome held that both logic and the book of Revelation indicated that it had been at the time that Satan fell from heaven. Gregory the Great dated the deed at the end of the world. Gregory's thought predominated until the twelfth century, but at that time Peter Lombard accepted Jerome's chronology, and Aquinas followed him. See the article "Anges" in the *Dictionnaire de spiritualité ascétique et mystique*, 1:584–585, 601–602, 610–615.

be repeated. In order to avoid this flaw, Gregory argued that the process can happen only once. Time is not cyclical. We are progressing through time toward a fulfillment in Christ that will be even better than the pristine state existing before the fall. We will be restored to God, and the cosmos will be renewed, but in a better state than before. God is using time to improve the world. The point in the past when all intelligences dwelt with God is a model for our return, but the point toward which we are moving is even more excellent. The omega is better than the alpha.[20]

Gregory of Nyssa's view was optimistic in the long run, because the cosmos is fully in the hands of God. But in the short run the Devil wields enormous power. The fall of Satan distorted the universe; the fall of humanity wrenched it further out of joint. God, working through Christ, moves the cosmos toward renewal, but though his ultimate success is sure, it takes a great length of time to accomplish. Christ dealt the kingdom of Satan its death blow, but its defeat is not yet completed. Those who are saved by the Passion of Christ will at the end of time be taken up by God to become one with him.[21] Those who lack the necessary goodness—and that includes Satan—will be destroyed.[22]

Saint Augustine of Hippo, one of the most influential Christians of all time, synthesized existing diabology and, adding new insights, constructed a relatively coherent approach to the problem of evil. Though Augustine's influence was largely limited to the western church, he dominated medieval, Protestant, and post-Reformation Catholic theology. Both Protestant and Catholic traditions still base many of their assumptions upon

20. This idea is very important both for the development of the theory of history and for that of the theory of reform. The idea of renewal for the better—*renovatio in melius* in the Latin church—is one of the seminal ideas of all time. On this see especially G. Ladner, *The Idea of Reform* (Cambridge, Mass., 1959). On Gregory of Nyssa's apocatastasis, see Daniélou, "L'apocatastase chez Saint Grégoire de Nysse."

21. Becoming God: θέωσις.

22. Philippou, p. 355. See this article in general for a resumé of Gregory of Nyssa's demonology.

the thought of Augustine. Born at Thagaste (modern Souk Ahras in Algeria) in 354, and strongly influenced by his Christian mother, Monica, he went when young to Carthage, in 371, to study the classics. He acquired a mistress and had a son by her, but women other than Monica played little role in his mental life; his closest attachments were to his intellectual male friends. Though Monica raised him as a Christian, his independence of mind and his classical education led him to look down on Christianity as intellectually and culturally inferior. He espoused a variety of religious philosophies including Neoplatonism and Manicheism before at last returning to the Christian community.

Augustine's intellectual and spiritual life flourished after he went to Italy in 383. He became professor of rhetoric at Milan in 384, and there the great archbishop Ambrose exercised strong influence over him. He finally reconverted to Christianity, the turning point being the mysterious moment in the garden when, hearing a child in the distance chanting "take up and read," he found in the Scriptures a passage that induced him to give himself up entirely to Christ. The turbulent, questing nature of his intellectual life was by no means reduced by his conversion. Indeed, most of his writing was done afterward and can be fully understood only in terms of responses to his theological opponents—Manicheans, Donatists, Pelagians, and others. Though closest to his heart was a quiet garden where he could walk with his friends and discuss philosophy, he allowed himself to be persuaded to pursue an active administrative career in the church and served as bishop of Hippo from 395 till his death in 430. Like Jerome and all politically aware contemporaries, Augustine experienced the fall of Rome to the Visigoths in 410—the first time in eight hundred years that Rome had been taken by a foreign enemy—as a shattering blow that forced him to shift his opinions about Christian society and the other world. The force of character and intellectual clarity that shone through his writings—and he was one of the most prolific writers of all time—ensured that he would loom over all subsequent western thought.

The problem of evil occupied him from an early age. His

sensitivity to sin as a child is clear in his story of the stolen pears; in his Manichean stage he grasped at a thoroughly dualist interpretation of evil; and the question continued to absorb him after he became a settled Christian. In dealing with evil he was more concerned with the sinfulness of human nature and its redemption by Christ than with the power of the Devil, but the Devil was an integral part of his theology; without his dark shadow Augustine's cosmos would have been unintelligible. "The problem of evil," noted R. M. Cooper, "is one which confronted St. Augustine at every point of his intellectual development; it is everywhere either to be openly seen or to be perceived lurking just beneath the surface of the question at issue."[23]

Augustine began his work "On the Free Choice of the Will" with the question of evil. Evodius, his partner in the dialogue, inquires, "Tell me, please, whether God is not the cause of evil."[24] Augustine "always believed in the vast power of the Devil," and that God permits evil powers to rule the world under his control. Each human being must struggle to defeat the demons within his or her own soul. "The human race is the Devil's fruit-tree, his own property, from which he may pick his fruit. It is a plaything of demons."[25] Augustine viewed the cosmos as a book composed by a perfect poet, God, who has

23. The quotation is from R. M. Cooper, "Saint Augustine's Doctrine of Evil," *Scottish Journal of Theology*, 16 (1953), 256. Peter Brown's *Augustine of Hippo* (London, 1967) is the best biography of Augustine. For editions and translations of Augustine's works, see the Essay on the Sources. The works cited here are "The Free Choice of the Will" (Free); "Order"; "True Religion" (True); "Commentary on the Psalms" (CPs.); "Christian Doctrine" (Doctrine); "Confessions" (Conf.); "The Trinity" (Trin.); "Commentary on Genesis (Gen.); "Demonic Divination" (Dem.); "The Nature of Good" (Good); "Against Faustus" (Faust.); "Against Maximus the Arian" (Max.); "On Holy Virginity" (Virg.); "The City of God" (City); "Against Julian" (Jul.); "Enchiridion" (Ench.); "Admonition and Grace" (Admon.); "Letters"; "Sermons"; "Retractions" (Ret.). For the dates of the works see the chronological tables in Brown.

24. Free 1.1; trans. A. S. Benjamin and L. H. Hackstaff, p. 3.

25. Brown, pp. 244–245; 395. R. Jolivet, *Le problème du mal d'après Saint Augustin* (Paris, 1936), observed that the question of evil dominated Augustine's whole thought, only a slight exaggeration. In Free 1.2 Augustine said that his preoccupation with evil drove him to Manicheism.

shaped his plot to his purpose from its beginning to its end, and who has chosen every word, syllable, and letter with perfect care.[26] God may be said to have sung the universe into existence, as C. S. Lewis' Aslan does in *The Magician's Nephew*, and to sustain it in counterpoint through its concluding coda. The conclusion, the ɔmega point, restates the whole and lends meaning to it.

God's perception of the plot's meaning presumably never changes, but Augustine's understanding of it shifted, especially after the terrifying fall of Rome in 410. Hitherto he had expressed a basically optimistic view of time. God is a narrator, whose world moves through time in stately measures according to his purpose. The meaning of time is to prepare the world, first for the incarnation of Christ and now for his return. We, moving with time toward the second coming, have the duty with God's help to build a Christian society in this world, to compose it in harmony with God's narrative. Pain and suffering are afflictions that God mercifully sends so that he may teach us wisdom, humility, and kindness to others. Because pain is part of the learning process preparing the way of God, God permits demons to afflict even children with disease, catastrophe, temptation, and pain. But the ancient pessimism that had nagged Augustine since childhood and caused him to accept Manicheism as a youth reemerged when Rome fell. Now he saw the cosmos as incurable; no viable Christian society could be constructed in a world so riddled with sin. Pain now appeared not as instruction but as punishment, a prelude to hell. Like Camus' Paneloux and Rieux facing the agonies of a small boy dying of the black death, Augustine found that he could offer no palliative. "This is the Catholic view," he wrote toward the end, "a view that can show a just God in so many pains and in such agonies of tiny babies." The stare he leveled unflinchingly at pain and death became so stark and somber that his biographer speaks of "the fearsome intensity with

26. I am indebted to Professor John Freccero of Stanford for this image, which he developed in a lecture presented at the University of Notre Dame in 1977.

which he had driven the problem of evil into the heart of Christianity."[27]

Where does evil come from? Why do pain and sin exist in the world? Augustine quickly abandoned the dualist solution he had once espoused as a Manichean. A principle of evil, a being absolutely evil in itself, a lord of evil independent of God— none of these can exist. No aspect of the cosmos, whether spirit or matter, no Devil, no unformed primal matter, can resist, deflect, or defer God's plan. God can in no way be limited. The book is written: God has devised its ending in all eternity no less than its beginning, and no letter that the moving hand has writ can be altered. Evil has no substance, no actual existence, no intrinsic reality. Nothing is by nature evil, and nothing is by nature evil. Both meanings of the phrase apply.[28] Evil is lack of good.[29]

But why is there this lack? Why did God make the cosmos with holes in it? Augustine distinguished between natural and moral evil. Natural or physical evils—tornadoes and cancer— are painful, frightening, terrible, but they are not really evils at all. They are part of a divine plan whose outlines are hidden from us but which, if only we could see clearly, we would understand. Natural evils only appear to be evil because we do not understand the cosmos.[30] Nonetheless, imperfectly though we see, we can understand even here and now some of the reasons for suffering and pain: they exist to teach us wisdom, or

27. Brown, pp. 395–397; R. A. Markus, *Saeculum: History and Society in the Theology of Augustine* (Cambridge, 1970), for Augustine's view of society. *Free* 1.1. reveals Augustine's early sense that pain was punishment.

28. *City* 11.22, 12.3; *Gen.* 11.13. See Hick, *Evil and the God of Love*, for a summary of the Augustinian approach to the problem of evil as opposed to the "Irenaean approach"; see also above, p. 85; D. M. Borchert, "Beyond Augustine's Answer to Evil," *Canadian Journal of Theology*, 8 (1962), 237–243; T. Clark, "The Problem of Evil: A New Study."

29. *Conf.* 7.12.18: "Quaecumque sunt, bona sunt; malumque illud, quod quaerebam unde esset, non est substantia, quia si substantia esset, bonum esset" (Whatever is, is good; evil is not a substance, for if it were, it would be good). *City* 11.9: "Mali enim nulla natura est; sed amissio boni mali nomen accepit (evil has no nature; what is called evil is merely lack of good).

30. Cooper, p. 257; *Order* 1.1.

to warn us of the danger of sin, or to ensure just punishment for sin. For sinners, adversity is a punishment; for the innocent, it is a divine gift of warning. God's providence assures that the book that is written is a good book. Natural "evil" is really part of God's plan for the greatest good, and he turns even moral sin to ultimate good.[31]

But why does moral evil exist? Natural evil hurts those who suffer, but that hurt is made good by God's love. Moral evil is different. It hurts its victims, but, far worse, it does grievous harm to the one who commits the sin, for it eats away at his very soul.[32] What is the cause of this moral evil? Augustine answers variously. One of his responses is incoherent: that evil is the *result* of a free-will choice on the part of intelligent beings such as angels or humans. Put this way, the answer requires a further question: what was it that caused the free-will choice of evil? Any answer to that question must be illogical, because nothing is able to cause a free-will choice. The coherent answer is that evil *is* the free-will choice to sin, and that free-will choices *have no* causes.[33]

31. Letter 210. The distinction between moral and natural evil is not so clear as it may first appear. If evil is harm done willingly and knowingly by one sentient being to another, then God may be held responsible for the natural evil he inflicts upon us. We do not hesitate to call a man evil who knowingly inflicts agony and torment on an old lady or a child; but God apparently inflicts agony and torment upon millions of old ladies and children. We evade the problem by *defining* God as good and then arguing that by definition God must have a good reason for his actions. In fact we simply do not know. But it is odd that we do not hold God to the basic moral standards to which we hold one another.

32. Everything that is called an evil is either a sin or a punishment for sin: True 12.23; Trin. 13.16; Gen. 1.1–4. On justice, Free 3.9: "When sinners are unhappy, the universe is perfect." Free 3.23: granted the alleged positive functions of natural evil, what about the suffering of infants and animals? Augustine answered defensively and lamely. Perhaps the suffering of children is to instruct their parents! In the long run God will make the children happy. Animal suffering is simply part of the natural order of the universe. Animals breed, eat one another, and die. Since they do not have rational souls, we need not concern ourselves with them. Perhaps suffering teaches beasts to hate corruption and to love perfect unity!

33. This discussion is drawn in part from R. R. Brown's article "The First Evil Will Must Be Incomprehensible: A Critique of Augustine," *Journal of the American Academy of Religion*, 46 (1978), 315–330.

Evil arising from free will is absolute; it must remain incomprehensible, since the movement of a free will cannot be analyzed causally. If sin arose from a prior deficiency in the intellect, then God would be the cause of that deficiency and the ultimate cause of sin. If sin arose from a prior deficiency in the will, then the same argument follows and God would again be responsible. If sin is the result of any prior fault, pride for example, then either the pride is God's work and responsibility, or it is itself the sin, and the whole argument revolves in endless circles. Statements that any beings created from nothing will inevitably fall, or that the whole thing is an unfathomable mystery, evade the question. Any explanation fails. If any prior cause at all exists, then God is to blame.[34] The Devil is partly responsible for the distortion of the cosmos, to be sure, but he has no power to force anyone else into sin, and in any event his own sin poses the same question of its causes.[35] To ascribe evil to the Devil requires that we ask why God permitted him to sin and why God continues to tolerate his evil activities after he sinned. The sole coherent position is that God gives intelligent creatures—humans and angels—free will in order to achieve the greatest good for the cosmos; that they freely abuse this

34. Free 2.20, 3.9, 3.17; City 12.7: "Nemo igitur quaerat efficientem causam malae voluntatis; non enim est efficiens sed deficiens, quia nec illa effectio sed defectio" (no one should ask the efficient cause of an evil will, for the cause is deficient, not efficient; an evil will is a defect). This of course avoids the question of where the defect comes from: Ret. 1.9: "Malum non exortum nisi ex libero voluntatis arbitrio" (evil does not arise except through free choice of the will). Cf. Admon. 10.27. Augustine distinguished between will (*voluntas*) and free will (*liberum arbitrium*), a distinction that comes through in French (*volonté* and *libre arbitre*) but not in English, where "will" serves for both. See R. R. Brown, p. 318: *voluntas* is not the decision-making faculty, but "rather the basic core of an individual as a moral personality. It has no specific cause for being as it is; it is the fundamental character from which all of one's actions proceed." *Arbitrium* on the other hand is the "conscious power of choosing among alternatives." You can move your *arbitrium* to make particular moral choices. "But at the level of *voluntas* the person is governed by the basic love which draws him or her one way or another." You cannot change your *voluntas* except by divine grace. The original sin of Adam and of Satan was to turn a wholly undetermined and free *voluntas* away from God; after original sin the *voluntas* was already bent.
35. Free 3.10: two sources of sin exist: the internal, unaided prompting of our own thoughts; and external persuasion.

freedom; and that their choice of sin has no cause beyond their absolute freedom. Freedom is the condition that makes their sin possible, but it is not the cause of sin. Sin is the free-will choice to evil that has no prior cause.

Augustine prolonged the old Christian confusion of moral evil with ontological privation. He used the theory of privation in opposition to dualism. Nothing can exist other than God and what he creates. Anything else is really not anything, but nothing, mere lack of good. Only one principle exists—God—and all real things come from him. One answer to why God permits holes in the cosmos is the moral answer: freedom of will entails real freedom to do evil. But Augustine did not stop at that answer. He posed the question in ontological terms, using a scale similar to that of Origen. God is at the top of the scale: absolute being, goodness, and spirit. Below him are angels, humans, animals, plants, inanimate objects, and unformed matter. Each step down in the scale is less real, less spiritual, and less good. The basic confusion of moral with ontological "good" appears immediately and breeds further problems. To ask, ontologically, why God permits evil is to ask why God did not create every being equally close to him. The answer Augustine gave derives from Neoplatonism. Plotinus viewed the successive emanations proceeding from God as filling the whole realm of possible forms all the way down to unformed matter. God wanted to write a complete, unabridged book, so he desired a cosmos full of forms. Augustine concurred: "You do not have a perfect universe except where the presence of greater things results in the presence of lesser ones, which are needed for comparison."[36]

The idea of plenitude is as much aesthetic as it is logical—the universe is a beautiful, apt expression of God's will, an ordered orchard filled with every kind of sweet fruit and bitter. In such a view, the least good must exist along with the most good, so pain exists to instruct, to right wrongs, and to balance justice. God permits the everlasting torment of hell to exist because hell is aesthetically as well as logically necessary in order to balance

36. Free 3.9.

justice. Animal pain can also be understood in the aesthetic context, for animals, eating one another and procreating, in the course of time fill up the universe. In a cosmos where inequality is both aesthetic desirability and logical necessity, no being can be blamed for its infirmity. Indeed, if we decry the defect of a being, we are by implication praising what is good in its nature.

But what about moral evil? Confusion again. We can properly blame beings for moral defects if not natural ones. We can blame a bad choice if not a bad back. But the suggestion that moral evil is the result of a defect in the will fails. It fails because it ascribes sin to ontological defect, which is by definition not blameworthy; and it fails because if a defect in the will can cause sin, the will is not truly free. In short, the ontological explanation of evil neither protects God from responsibility nor responds to our experience of radical evil.[37]

Augustine's most important contribution to diabology was his discussion of free will and predestination. The problem is this: Experience and revelation both tell us that we are free. We experience the sense that we are free to choose, and the Bible implies that we are responsible for choosing. Yet both reason and revelation also indicate that God is the all-knowing and all-powerful ruler of the cosmos. If God has written every word of the book in all eternity, we are incapable of changing one letter. If God is omnipotent, how can angels and humans be really free to choose, or be responsible for their choices? Augustine was the first to pose the question in all its complexity. He never resolved it, and the debate continues today among philosophers, physicists, biologists, and psychologists, as well as theologians. Einstein observed, "what I am really interested in is whether God could have made this world in a different way; that is whether the necessity of logical simplicity leaves any freedom at all."[38]

37. Free 3.1, 3.9, 3.13, 3.15; City 19.3; Conf. 7.12. Free 3.1; the "defective movement of the will," the decision to sin, does not arise from the nature of the will itself. It is not necessary and has no cause. Augustine should have stuck with that point of view rather than searching for causes.

38. Quoted in P. Munz, *The Shapes of Time* (Middletown, Conn., 1977).

Augustine always asserted the truth of both propositions: that humans and angels are free, but that God's power is unlimited by any principle, including freedom. Augustine never achieved consistency, and his views changed as he grew older. In early life, when he was a Manichean, he tended toward the determinism typical of Gnostic dualism. Then, after converting to Christianity, he wrote "The Free Choice of the Will," in which he affirmed, against both pagans and Manicheans, a definite role for free will. God's purpose in creating the world is to increase the opportunity for real goodness; goodness depends upon moral choice; free choice is necessary to God's plan. Later, when he found that his views were more threatened by the Pelagians, who emphasized free will, he took a much more deterministic stance, affirming predestination with such severity that Faustus of Riez, one of his free-will opponents, accused him of reverting to a variant of pagan fatalism. Only his dogged insistence that free will must somehow exist, even in a totally determined universe, saved it at all, and then at the cost of naked inconsistency. Augustine held both positions at one time or another, and both continued to appear, though his predestinarian views were more influential with later writers such as Aquinas, Calvin, and Luther.

The most important options concerning freedom and determinism are: (1) the cosmos is meaningless, random, moving in no planned or discernible direction—a position favored by modern quantum theory; (2) the cosmos is determined—moving in accordance with fixed natural laws that are the product of coherent and explainable—albeit extraordinarily complex—material forces, a position favored by Einstein; (3) the cosmos is determined by one or more unexplained, mysterious forces, such as "fate" in Greek and Roman historiography or "history" in Marxism; (4) the cosmos is predetermined and completely mapped by God; (5) intelligent beings have the power to shape, to some extent, the cosmos according to their free will. Options four and five were open to Augustine.

Within the framework of these two options a variety of positions is possible, depending upon one's view of time. First: time is the fourth dimension. All time and space exist eternally in an "unchanging four-dimensional whole," though we are able here on earth to see only one position at a time. The terminology is Einsteinian, but the notion behind it is consistent with Augustine. Second: the future does not yet exist, but "each state of the universe uniquely determines the next state, so that if one knew all the causes operating at any one time, one would know precisely what their outcome would be in the future." This view is only a slight modification of the above, for with a "temporally structured deterministic universe" God will know "precisely what will come to pass, since a deterministic universe is . . . present in its causes." Third: God's omniscience can be conditional: he may know all there is to know, without knowing a future which does not yet exist to be known. This allows both for the freedom of intelligent beings and for the randomness of quantum theory. Though God knows "every possibility and what to do in respect of each eventuality," he leaves this "a genuinely open-structured world."[39]

Augustine's views were based upon traditional Christian theodicy: God does only good; evil is therefore done by others; God tolerates the evil done by others for the greater good.[40] The greater good is the presence of freedom in the cosmos. God created the cosmos for the purpose of increasing the amount of goodness in existence; it could be increased only if he created

39. The quotations and general discussion of the problem are drawn from B. L. Hebblethwaite, "Some Reflections on Predestination, Providence, and Divine Foreknowledge," *Religious Studies*, 15 (1979), esp. 435–439, 448.

40. N. Pike, "Plantinga on Free Will and Evil," *Religious Studies*, 15 (1979), 473, observes that "a suitably formulated version of this theodicy is free of logical incoherence." Pike notes that we need not use the theory of the greater good. God may simply, having made the decision to grant freedom, be logically powerless to prevent evil. But of course then freedom itself is the greater good. G. B. Wall, "A New Solution to an Old Problem," *Religious Studies*, 15 (1979), 511, finds some problems with the traditional position. We excuse God from obligations that we are accustomed to expect from other people. For example, "freedom ought to be limited when doing so would avoid or reduce the loss or degradation of life. . . ; suffering due to natural causes ought to be prevented or eliminated, even though the suffering might lead to the expression or development of some moral virtue or other."

beings with true freedom to choose the good. Free will is necessary: without it no righteous act can be performed. The argument of "Free Choice of the Will" set forth this necessity and excused God from responsibility for evil by laying it upon the free will of angels and humans.[41] God knows, completely, the pattern of the cosmos whose script he has written, but the script includes room for real freedom, and his foreknowledge of the free choices that we make does not cause us to make those choices.[42]

Evil is a product of the free choice by intelligent beings to turn away from eternal good toward limited, temporal goods—to reject God in favor of passing pleasures. This misstep is the result of a "defective movement" of the will. The defective movement does not spring from the nature of the will; the will's defect is the product of its freedom.[43]

God grants free will to intelligent beings and supports them in their search for the good by giving them a special energy that Augustine called grace. Grace helps us to choose the good; in his more predestinarian moods Augustine argued that it obliges us to choose the good. This difference became the basis of an enduring theological dispute. That dispute should not be viewed in terms of a simplistic opposition between free will and predestination. Rather, a spectrum of views exists. Pelagius took the extreme view that salvation might be achieved without the help of divine grace. Most of those on the free-will side took the more moderate position that God gives his grace to all, that we are wholly free to reject it, and that some, accepting it, are saved, while others, rejecting it, doom themselves. Augustine began with a moderate position but later shifted to a strongly predestinarian view. Even this reserved a place, however

41. Free 3.3. Augustine here clearly saw that a strong emphasis on predestination weakens this central Christian explanation for the creation of the world. Free 2 is devoted to an attempt to reconcile freedom with God's will.

42. Free 3.3–4; City 14.27; Letter 246.

43. Defective motion: *defectivus motus*: Free 2.20, 3.1. In using this term Augustine avoided speaking of a defective *voluntas* or a defective *arbitrium*; but even a defective *motus* seems to require an explanation. In using the term "defective" he again fell into the trap of confusing ontology with morality.

cramped, for free will. The extreme position, which Augustine himself condemned, was to deny any real freedom of the will at all.[44]

Augustine described the original state of Satan and of Adam as being similar: before their sins each was wholly and completely free. As an angel, an intelligent being, Satan possessed basic character and will (*voluntas*) that were free, undistorted, and unbent. Adam was similarly free. But whereas Adam's original sin twisted his will and that of all humanity, inclining us to evil, Satan's sin, the original sin of the angels, did worse; it tied him to sin and ruin forever.

Augustine was unclear as to why the Devil and his followers were eternally chained to their sin, and he spent a good deal of time trying, unsuccessfully, to cope with the question. Every nature that God creates remains forever good. After the angels sinned, their wills were distorted and bent, but their natures remained unspoiled. The fallen angels are good insofar as they are angels, evil insofar as their will is bent.[45] Once having sinned, the Devil and the other fallen angels are bound forever to the shadows and can never more do good. No possibility exists that they will ever repent. This loss of freedom and servility to sin are a just punishment for their original transgression. Another reason for the permanence of their ruin is that angels deserve worse treatment than humans because they were originally higher beings and entrusted with greater responsibility. Sinning, their sin was graver than ours, and they were justly plunged into lower levels of decay.[46] In fact, the eternal harden-

44. Four traditional aspects of grace exist: prevenient grace, by which God initiates and sustains every good motion of our will; cooperating grace, by which he assists our will; sufficient grace, the assistance *without* which we cannot do good; and efficient grace, the assistance *by* which we do good.

45. Good 33: "Quia vero et ipsi mali angeli non a Deo mali sunt conditi; sed peccando facti sunt mali" (because even the evil angels were not created by God, but became so by sinning). True 13.26: "Ipse in quantum angelus est non est malus, sed in quantum perversus est propria voluntate" (even [the Devil] is evil not insofar as he is an angel but insofar as he was bent by his own free will). Cf. Free 3.25; City 12.1; Gen. 11.21.

46. Letter 217. Sometimes it is thought that angels cannot repent because they are purely spiritual bodies and that humans can repent in life because

ing of the angels' hearts and their consequent endless punishment has never received adequate explanation in Christian tradition; Augustine's efforts to resolve the drama were unsatisfactory. The basic idea was that original sin, whether angelic or human, bends the will in such a way that it cannot be straightened again without God's grace. But there seems no compelling reason for God to withhold the necessary grace from the fallen angels.

The problem of free will in humans further illuminates the question of the angelic fall. Adam, like Satan, originally had a will that was absolutely free to choose either good or evil. He was able, even without God's grace, to choose not to sin.[47] But ever since Adam's and Eve's fall, in which we all participate, humans have lost that metaphysical freedom. We are now incapable of considering good and evil courses of action and choosing one or the other. The sin we all share in has so twisted us that we are incapable of choosing the good without the help of divine grace, but the same twisting of our will keeps us entirely free to choose to sin, serve the Devil, and dwell in the earthly city and the old eon. Indeed, it bends us in that direction. The freedom that we now apparently enjoy is spurious; it only disposes us to doom. Grace must free us from this false freedom; grace, which makes us servants of God (*servi Dei*), gives us true freedom, the freedom not to sin.[48] Augustine did not always take the hard line that all virtue was wholly caused by grace and that our own cooperation with grace therefore had no merit, but he saw our responsibility as severely limited.

---

attached to bodies but cannot repent after death because separated from their bodies. But if the angels were able as purely spiritual beings to have an original free motion of the will toward sin, then a new motion toward goodness should also be possible.

47. J. M. Rist, "Augustine on Free Will and Predestination," *Journal of Theological Studies*, ser. 2, 20 (1969), 433. Adam was able not to sin (*posse non peccare*); after original sin humans are unable not to sin (*non posse non peccare*) except when saved by grace; once saved by grace they are unable *to* sin (*non posse peccare*).

48. Rist, pp. 424–425. We are free (*liberi*) to sin but must be freed (*liberati*) by grace in order to obtain the true freedom to love God. Admon. 11.31: "liberum arbitrium ad malum sufficit" (our freedom means that we are free to do evil if left to ourselves). Cf. Letter 217; Jul. 2.8.23.

Augustine's strong predestinarian emphasis was attacked from two quarters. Pelagius, a Briton who spent most of his life in Rome before the catastrophe of 410 drove him out, and who briefly and unhappily visited Augustine at Hippo on his way to Palestine, was the strongest defender of free will. A powerful moralist, he argued that we could attain salvation by practicing an ascetic life without necessarily having the assistance of grace. We could, in other words, pull ourselves up to God by our own bootstraps.[49] Julian of Eclanum, Pelagius' most intelligent supporter, argued that humans are good by nature and that grace, though it helps us, is not necessary for salvation. The fact that Pelagius and his supporters drew comfort from "The Free Choice of the Will" caused Augustine to reconsider that book and retract some of what he had said so as to take a sterner stance. When he moved in this direction he was opposed by a number of moderate theologians who rejected both Pelagius' indifference to grace and his own extreme limitation of free will. Opposition to Augustine centered in southern Gaul, where Vincent of Lérins, Faustus of Riez, Cassian, and Prosper of Aquitaine argued that his views went beyond tradition, that grace was necessary but was offered to everyone, and that we are free either to accept it or to reject it. Augustine himself intended to be moderate, always insisting on "both free-will and divine grace."[50] But by the end of his life he had written himself into a predestinarian corner. Pelagianism was condemned at the local Council of Carthage in 418 and in Gaul at the local Council of Orange, in 529, but the Council of Orange also refused to accept Augustine's views, leaving the whole question open permanently.

Augustine confirmed the tradition that the demons were not a separate species but angels. Angels are the only known intelli-

49. For the works of Pelagius, see the Essay on the Sources. Augustine's Letter 179 attacked Pelagius for arguing that "per solum liberum arbitrium sibi humanam sufficere posse naturam ad operandam justitiam et omnia Dei mandata servanda" (human nature is sufficient through the free action of the will alone to do right and to follow all the commandments of God).

50. In Letter 214 Augustine showed his own intention to be moderate by admonishing a monastery where the monks were emphasizing grace to the point of excluding freedom of will.

gent beings in the cosmos other than humans. The Devil and the other demons are fallen angels.[51] Why did the angels fall? The simplest and best answer is that they sinned because they were free to sin. Only God is perfect and unchanging. The angels are not coeternal with God but creatures whom he made at the beginning of time, and all created beings are prone to change, decline, and corruption.[52] Further, God's purpose in making the cosmos was to create free beings capable of moral choice, and freedom entails the possibility of sin. The angels were thus logically prone to change and specifically created capable of sin.[53]

But why did some angels sin and others remain in God's grace? During his moderate free-will period, Augustine as-

51. City 8.14–17 indicates that Augustine considered treating demons as a separate species. The pagan Neoplatonists had suggested a threefold division into three species: gods, demons (both good and bad spirits), and humans. Augustine pondered a modified division into angels, humans, and demons. But since Christians defined demons as being evil, Augustine could not very well defend the idea that the demons were a separate species since that would mean that God had either created the whole species evil or else permitted the whole species to fall. Emphasizing that *angelus* meant *nuntius*, a "messenger" of God rather than a species in itself, Augustine preferred to define both angels and demons as spirits. In so doing, he encouraged the practice of using the term "angel" to refer only to good spirits and "Devil" and "demon" to refer to evil spirits: City 5.9, 5.19, 9.2; Gen. 5.19; CPs. 103.1.18), though the demons were still referred to as "fallen" or "evil" angels. The Devil is an angel and the chief of the fallen angels, and he and the other evil angels fell at the same .time and for the same reason: Admon. 10.27; Trin. 4.10; Gen. 3.10, 11.26; City 14.3. Augustine rejected the Watcher story decisively. Angels, being spirits without bodies, are incapable of coitus (though Augustine was ambivalent on the point, since he also accepted the notion that the demons, falling into the *zophos, caligo,* or thick lower air, became *aeria animalia,* spirits with bodies made of gross air: Gen. 3.10; City 15.23). Augustine explained the "sons of God" passage of Genesis 6:2 as a reference not to angels, but to the descendants of Cain and of Seth. For the names that Augustine assigned to the fallen angels, see H. J. Geerlings, *De antieke daemonologie en Augustinus' geschrift* De divinatione daemonum (The Hague, 1953), p. 51, where the names given the Devil are listed: diabolus (also zabulus), Satanas, serpens, draco, Lucifer, deceptor, hostis, princeps mundi, pater mendacii: the Devil, Satan, the serpent, Lucifer, the deceiver, the enemy, the prince of this world, the father of lies.

52. City 12.15.

53. Good 1; City 11.10, 12.1; Max. 2.29; Geerlings, p. 67.

sumed that no cause existed other than the free-will choice of the angels themselves. Later, when God's will and the power of grace seemed irresistible to him, he wondered whether God really had created two classes of angels. His dilemma was this: on the one hand, both sets of angels (that is, all the angels) must have been created absolutely equal, or else God would be responsible for their inequality and hence for the sin of those who fall. But on the other hand, if there was no difference between them, no cause of the fall could be discerned, and the only explanation would be absolute freedom, which at that point he was not willing to accept.[54]

Augustine reasoned as follows. The angels, being limited and fallible as well as free, are capable of sinning if left to their own devices. But God did not wish them to fall. He therefore decided to strengthen them, to confirm them in their goodness by a gratuitous act of grace.[55] He confirmed some of the angels in their blessed state, giving them a "fullness of goodness." This confirmation brought with it a deep understanding of God, of the cosmos, and of their own condition. Thus illumined, they became incapable of sinning, unable to fall. They became fully free by losing their freedom to sin, by freely submitting to the service of God, a free choice that God's grace made inevitable.[56] These angels formed one group. God created another group as well. Both groups were good in nature and both had the freedom to choose. But to one group God freely gave the gift of grace, and from the other group he withheld it. The second group of angels were left free to sin. And they did sin, and thereby became demons.

God may have made this selection directly after he had created the angels, though Augustine thought it likely that the Devil and his companions lived happily in heaven for a while be-

54. R. R. Brown, p. 320. Augustine's search for a causal explanation for the fall of the angels seems to have begun about 417. For his various views on the subject see Gen. 3.10, 11.13, 11.17, 11.19, 11.26–30; Good 33; City 11.11.

55. Jul. 5.57; Geerlings, p. 68; R. M. Brown, p. 320.

56. Admon. 10–11, esp. 10.27. Fullness of grace: plenitudo bonitatis. Cf. City 22.1; Letter 217.

fore they fell.[57] The evil angels were created good and lost their goodness by a defect of will. God did not will their defect, but he did permit it.[58] God could have confirmed more of the angels in goodness, but he did not choose to, preferring to leave them to their own devices.[59]

This analysis does not work. The first problem is that it closely follows the lines of Augustine's argument for the predestination of humans, ignoring the fact that the pristine state of the angels was quite different from that of already fallen humans. Augustine argued that Adam's fall constituted a breach of contract with God, so that in strict justice God could have abandoned us all to pursue our own twisted path to doom. In his mercy, however, he decided to save some of us; the rest he leaves to our own devices. Since we are all guilty, the salvation of only one person would be an act of mercy beyond justice; the salvation of many is a great wonder of mercy. That God leaves most of us to destruction is both just and apt, for we ourselves have chosen destruction. Such a scenario is arguable for humanity but wholly implausible for the angels, because in their pristine state the angels were not yet fallen, not yet bent to sin. For God to decide to save some of the angels and not others would therefore be an inexplicable act apparently lacking in justice. Another problem is that the analysis does not succeed in shift-

57. Augustine was not consistent, sometimes arguing that the Devil had sinned at the beginning of his existence, sometimes that he had lived a blessed life in heaven with the other angels at least for a short while. City 11.13: "Ab initio suae conditionis in veritate non stetit [John 8:44]. Ideo numquam beatus cum sanctis angelis fuerit" (from his very beginning he did not dwell in truth, and therefore he never dwelt with the holy angels). City 11.15 takes a different tack: "in veritate fuerit, sed non permanserit" (he was once in the truth but did not persevere). Cf. Gen. 11.16, 11.23: whether or not he was depraved right from the beginning of his existence, it is clear that his defect lay not in his nature but in his will.

58. City 12.9; cf. Conf. 7.3.5: "Si diabolus auctor [malorum], unde ipse diabolus? Quod si et ipse perversa voluntate ex bono angelo diabolus factus est, unde et in ipso voluntas mala, qua diabolus fieret, quando totus angelus a conditore optimo factus esset?" (Granted that the Devil is the cause of evils, the question remains how it happens that he is the Devil. Because if he changed from a good angel to the Devil, where did that evil will arise in him that changed him, when God created every angel equally good?)

59. City 11.11, 14.27.

ing the responsibility for evil away from God, as Augustine intended that it should. His argument did not benefit from his insistence that God did not *create* two varieties of angels, since it assumed that God, immediately upon creating them, chose for no discernible reason to discriminate between them. The whole blundered argument might have been avoided had Augustine stuck to the simplest possible explanation: some angels choose God and others choose sin, both with an absolutely free motion of the will having no cause.

When the angels fell, they became demons, and when the angel named Satan fell, he became the Devil.[60] The good angels, remaining with God, retained an illuminated understanding, but the evil angels, shadowed by sin, lost the light of intelligence as well as the light of love. Though they retained at least some rational powers, those powers were "darkened by folly."[61] The demons became stupid as well as evil—providentially for us, because God takes advantage of their stupidity to protect the world from them. The higher an angel stood in the ranks of heaven, the lower it plunged into hell; this accounts for the fact that Satan, prince of angels, sank to the center of hell, the very lowest point of the universe.[62] From their ruin they never more can rise. "No new devil will ever arise from among the good angels . . . this present Devil will never return to the fellowship of the good."[63]

60. Max. 2.12: "Nam et angeli peccaverunt et daemones facti sunt quorum est diabolus princeps" (the angels sinned and became demons; their chief is the Devil). CPs. 121.6: "Cecidit angelus, et factus est diabolus" (an angel fell and became the Devil). Cf. Admon. 11.32; City 11.33, 18.18; CPs. 103.4; Jul. 3.26.

61. City 11.11, 21.6; Dem. 6.10.

62. Augustine divided the angels into more closely defined ranks than Evagrius had done. There were cherubs, *sedes* (thrones), *dominationes* (dominions), *principatus* (principalities), *potestates* (powers), *archangeli* (archangels), and *angeli* (angels). Further refinements were offered later by Pseudo-Dionysius and Gregory the Great. As a result of their sin, the falling angels lost their ethereal bodies and were converted into "crassus et humidus aër" (gross and thick air), one result of which is that they can feel the pain of hellfire: Gen. 3.10; City 15.23, 21.10. The Devil is lessened by his fall: "eo enim, quo minus est quam erat, tendit ad mortem": True 13.26.

63. City 11.13.

Regardless of the *cause* of the Devil's fall, the *reason* for it was pride. That is, when his will moved to sin, the sin it seized first was pride. This pride consisted of love of self above love of God; Satan wished not to owe anything to God, preferring to be the source of his own glory. From pride sprang envy of God, and, later, after humanity was created, of humans as well.[64] It was the envy that Satan and the other evil angels felt for our own original happy relationship with God that led them to mar that relationship by tempting us to sin. Satan's temptation of humanity was inevitable given the fact that he was confirmed in sin.[65] Lies, like envy, followed naturally from pride.[66] Pride was now firmly fixed in the tradition as the first sin.[67] The evil angels, once fallen, hate all good with a prideful, envious hatred, for the sole and simple reason that it is good.[68]

The Devil, proud and envious, exerted himself to encompass the ruin of the human race. His success in tempting Adam and

64. Pride: CPs. 58.2–5; Gen. 11.16, 11.23. City 11.15: "ab ipsius superbia coeperit esse peccatum" (sin began with the Devil's pride). Cf. City 11.13–14; Gen. 11.16–30. City 12.6: "initium quippe omnis peccati superbia" (truly the origin of all sin is pride). CPs. 58: Diabolus "sola superbia lapsus est" (the Devil fell through pride alone). True 13.26: "ille autem angelus magis se ipsum quam Deum diligendo subditus ei esse noluit et intumuit per superbiam et a summa essentia defecit et lapsus est" (that angel [the Devil], loving himself more than God, wished not to be his subject, and, swelling with pride, he declined from his high essence and fell). Pride and envy: Free 3.25; Virg. 31: "quibus duobus malis, hoc est superbia et invidentia, diabolus est" (it is through these two sins of pride and envy that he is the Devil). CPs. 58: it is not possible for a proud person not to be envious, so that the second sin follows from the first. Cf. Gen. 11.13–30; City 11.15, 12.5–9.

65. City 15.23: "Qui primum apostantes a Deo cum zabulo suo principe ceciderunt, qui primum hominem per invidiam serpentina fraude deiecit" (the angels, apostasizing from God, fell along with their leader the Devil, who because of envy brought down the first humans with his snakelike lies). Cf. City 14.3, 14.6, 14.13. Trin. 4.10: "Sicut enim diabolus superbus hominem superbientem perduxit ad mortem" (thus the proud Devil brought prideful man down to death).

66. Faust. 22.17: "praevaricatores angeli, quorum duo maxima vitia sunt superbia atque fallacia" (the deceitful angels, whose two greatest vices are pride and lying). Cf. Doctrine 2.23.

67. Avarice had its turn for a while later on. See L. K. Little, "Pride Goes before Avarice," *American Historical Review*, 76 (1971), 16–49.

68. City 14.28, 15.5. The idea that demons can hate good just because of its goodness, whether it really applies to angelic beings or not, derives from an acute observation of human nature.

all of us to imitate him in preferring our own pleasures to the love of God set in motion the events leading to the Incarnation and Passion of Christ. Before our original sin, the Devil had no power over humanity. But after we freely chose to break our contract and covenant with God, God permitted the Devil to exercise certain rights over us. The Devil could not have claimed such rights on his own—he, a sinner and the greatest of sinners, possessed no rights of any kind—but God in his justice gave him power over humanity for a while to punish us and test us. Thus God can use even the Devil to providential purposes. Because we had violated our contract with God, God could in strict justice have left us—all of us—in Satan's power forever. Not in justice obliged but in mercy sustained, he took on a human body in order to reconcile us with him. God had no need of such a device. He had given us into the hands of Satan and could have taken us back by any means he chose. But he preferred not to use force when justice sufficed. He preferred to pay the Devil his due, and so he delivered himself to Satan, who hastily and greedily seized him.

In seizing Jesus, Satan lost all his rights over humanity, for Jesus, being sinless and divine, was in no way the Devil's due. In seizing him, Satan transgressed justice, tore up the contract he had held with God, and, once that contract had been voided, lost his claim on us. This, of course, was according to God's strategy. Though Augustine did not crudely state the bait-and-hook conception, he used an equally vivid image: Christ was the cheese in the mousetrap, placed there by God to induce the Devil to make the grab and lose the prize. It was not really so much that God planned to trick Satan as that Satan, according to his nature, was overwhelmed with hatred and envy at the thought of God's love for humanity, and hurled himself against Christ with careless fury. It might almost be said that Satan's attack on Christ was the inevitable by-product of God's decision to take human nature upon himself. Augustine, like his predecessors, took a number of soteriological tacks—arguing the ransom and the sacrifice theory at one and the same time.[69]

69. Cheese (literally "food") in the mousetrap: *esca in muscipula*. *Trin.* 4, 13.14–18; *Ench.* 108; *Sermon* 263.1; See E. Te Selle, *Augustine the Theologian*

Christ's sacrifice was an act of infinite generosity having infinite potential effects. Yet its effects were immediately limited: it saved some but not others. Two cities exist. One is the heavenly city, whose inhabitants long for God. They view the world as a temporary lodging on the road to their true native land. The other is the earthly city, whose inhabitants scuttle about after the pleasures fetched by greed, lust, envy, and the other sins, deluding themselves that such poor food provides true nourishment. The cosmos was first divided into these two distinct communities when the angels fell; later Adam, and then Cain, inducted humanity into the earthly city. The evil angels and evil humans together occupy that city, while the heavenly city is inhabited by the good angels and humans.[70] The world in which we live is a mixture. Some of us are citizens of heaven and some of hell, and it is often difficult to discern saints from sinners, difficult even to know to which city we ourselves belong.[71]

Though Christ died for all and therefore wishes that everyone lived in the heavenly city, many people are so perverse that they do not choose to live there and actually prefer the things of this world. Therefore Christ's Passion does not realize its full potential: it does not deplete the earthly city and fill the heavenly one. There are those who remain unsaved.

First among these are the fallen angels. Jesus, a man, died for his brothers and sisters, but he did not die for the fallen angels, who were set immovably in their sin. His death helped remove some of the consequences of their fall, but not their own aliena-

---

(New York, 1970); Kelly, *Early Christian Doctrines*, pp. 390–394. Trin. 13: "Nescit diabolus quomodo . . . utatur ad salutem" (the Devil is ignorant how Christ would be used for our salvation). Trin. 4.13: "Christ's free willingness to pour out his innocent blood" and Satan's blind, eager greed to seize Christ "tore up the contract" (chirographum delens) that God had made with Satan. Free 3.10 put Augustine's position most clearly.

70. City 12.1; 15.5. See Markus, passim.

71. From Evagrius of Pontus to Flannery O'Connor, the Christian's chief problem and first duty has been seen as the discernment of spirits, the effort to pierce through lies and façades to the true good and evil that lies at the heart of the matter. The "mixed society" of this world: civitas permixta.

The face of a damned soul shows utter horror, hatred, and despair. Detail from a Michelangelo fresco in the Sistine Chapel.

tion from God. Why Christ's sacrifice should not have helped the angels, or why (if that were impossible) the angels should not have been vouchsafed their own savior, is unclear.[72] Neither are human sinners saved. Sinners, including infidels and heretics, are citizens of the earthly city; they walk the downward way; they are cells of Satan's body. Over these Satan did not lose his rights; he holds them firmly, justly, and for as long as their sin shall last.

Fallen angels and fallen humans may recognize that Christ is God, but if they do, their understanding springs not from love but from fear, and they derive no benefit from it. They understand the cosmos only to hate it and its maker.[73]

The clarity, power, and sheer quantity of Augustine's work ensured that most of his ideas would be fixed in the diabology of the western church. Yet some of his arguments were weak, even incoherent. This weakness raises an enormously important question about the validity of the process of formation of the concept. If Augustine, being incoherent on a given point, fixed the tradition on that point, how valid can the tradition be? No concept resting upon shifting ground can endure.

72. Ench. 61: "Non enim pro angelis mortuus est Christus" (for Christ did not die for the angels). City 14.27: the sins of men and angels do not impede God's work, for his Providence adjusts for everything.
73. Sermon 183.9: "Laudatur amor; damnatur timor" (love is to be praised, fear condemned).

8   Conclusion: Satan Today

The diabology of Augustine represented the general state of the concept as it existed in the mid-fifth century and the general lines of the development it would take in the future. What were the dynamics of the concept? It had departed from the original pre-Christian monism in which good and evil were conceived as being two sides of the God. Although it had moved in the direction of dualism, it had stopped well and emphatically short of the pure dualist view that God and the Devil were two independent principles, instead taking the middle position that the Devil was both God's creature and his adversary. The Devil's function in Christian theology was to provide an explanation of evil which avoided laying responsibility upon the good Lord. God is ultimately responsible for the cosmos, for he was not obliged to create it and is not obliged to maintain it in existence. Thus he is indirectly responsible for evil. But he does not will evil; he does not wish it to exist. He tolerates evil for the greater good. But some of the intelligences that he has created will evil actively. Some angels and some humans deliberately choose to hurt rather than help, to envy rather than to love. These creatures hate the good for its own sake and do evil for its own sake. As the angels' power is immensely greater than ours, so is the malevolence of the fallen angels. The Devil, the greatest of the fallen angels, extends his enormous hateful will so that it penetrates every corner of the cosmos, from the stones to the stars.

Thus three complementary explanations of evil exist: God tolerates it; the Devil wills it and promotes it; individual wills freely choose it. But because God's part in this scheme is permissive rather than active, the guilt is shifted from him to sinners, and especially to their leader, the Devil.

The history of the concept of the Devil can be a test case for historical theology. The history of concepts, independent of theology, sets forth how the concept has developed. But historical theology asks a further question: is the development legitimate? A concept, in order to be valid, must possess the following characteristics: (1) continuity through time; (2) trueness to type; (3) correspondence to living perceptions; (4) coherence. Augustine and his contemporaries left many points unclear, and some incoherent. The later development of diabology would remove some of these problems, but some remain obscure. The central question is whether the degree of unclarity and incoherence among the fathers on a number of points—for example, the nonbeing of evil, the role of Satan in the theory of redemption, and the predestination or free will of the angels—invalidates the development of the concept. For this difficult question, with its wide implications for historical theology in general, I have no ready answer.

Perhaps the solution may proceed as follows. The main lines of the concept are clear: the Devil as created, fallen through his own free choice, the chief of evil forces in the cosmos, mortally wounded by Christ, and doomed to ruin at the end of the world. It is in the details that the fathers tried to work out that the system appears to break down. In every theological question there is a limit to how far the "positive way"—assertions based upon the rational analysis of nature, revelation, and tradition—can take us; beyond lies mystery. It may be that the fathers were attempting to take theology beyond its natural limitation and thus inevitably fell into incoherence.

Seven major objections to belief in the Devil are common today. The first arises from general disbelief in theology and metaphysics, usually (though not always) from the position of positivism, the belief that only scientific knowledge is true

knowledge. This is an objection based upon fundamental epis-
temological difficulties that cannot be discussed here. I have
argued throughout (along with many other people) that there
are many roads to truth and that history and theology are inherently valid systems independent of science. The second is
that belief in the Devil is not progressive or up-to-date. This is
probably the most common objection, and it is totally without
merit, since it arises from hunches and fads rather than careful
or coherent thought. The question is not whether belief in the
Devil is liberal but whether it is true. A third arises from a
theological viewpoint outside the tradition that we have been
investigating—from rabbinical Judaism, for example, or from
Buddhism. Almost all religious points of view deal with the
problem of evil in one way or another, but many have no figure
comparable to the Christian Devil. Obviously, then, there are
ways to deal with the problem of evil in theological terms without recourse to the Devil, and those ways may be entirely valid.
It would be vain at this point to launch into a discussion of the
relative merits of the Christian view of evil and, for example,
the Buddhist view. I have argued throughout, however, that
the Christian view seems to meet the question head on and
more frankly than other traditions.

Those adopting a general Christian view, or something like
it, on the nature of evil, can raise other objections. A fourth is
that belief in the Devil is inconsistent with the main lines of
Christian tradition; but that is manifestly and demonstrably un-
true. A fifth is that it is inconsistent with Scriptures, specifically with the New Testament. As I argued in my earlier book,
The Devil, this position is very difficult to maintain without
wrenching the New Testament violently away from the meaning its authors wished to give it. A sixth is that it is inconsistent
with experience. I will address this point more fully below;
here it is enough to say that even today, despite a generally
shared world-view that is powerfully and dogmatically mater-
ialistic, a great many people still experience what they take to
be the Devil, and that at other times when not repressed by
materialist preconceptions the experience has been quite gener-

al. The seventh is that diabology is inconsistent. This last is a ticklish point, because diabology is no more incoherent than many other central points of Christian theology.

The question is to what degree it is incoherent. The inconsistencies, though real, are not at the heart of the concept. The heart of the concept is that a cosmic power exists other than the good Lord, a power that wills and urges evil for its own sake and hates good for its own sake, a power that is active throughout the cosmos, including human affairs. This power is not a principle independent of God but rather a creature of God. The evil in him proceeds not from his nature, which was created good, but rather from his free choice of hatred. God permits him to choose evil and to remain evil because true moral freedom is necessary to the divine plan: God creates the cosmos for the purpose of increasing moral goodness, but moral goodness entails freedom to do evil. The Devil, whose will is wholly given over to hatred, wishes to distort the cosmos as much as he can; to this end he tries to corrupt and pervert the human race. This is the center of the concept, and the crucial judgment must be made upon it.

To revert to the question of experience: a concept that does not respond to human experience will die. But the concept of the Devil is very much alive today, in spite of opposition from many theologians as well as from those hostile to all metaphysics. Indeed, the idea is more alive now than it has been for many decades, because we are again aware of the ineradicable nature of perversity in our own behavior, a perversity that has perhaps been more evident in the twentieth century than ever before. Well-intentioned efforts to reform human nature by education or legislation have so far failed, and rather spectacularly, as they break like waves against the rock of radical evil. We have direct perception of evil, of deliberate malice and desire to hurt, constantly manifesting itself in governments, in mobs, in criminals, and in our own petty vices. Many people seem to have the additional experience that behind all this evil, and directing it, is a powerful, transhuman, or at least transconscious, personality. This is the Devil.

A stereotype of the Devil, from the "Codex Gigas," about 1200. The Devil's
bestial horns and talons, his leering eyes and grimacing mouth, and his livid
face were generally thought to represent the most appropriate form a demon
might assume. Though the figure appears comic, it is intended to be frightening.
Courtesy of the Royal Library, Stockholm, owner of the manuscript.

In what direction is the concept moving? I suggested in *The Devil* that it may be moving toward the integration of good and evil within the God. Having passed from belief in a vague, barely differentiated melding of good and evil within the God, past a sense of dualist total separation of good and evil, we might turn to an understanding of evil in which the God integrates the dark side of his nature without actualizing it. That is one of the options. The concept will not return to either extreme monism or dualism. It will take one of three possible courses: (1) it will die; that is to say, people will cease to have direct experience of evil; (2) it will move toward integration; (3) it will continue to be refined within the basic outlines it had taken at the time of Saint Augustine. Of these three possibilities, perhaps the last is the most likely. The first is improbable on the basis of the entire history of the human experience, and the second represents such a radical new course in the development of the concept that it too is unlikely.

Yet the option of integration should not be dismissed too quickly. To say that the concept may integrate good and evil within the God is not to say that God actually integrates good and evil, but only that our human concept of God may move in that direction. Second, the idea that God integrates evil does not mean that God yields to evil, or in any way becomes evil, or actualizes evil. Rather it means that God accepts and incorporates evil in such a way as to transform it into a higher good. Innocence is not the only mode appropriate to God. God may be said to be innocent in the sense that Jesus was offered up without sin for the salvation of humanity. But God's innocence is not ignorance. When an adult remains innocent in the same way as a child, innocence becomes ignorance, and if ignorance is maintained deliberately, it becomes culpable. The higher state is wisdom, which recognizes that evil exists within oneself, and then grasps it, overcomes it, and transforms it into something better and more powerful. The need to integrate evil is not often understood. The figure of the Blessed Virgin Mary, for example, has in the last few centuries been sentimentalized in such a way that the Virgin is portrayed as innocent to the point of vapidity. Such a woman could not have borne Christ, raised him, and suffered through his Passion. The immaculate conception of the Virgin would have made her, not meek and mild, but rather deep, strong, wise, and powerful. Only thus able to confront and transform evil could she bear God and God's death. An integrated idea of God is not an idea of a morally mixed God, but of one whose wisdom has integrated the evil of the cosmos in such a way that the evil is transformed.

Nonetheless, it is more consistent with the theory of the history of concepts to return to the view that the chief evil is separate from, and subsidiary to, the benevolent Lord. All things considered, the concept will probably continue along the general lines formulated in the fifth century, though it will be deepened and broadened as Christian theology reaches out to embrace what is valid in depth psychology and in other religions. The traditional concept is deep and subtle enough to accommodate the most complex human understanding of evil. The subordinate nature of evil also accords best with the experience of most people. Few societies or individuals have perceived evil as equal to good. Rather, they sense that evil is a misshapen copy, a distorted imitation, of good.

The final question is the most immediate; what, if anything, does the Devil mean today? What grounds exist today for believing in the Devil? The most fundamental answer is that we are incapable of knowing whether the Devil exists "objectively" or "transcendently." Absolute knowledge is not obtainable. But we can know in a secondary sense. Human experience is the basis of this "secondary knowledge." When we have set rationalization and embarrassment aside, most of us will recognize that we have experience in our lives of real evil, not just maladjustment or some other euphemistic dodge of reality, but real, conscious, purposeful hatred of the good and beautiful for their own sake and love of the ugly and twisted for their own sake. And we have the sense that the depth and intensity of this evil, though responding to the corruption that is in all of us, exceeds and transcends what could be expected in an individual human. The persistence of the idea of the Devil indicates that it continues to generate a resonance of experience in many people.

The next level of understanding beyond individual experience is collective human experience. Whether or not the Devil
exists objectively, it is certain that the Devil exists in the sense
that the phenomenon Devil, the concept Devil, exists and can
be defined historically with a reasonable degree of coherence.
The historian can trace the development of the concept, which
appears in Judaism, Islam, and other religions but reaches its
fullest development in Christianity. People who are not Christians must cope with the problem of evil, but they are not
obliged to cope with the problem of the Devil; they can define
evil in different ways. The historian may rest content, as a
historian, with describing the development of the concept. But
the historical theologian is obliged to cope with the problem of
the Devil, for the reason that the Devil has always been a central Christian doctrine, an integral element in Christian tradition. Theologians who exclude Satan in the interests of their
own personal views run the risk of holding an incoherent view
of Christianity.

What, according to the historical theology of concepts, is one
to believe regarding the Devil? We should be willing to face the
problem of evil squarely without trying to dodge it intellectually. We should be open to the possibility of the existence of
an evil spirit or spirits beyond humankind. The metaphysical
assumptions of our present age may lead many to prefer to interpret the diabolical in terms of depth psychology, arguing
that the demonic exists within the human mind, or perhaps col-
lectively among human minds. But on no account is one entitled to dismiss the idea of the Devil as irrelevant.

The Devil's place in Christian theology is best fitted into a
credible theodicy. The problem of evil can be stated as follows:

God exists.

God is all-powerful: God is capable of creating a cosmos that
is benign.

God is all-good: God desires a cosmos that is benign, that is,
one in which cruelty and suffering do not exist.

Therefore evil—cruelty and suffering—cannot exist.

But we observe that in fact evil exists.

Therefore God does not exist.

But the alternative to this conclusion is that the statement itself is faulty, and God is either not all-powerful or not all-good (or even neither). The atheist attack on Christian theodicy is ineffective if God can be conceived as either not all-powerful or not all-good.

The hypothesis that God is not all-powerful is a dualist religious position. Its assumption is that God is limited by a principle outside himself, whether that principle is matter, the Devil, or nothingness, or any other force, being, or principle. Ancient Gnostics and medieval Cathars limited God by the Devil. Modern process theologians tend to limit him by matter, arguing that he is gradually forming a good cosmos out of eternal, unformed matter and that evil arises from the resistance of matter to his will. But dualism of any kind is difficult to maintain. If two principles—God and another principle—exist, do they derive from a prior, ur-principle? If the two powers are coeternal and equally balanced, the universe would have to be static. Or, if they are not equally balanced, then one must be greater than the other in all eternity and must prevail; but if the balance is tipped in essence and eternity, the greater principle would require no time to prevail, and the observed delay would not be taking place. Nor does an argument that God may not be all-powerful in our sense of the term help, for if omnipotence means anything it means the power to create or not create a cosmos. God's omnipotence cannot be defined in a way that makes him not responsible for the cosmos he creates.

The hypothesis that God is not all-good is disquieting, even frightening, but it is logical and coherent. The alleged goodness of God must be examined in the context of the observed existence of evil. If by God we mean a being that would not permit torture, genocide, and concentration camps, that being obviously does not exist. If we observed a human being—let us say a head of state—who had the power to prevent torture, genocide, and concentration camps in his nation and refused to do so, we would not call such a ruler good. We can scarcely hold God less accountable than a human. Thus, if God exists, he cannot be good in our sense of the word.

Traditional Christian theodicies do not succeed. For example, the argument from free will does not ultimately help. The existence of free-will creatures may be necessary in order that moral good may exist. But it is possible to imagine a cosmos where free-will creatures choose to do only limited harm to one another. It is even possible to conceive of a cosmos in which all creatures endowed with free will freely choose only the good. The absolute omnipotence of God must embrace such cosmoses. Yet it is this cosmos, with all its evil, that God creates. Neither does the argument that evil is essentially nonbeing or lack of being really help. For a world is conceivable in which such a lack is not present. It does not help to say that God does not create (or will) the napalming of children on the grounds that the act of naplaming a child is an act lacking essential being, or even on the grounds that the act is willed directly by a human being rather than by God. The undeniable fact is that God creates, and maintains, a world such that it contains the napalming of children. All that one would need to challenge the goodness of God is the existence of one person needlessly suffering—and in reality we observe hundreds of millions.

If God exists, then, he is not good in the sense that we traditionally use the word good. If we wish to call God good, we must accept that his goodness is different from ours. This kind of argument has long been put forward by mystically inclined theologians. In theology, the *via positiva*, the "positive way," can take us only so far in saying what God *is*; we are then forced to the *via negativa*—statements about what God is not, and then the abandonment of any assertion about God's nature in either positive or negative terms. Among other things that God is not, he is not much like a human being, and qualities that we call "good" or "beautiful" can be applied to him only through remote analogy.

That God cannot be good in our sense of the word is borne out by observation, by comparison with other religious traditions in which the God is perceived as combining sun and shadow, good and evil, and by a reference to the Judeo-Christian tradition itself particularly the Book of Job. God tells Job that no human being has any way of understanding the reason for his suffering: "Then the Lord answered Job out of the whirlwind and said, Who is this that darkens counsel by words without knowledge? . . . Where were you when I laid the foundations of the earth? declare, if you have understanding?" And God tells Isaiah, "As high as the heavens are above the earth are my ways above your ways, and my thoughts above your thoughts." (Job 38; Isaiah 55.)

The problem of theodicy can thus be restated:

God exists.

God is all-powerful.

God is all-good; but the goodness of God is not equivalent to goodness as we understand it; God creates a universe in which evil, in our sense of the word, exists.

The existence of evil therefore does not contradict the existence of God.

A ready objection to such an argument is that if God is "good," but in another sense than "good" as we know it, the goodness of God is a word-game devoid of linguistic meaning. But here negative analogical theology enters. God's goodness is not wholly unlike our goodness. We may assume that God ultimately loves his creatures, though in ways beyond our grasp. The traditional argument that this must remain a mystery is patently true, but for Christians this shadowed mystery is alleviated by the fact that Christ—the Son of God and true God himself—is willing to suffer as humans do, and indeed more than most humans have to. The Incarnation liberates God from the charge of cruelty and shows that he takes the cosmos both seriously and lovingly. He shares the suffering of the suffering world that he creates. The goodness of God is as high above our goodness as the heavens are above the earth, but an analogy exists between the two.

Two levels of understanding God and evil exist. On the first level, God is not all-good in our sense. He creates a cosmos such that evil exists, in our sense of the word evil. Ultimately God is responsible for this evil.

On the second level, God rejects evil and desires us to fight it. He creates the cosmos such that good also exists; he creates it such that we have the power to resist evil; he creates it such that he wishes us to resist evil and loves us for doing so. Thus the standards of human goodness taught by Jesus are completely good in themselves: they do not contradict, but complement, the goodness of God. They are analogous to the goodness of God. Just as God presents himself to humanity as a man, to whom we can relate, rather than as, say, a luminous polyhedron, so God presents goodness to us in a form that we can understand and implement rather than in a form that we could not understand or implement.

The relationship between the "goodness" of God on the first level and the "goodness" of the second level is the location of the mystery, the eternally ungraspable by the human intellect. Yet human goodness is analogous to that of God, and the two are not divorced. Further, both levels should be understood. Failure to understand the first level leads to atheism; failure to understand the second leads to indifference to suffering. Though God creates a world in which evil exists, he insists that we reject it and fight it.

The corollary for the Devil is as follows: the Devil is not a principle; the Devil does not limit God's power; the Devil is a creature; the Devil is permitted by God to function; the Devil has some purpose in the cosmos that we cannot grasp; the Devil is God's enemy and our enemy and must be resisted with all our strength. This is true whether the Devil is an ontological entity or the personification of the "demonic" in humanity.

Essay on the Sources

Reasonably up-to-date bibliographies of the writings of the church fathers are: Eligius Dekkers, ed., *Clavis Patrum Latinorum*, 2d ed. (The Hague, 1961) and Maurice Geerard, ed., *Clavis Patrum Graecorum*, 2 vols. (Turnhout, 1974–1977). Most of the editions used in *Satan* appear in one of the following series collections of sources:

Corpus Christianorum Series Latina (CCSL)

.Corpus Scriptorum Ecclesiasticorum Latinorum (CSEL)

Griechische Christliche Schrifsteller (GCS)

Migne: Patrologia Latina (MPL)

Migne: Patrologia Graeca (MPG)

Sources chrétiennes (SC)

New editions and translations of patristic works continue to appear frequently. I indicate below the latest (or best) editions of the works that I have used, and their latest (or best) translations. The authors appear here in roughly the same order as they do in the text.

The best edition generally of the writings of the apostolic fathers is K. Bihlmeyer, *Die apostolischen Väter* (Tübingen, 1924); see also the translation by K. Lake, *The Apostolic Fathers*, 2 vols. (London, 1950).

For Epiphanius, see K. Holl, ed., *Epiphanius: Amoratus und Panarion*, 3 vols. (Leipzig, 1915–1933).

On Justin Martyr, see L. Barnard, *Justin Martyr: His Life and Thought* (Cambridge, 1967); E. Osborn, *Justin Martyr* (Tübingen, 1973); H. A. Kelly, *The Devil, Demonology, and Witchcraft*, pp. 27–31; F. Andres, *Die Engellehre* (Paderborn, 1914), pp. 1–35. The best edition of Justin's works is in E. J. Goodspeed, ed., *Die ältesten Apologeten* (Göttingen, 1914). On the dating of Justin's work and that of the other apologists, see R. M. Grant, "The Chronology of the Greek Apologists," *Vigiliae Christianae*, 9 (1955), 25–33.

Tatian's "Discourse" is edited in *Texte und Untersuchungen*, 4:1 (1880) and in Goodspeed, pp. 268–313.

Athenagoras' "Plea for the Christians" is often known as the Apology; in Latin it is known as the *Supplicatio* or *Legatio*; in Greek the πρεσβεία περὶ χριστιάνων. It is edited and translated by W. R. Schoedel, *Athenagoras: Legatio and De Resurrectione* (Oxford, 1972).

Theophilus' tract "To Autolycus" is edited by R. M. Grant, Theophilus of Antioch: *Ad Autolycum* (Oxford, 1970).

The standard edition of Irenaeus' chief work, "Against the Heresies," is W. W. Harvey, ed., *Sancti Irenaei episcopi Lugdunensis libros quinque adversus haereses*, 2 vols. (Cambridge, 1857). A new edition and translation has appeared: A. Rousseau and L. Doutreleau, eds., *Irénée: Contre les hérésies*, SC 263–264 (1979). The original Greek version is mostly lost. I use the book and chapter numbering of MPG, vol. 7. On Irenaeus and this theology of evil, see J. Hick, *Evil and the God of Love* (New York, 1966), and the critique of Hick by T. Clark, "The Problem of Evil: A New Study," *Theological Studies*, 28 (1967), 119–128. During the twentieth century, a previously lost work, "Proof of the Apostolic Preaching," has been rediscovered and edited. See J. P. Smith, trans., *Saint Irenaeus: Proof of the Apostolic Preaching* (Westminster, Md., 1952).

The relevant works of Tertullian are: E. Castorina, ed. *Tertulliani De spectaculis*, Biblioteca di studi superiori, 47 (1961); E. Evans, ed. *Tertullian adversus Marcionem*, 2 vols. (Oxford, 1972); *De praescriptione haereticorum*, F. R. Refoulé and P. de Labriolle, eds., *Tertullien: Traité de la préscription contre les hérétiques*, SC 46 (1957); J.-P. Waltzing, ed. *Tertullien: Apologétique* (Paris, 1961); C. Tibiletti, *Q. S. F. Tertulliani De testimonio animae*, Pubblicazioni della Facoltà di Lettere e Filosofia dell' Università di Torino, 11.2 (1959); J. H. Waszink, ed., *Tertulliani De anima*, CCSL 2 (1954), 779–869; A. Kroymann, ed., *Q. S. F. Tertullian: Adversus Valentinianos*, CCSL 2 (1954), 751–778; A. Kroymann, ed., *Q. S. F. Tertulliani De corona*, CCSL 2 (1954), 1037–1065; A. Kroymann and E. Evans, eds., *Q. S. F. Tertulliani Adversus Praxean*, CCSL 2 (1954), 1157–1205, or G. Scarpat, ed., *Adversus Praxean* (Turin, 1959); J. G. P. Borleffs, ed., *Q. S. F. Tertulliani De patientia*, CCSL 1 (1954), 297–340; E. Evans, ed., *Tertullian's Homily on Baptism* (London, 1964); A. Reifferscheid and G. Wissowa, eds., *Q. S. F. Tertulliani De idololatria*, CCSL 2 (1954), 1099–1124; J. J. Thierry, ed., *Q. S. F. Tertulliani De fuga in persecutione*; M. Turcan, ed., *Tertullien: La toilette des femmes* (Paris, 1971); R. Willems, ed., *Q. S. F. Tertulliani De testimonio animae*, CCSL 1 (1954), 173–183; J. G. P. Borleffs, ed., *Q. S. F. Tertulliani De resurrectione mortuorum*, CCSL 2 (1954), 919–1012; G. F. Diercks, ed., *Q. S. F. Tertulliani De oratione*, CCSL 1 (1954), 255–274; E. Dekkers, ed., *Q. S. F. Tertulliani De virginibus velandis*, CCSL 2 (1954), 1207–1226; E. Dekkers, ed., *Q. S. F. Tertulliani Ad scapulam*, CCSL 2 (1954), 1125–1132; A. Stephan, ed., *Tertulliani Ad uxorem libri duo* (The Hague, 1954); A. Reifferscheid and G. Wissowa, eds., *Q. S. F. Tertulliani Scorpiace*, CCSL 2 (1954), 1067–1097; J. G. P. Borleffs, ed., *Q. S. F. Tertulliani De paenitentia*, CCSL 1 (1954), 319–340; E. Dekkers, ed., *Q. S. F. Tertulliani De pudicitia*, CCSL 2 (1954), 1279–1330; A. Kroymann, ed., *Q. S. F. Tertulliani De carne Christi*, CCSL 2 (1954), 871–917.

"The Octavius" of Minucius Felix was edited by M. Pellegrino, *M. Minucii Felicis Octavius*, 2d ed. (Turin, 1963).

The relevant works of Cyprian are the *Epistulae*, "Letters," CSEL 3; *De catholicae ecclesiae unitate*, "The Unity of the Christian Church," M. Bévenot, ed. (Oxford, 1971); *De zelo et livore*, "Jealousy," M. Simonetti, ed. (Turnhout, 1976).

The chief extant works of Clement are: *The Tutor* or *Paedagogus*; the *Miscellanea* or *Stromata; The Rich Man's Salvation* or *Quis dives salvitur?*; the *Protrepticon*; surviving fragments of the *Theodotus*, which consists largely of excerpts from Theodotus, the exponent of Valentinian Gnosticism; an *Exhortation to the Greeks*; and a recently discovered letter. For the letter, see Morton Smith, *Clement of Alexandria and a Secret Gospel of Mark* (Cambridge, Mass., 1973). Though Clement wrote in Greek, many of his works are familiar in the West under Latin titles. The standard edition is Otto Stählin, ed., *Clemens Alexandrinus*, 3 vols. (Leipzig and Berlin, 1905–1970). See also H.-I. Marrou and M. Harl, *Clément d'Alexandrie: Le Pédagogue*, I, SC 70 (1960); C. Mondésert and H.-I. Marrou, trans., *Clément d'Alexandrie: Le Pédagogue*, II, SC, 108 (1965); C. Mondésert and M. Caster, ed. and trans., *Clément d'Alexandrie: Les stromates, Stromaton I*, SC 30 (1951); C. Mondésert and Th. Camelot, ed. and trans., *Clément d'Alexandrie: Les stromates, Stromaton II*, SC 38 (1954); F. Sagnard, ed. and trans., *Clément d'Alexandrie: Extraits de Théodote*, SC 23 (1948); C. Mondésert, ed. and trans., *Clément d'Alexandrie: Le protréptique*, SC 2 (1949); G. W. Butterworth translated Clement's works in *Clement of Alexandria* (London, 1919).

The relevant works of Origen are: A. Méhat, trans. *Origène: Homé-*

lies sur les Nombres, SC 29 (1951); ed. MPG 12, 575–806; H. Crouzel, ed. and trans., *Origène. Homélies sur Saint Luc*, SC 87 (1953); L. Doutreleau, trans., *Origène: Homélies sur la Genèse*, SC 7 (1943); ed. MPG 12, 145–262; O. Rousseau, ed. and trans., *Origène: Homélies sur le cantique des cantiques*, SC 37 (1953); P. Fortier and H. de Lubac, trans., *Origène: Homélies sur l'Exode*, SC 16 (1947), ed. MPG 12, 297–396; E. Klostermann, ed., *Origenes Matthäuserklärung*, part 2 (Berlin, 1976); H. Chadwick, trans., *Origen: Contra Celsum* (Oxford, 1965); M. Borret, ed. and trans., *Origène: Contre Celse*, 4 vols., SC 132, 136, 147, 150 (1967–1969); H. Crouzel and M. Simonetti, eds. and trans., *Origène: Traité des principes*, 4 vols. SC 252–253; 268–269 (1978–1980); P. Koetschau, ed., *Origenes: De oratione*, GCS 2; P. Koetschau, ed., *Origenes: Exhortatio ad martyrium*, GCS 2 (on the Exhortatio see also E. Früchtel, *Origenes: Das Gesprach mit Herakleides und dessen Bischofskollegen über Vater, Sohn, und Seele; die Aufforderung zum Martyrium* [Stuttgart, 1974]); Commentary on John, MPG 14, 21–830; Commentary on Romans, MPG 14, 837–1292; Homilies on Judges, MPG 12, 951–990; Homilies on 1 Kings, MPG 12, 995–1028; Homilies on Jeremiah, MPG 13, 253–544; Homilies on Leviticus, MPG 12, 405–574; Homilies on Ezechiel, MPG 13, 665–826; Homilies on Joshua, MPG 12, 825–948. The commentary on the Psalms previously attributed to Origen is now ascribed to Evagrius of Pontus. See M. J. Rondeau, "Le commentaire sur les Psaumes d'Evagre le Pontique," *Orientalia Christiana periodica*, 27 (1961), 241.

Julius Africanus (c. 180–240?), who wrote a "Chronicle" (MPG 10, 63–94), interpreted Genesis 6:2 by distinguishing between the "sons of God," whom he identified as the sons of Seth, righteous humans, from the "angels of God," whom he identified as the Watchers. This distinction did not endure, but the idea that all the beings of Genesis 6:2 were the sons of Seth persisted, helping to dislodge the story of the Watchers from the tradition.

Commodian, a mid-third-century writer, wrote "Poems," ed. J. Martin, CCSL, 128 (1960); cf. Daniélou, pp. 99–100. Commodian repeated the idea that God hid the true nature of Christ from the Devil so that he might trick him and by his Passion cast the ancient enemy down.

Victorinus of Pettau, an Illyrian who was martyred about 304 during the persecution of Diocletian, developed millenarian ideas, arguing that the Devil would be eliminated (*dismisso diabolo*) when divine providence had completed its establishment of the kingdom of the saints. *Opera*, ed. J. Haussleiter (Vienna and Leipzig, 1916); see pp. 11–154 for the "Commentary on the Apocalypse." Cf. also P. Henry and P. Hadot, eds., *Traités théologiques sur la Trinité*, 2 vols., SC 68–69 (1960)

Methodius' most important surviving works are περὶ τοῦ αὐτεξουσίου, "Free Will," and Ἀγλαοφῶν, ἢ περὶ ἀναστάσεως, "The Resurrection," both edited by G.N. Bonwetsch, GCS 27 (1917), 143–206 and 217–424. Methodius (c. 260–311) insisted on the traditional position that God had made the world good but that it had been deformed by the free-will sin of angels and of men. Something of a throwback in his diabology, he reverted to the Watcher story, arguing that the Devil fell because of envy of humanity and the other angels because of lust for women. Methodius was the first Christian author to apply the term μισόκαλος to the Devil: Resurrection 1.36.2 Bartelink, "Μισόκαλος, épithète du diable." *Misokalos*, "hater of the good," is associated with the Devil's envy, φθόνος. Eusebius of Caesarea later used the term frequently, associating it with heretics as well as the Devil.

Arnobius, a North African rhetorician, wrote *Adversus nationes*, "Against the Pagans," ed. C. Marchesi (Turin, 1953); MPL 5, 718–1288; cf. G. E. McCracken, trans., *The Case against the Pagans* (Westminster, Md., 1949). Here he took the position that the gods, rather than being demons, may not exist at all, or if they do, they derive their being and function from God. Demons are made *materiis ex crassioribus* (4.12), from "thicker and grosser matter" than are the angels.

Eusebius of Caesarea (c. 265–340), the great chronicler and biographer of Constantine, wrote voluminously. His works are in MPG 19–24; *The Ecclesiastical History*, ed. and trans. K. Lake (Cambridge, Mass., 1926); A. Schoene, ed. *Eusebi chronicorum libri duo*, 2 vols., 2d ed. (Berlin, 1967); F. Winkelmann, ed. *Vita Constantini*, (Berlin, 1975); G. Bardy, ed., *Eusèbe de Césarée: Histoire ecclésiastique*, 4 vols., SC 31, 41, 55, 73 (1952–1960); N. K. Mras, ed., *Praeparatio evangelica*, 2 vols., GCS 43 (1954–1956). The Devil fell through his free will; he is the leader of the demons and the source of sin and temptation; under his power the demons incite persecutions, heresy, and idolatry; Christ has overthrown the power of the Devil, who at the Passion suffered his "first death," his second and final death to occur at the second coming. See H. Berkhof, *Die Theologie des Eusebius von Caesarea* (Amsterdam, 1939).

The works of Lactantius are edited by S. Brandt in CSEL 19 and

27 (1890–1897). His first Christian book, "The Work of God," *De opificio Dei*, was composed shortly after 300 and was edited by Brandt, CSEL 19, pp. 3–64. Books 1 and 2 are edited and translated by M. Perrin, *Lactance: L'ouvrage de Dieu créateur*, SC 213–214 (1974). The "Divine Institutes," *Divinae institutiones*, were first written in 311 and then revised about 324; they are edited by Brandt, CSEL 19, but see note 5 to Ch. 6. Book 5 is edited and translated by P. Monat, *Lactance: Institutions divines*, SC 204–205 (1973); see also the English translation by M. F. McDonald (Washington, 1964). About 320 Lactantius produced a shortened version of the "Divine Institutes" called the "Epitome": see E. H. Blakeney, ed. and trans., *Epitome institutionum divinarum: Lactantius' Epitome of the Divine Institutes* (London, 1950); J. Dammig, *Die Divinae Institutiones des Laktanz und ihre Epitome* (Münster, 1957). The "Anger of God," *De ira Dei*, appeared about 313–315: CSEL 27, pp. 67–132, and "The Death of the Persecutors," *De mortibus persecutorum*, CSEL 27, pp. 171–238, about 315. On Lactantius' diabology see R. M. Ogilvie, *The Library of Lactantius* (Oxford, 1978); E. Schneweis, *Angels and Demons according to Lactantius* (Washington, 1944); V. Loi, "Problema del malo e dualismo negli scritti di Lattanzio," *Annali delle facoltà di lettere . . . Cagliari*, 29 (1961–1965), 37–96; K. E. Hartwell, *Lactantius and Milton* (Cambridge, Mass., 1929, repr. 1974); E. F. Micka, *The Problem of Divine Anger in Arnobius and Lactantius* (Washington, 1943).

The following writers are especially significant for the history of the Devil in monastic literature. Rufinus wrote his *Historia monachorum* about 400 (MPL 21, 391–462). Palladius (a disciple of Evagrius), wrote the *Historia Lausiaca* about 420: C. Butler, ed., *The Lausiac History of Palladius*, 2 vols. (Cambridge, 1898–1904). For a critique of Butler's edition see R. Draguet, "Butleriana: Une mauvaise cause et son malchanceux avocat," *Le Muséon*, 68 (1955), 238–258. See W. L. Clarke, trans., *The Lausiac History of Palladius* (London, 1918). On Pachomius, see A. Boon and L. T. Lefort, *Pachôme: Le Règle* (Louvain, 1932); L. T. Lefort, ed. and trans., *Oeuvres de S. Pachôme et ses disciples*, Corpus scriptorum Christianorum orientalium, scriptores Coptici, 23–24 (Louvain, 1964–1965). The lives of Paul, Malchus, and Hilarion by Saint Jerome appear in MPL 23, 17–60. On Shenuti, a fourth- and fifth-century monk, see K. Koschorke, S. Timm, and F. Wisse, "Shenute: *De certamine contra diabolum*," *Oriens christianus*, 59 (1975), 60–77. On the holy man, see P. Brown, "The Rise and Function of the Holy Man in Late Antiquity," *Journal of Roman Studies*, 61 (1971), 80–101; W. H. C. Frend, "The Monks and the Survival of the East

Roman Empire in the Fifth Century," *Past and Present*, 54 (1972), 3–24.
The most important monastic source is Athanasius' "Life of
Anthony." Athanasius' most significant works are: R. W. Thomson,
ed., *Athanasius Contra gentes and De incarnatione* (Oxford, 1971); G. J.
Ryan and R. P. Casey, trans., *The De incarnatione of Athanasius*, 2 vols.
(London, 1945–1946); *Epistula encyclica ad episcopos Aegypti et Libyae*,
MPG 25, 537–594; *Orationes contra Arianos*, MPG 26, 11–526; W.
Bright, trans., *The Orations of St. Athanasius according to the Benedictine
Text* (Oxford, 1873); P. T. Camelot, ed. and trans., *Athanase d'Alex-
andrie contre les païens*, SC 18bis (1977); *De virginitate*, MPG 28, 251–
282; J. Lebon, trans., *Athanase d'Alexandrie: Lettres à Sérapion*, SC 15
(1947); *Vita Antonii*, MPG 26, 835–976; R. Mayer, trans., *Life of Saint
Antony* [*sic*] (Westminster, Md., 1950). See J. Stoffels, "Die Angriffe
der Dämonen auf den Einsiedler Antonius," *Theologie und Glaube*, 2
(1910), 721–732; 809–830; Daniélou, "Les démons de l'air dans la 'Vie
d'Antoine."
The dialogue of Ephraim the Syrian is in the Nisibene hymns:
Ephraim Syrus, "Nisibene Hymns," E. Beck, ed. and trans., *Des heili-
gen Ephraem des Syrers Carmina Nisibena*, 2 vols. in 4 (Louvain, 1961–
1963); F. Graffin and R. Lavenant, trans., *Ephrem de Nisibe Hymnes sur
le Paradis*, SC 137 (1968); G. Garitte, "Homélie d'Ephraim sur la mort
du diable: Version arabe," *Le Muséon*, 82 (1969), 123–163.
The relevant works of Evagrius of Pontus are: A. and C. Guillaumont, ed. and trans., *Evagre le Pontique: Traité pratique ou le moine*,
SC 170–171 (1971); trans. J. E. Bamberger; A. and C. Guillaumont,
eds., "Le texte véritable des 'Gnostica' d'Evagre le Pontique," *Revue de
l'histoire des religions*, 142 (1952), 156–205; A. Guillaumont, ed., *Les
"Kephalaia gnostica" d'Evagre le Pontique* (Paris, 1958); *De oratione*, MPG
79, 1165–1200, attributed falsely to Nilus; W. Frankenberg, ed.,
Evagrius Pontikus: Antirrhetikos, Abhandlungen der königliche Akademie
der Wissenschaften zu Göttingen, philosophisch-historische Klasse,
n.s. 13.2 (Berlin, 1912): Syriac text with Greek facing; the "Eight
Spirits of Malice," *De octo spiritibus malitiae*, falsely attributed to Nilus
and published in MPG 29, 1157–1160: this is actually part of the
Antirrhetikos; *De malignis cogitationibus*, attributed to Nilus, MPG 79,
1199–1228—probably a work of Evagrius. See J. Muyldermans, *A
travers la tradition manuscrite d'Evagre le Pontique* (Louvain, 1932). See
also R. Draguet, "'L'histoire lausiaque,' une oeuvre écrite dans l'esprit
d'Evagre," *Revue d'histoire ecclésiastique*, 41 (1946), 321–364, and 42
(1947), 5–49.
Cyril of Jerusalem, c. 315–386, was bishop of Jerusalem. His works

appear in MPG 33. They have been translated by L. P. McCauley and A. A. Stephenson, *The Works of Saint Cyril of Jerusalem*, 2 vols., Washington, 1969. On the Devil: *Catechesis illuminandorum*, 1; *Catechesis de providentia Dei*, 4; *Catechesis de penitentia*, 3–4; *Cathechesis de Christo incarnato*, 15; *Catechesis mystagogica*, 4.

Basil of Caesarea, c. 330–379, a Cappadocian, was the brother of Gregory of Nyssa. His works appear in MPG 29–31; see also S. Giet, ed. and trans., *Homélies sur l'Hexaémeron*, SC 26 (1949); Y. Courtonne, ed. and trans., *Lettres*, 3 vols. (Paris, 1957–1966); E. Amand de Mendieta and S. Y. Rudberg, *Eustathius: Ancienne version latine des neuf homélies sur l'Hexaémeron de Basile de Césarée* (Berlin, 1958). On the Devil, Homily 2.4, 9.4–10, 11.1–4, 13.8, 20.1–5; *Commentarium in Isaiam prophetam*, 97, 116–117, 278–279; *In Psalmos* 7.2.

The works of the Cappadocian Gregory of Nyssa (c. 335–394) were edited by W. Jaeger et al., *Gregorii Nysseni opera*, 11 vols. (Leiden, 1960–1968); see also J. Daniélou, ed. and trans., *La vie de Moïse*, 2d ed., SC 1:2 (1955); P. Maraval, ed. and trans., *La vie de sainte Macrine*, SC 178 (1971); *La création de l'homme*, SC 6 (1943); A. J. Malherbe and E. Ferguson, trans., *The Life of Moses* (New York, 1978). See A. J. Philippou, "The Doctrine of Evil in Saint Gregory of Nyssa," *Studia Patristica*, 9 (1966), 251–256; M. Canévet, "Nature du mal et économie du salut chez Grégoire de Nysse," *Recherches de science religieuse*, 56 (1968), 87–95; B. Otis, "Cappadocian Thought as a Coherent System," *Dumbarton Oaks Papers*, 12 (1958), 95–124. *Oratio catechesis*, 6; *Oratio dominica* 5, where the Devil appears as "the tempter and the evil one:" ὁ πειρασμός τε καὶ ὁ πονηρός.

Gregory Nazianzenus, c. 330–390, the opponent of Gregory of Nyssa. His works appear in MPG 35–38; see also J. Benerdi, ed. and trans., *Discours 1–3*, SC 247 (1978); *Discours 20–23*, SC 270 (1980). P. Gallay and M. Jourjon, eds., *Discours, 27–31*, SC 250 (1978); A. Tuilier, ed. and trans., *La passion du Christ*, SC 149 (1969); P. Gallay, ed. and trans., *Lettres*, 2 vols. (Paris, 1964–1967).

John Chrysostom, patriarch of Constantinople, lived c. 347–407. His works appear in MPG 47–64; see also A. M. Malingrey, ed. and trans., *Sur la vaine gloire et l'éducation des enfants*, SC 188 (1972); Malingrey, ed., *Sur la providence de Dieu*, SC 79 (1961); F. Cavallera and J. Daniélou, eds. and trans., *Sur l'incompréhensibilité de Dieu*, SC 28 (1951); Malingrey, ed., *Lettres à Olympias*, SC 13 (1947); A. Wenger, ed. and trans., *Huit catéchèses baptismales*, SC 50 (1957); G. Ettinger and B. Grillet, eds. and trans., *A une jeune veuve*, SC 138 (1968); see D. Attwater, *Saint John Chrysostom* (London, 1959) and A. Moulard,

Saint John Chrysostome: Sa vie, son oeuvre (Paris, 1941). On the Devil, see *Ad Stagyrium*; *Ad Theodorum*, 1.9; *In Matthaeum homilia* 28.2–3; *De Lazaro concio*, 2.2; *In Epistolam ad Colossenses homilia* 3.4; *Expositio in Psalmum* 41; 44.

Cyril of Alexandria, who died in 444, was patriarch of Alexandria and an opponent of the Nestorians. His works appear in MPG 68–77. See also Rivière, "Rôle du démon au jugement particulier chez les pères"; J. Liébaert, "Saint Cyrille d'Alexandrie et la culture antique," *Mélanges de science religieuse*, 12 (1955), 5–26. On the Devil see *In Joannis evangelium* 10.14, P. E. Pusey, ed. *Cyrilli Archiepiscopi Alexandrini in S. Ioannis evangelium*, 3 vols. (Oxford, 1872); *In Psalmos* 9.29; *Contra Julianum Imperatorem* 9; *Glaphyra in Genesin* 1.3, 2.2; *De Incarnatione Domini*, ed. G. M. Durand, *Deux dialogues christologiques*, SC 97 (1964).

Theodoret, c. 393–466, was bishop of Cyrus. His works are in MPG 80–84; see also P. Canivet, ed., *Thérapeutique des maladies helléniques*, SC 57 (1958). On the Devil see *In Genesim quaestiones* 34; 36; *In II Corinthios* 2.11; *In Ephesios* 2.2; 6.12; *Compendium haereticarum fabularum* 5.8; *Graecarum affectionum curatio* 3.100–101.

Jerome, c. 331–419, was one of the most influential Latin fathers and the translator of the Vulgate Bible. See J. N. D. Kelly, *Jerome*. His works are in CCSL 72–78; F. Bonnard, ed. and trans., *Commentaire sur Saint Matthieu*, SC 242 (1977) and 259 (1979). On the Devil see *Commentarioli in Psalmos* 16–20; *In Isaiam* 14.53.5–7; 15.54.16–17; Letter 14.5; Letter 22.3–4; *Commentarium in Ecclesiasten* 8.1–4; *Vita Malchi* 6; *Liber quaestionum hebraicarum in Genesim* 3.1–15; *Commentarium in Matthaeum* 2.15.19–20; *In Ephesios* 1.2.2; 3.6.11.

Ambrose, c. 333–397, another influential Latin father, was the teacher of Saint Augustine. His works are in CSEL 32, 62, 64, and CCSL 14; see also Gabriel Tissot, ed. and trans., *Traité sur l'évangile de Saint Luc*, 2 vols., SC 45, 52 (1956–1958); B. Botte, ed. and trans., *Des sacrements*; *Des mystères*, SC 25 (1949); J. J. Savage, trans., *Letters* (New York, 1967); R. Gryson, ed. and trans., *La Pénitence*, SC 179 (1971); M. P. McHugh, trans., *Seven Exegetical Works* (Washington, 1972). See A. Paredi, *Saint Ambrose: His Life and Times* (Notre Dame, Ind., 1964), and McHugh, "Satan and Saint Ambrose," which gives a thorough account, with many references, of Ambrose's diabology.

Bishop Hilary of Poitiers died about 367. His works appear in CSEL 22 and 65; see also J.-P. Busson, ed. and trans., *Traité des mystères*, SC 19 (1947). On the Devil see *Tractatus in Psalmos*, 9, 51, 62, 64, 67, 118, 120, 124–125, 128, 133–143, 148.

The relevant works of Augustine are: *De libero arbitrio*, "The Free

Choice of the Will," written 38⌐–395, ed. CSEL 74 (1956); A. S. Benjamin and L. H. Hackstaff, trans., *On Free Choice of the Will* (Indianapolis, 1964). *De ordine*, "Order," written 386, ed. W. M. Green, CCSL, 29 (1970). *De vera religione*, "True Religion," written 389–391, ed. K. D. Daur, CCSL 32 (1962); J. H. S. Burleigh, trans., *Augustine: Earlier Writings* (London, 1953). *Enarrationes in Psalmos*, "Commentary on the Psalms," written 392–420, ed. E. Dekkers and J. Fraipont, 3 vols., CCSL, 38–40 (1956); S. Hebgin and F. Corrigan, trans., *Saint Augustine on the Psalms*, 2 vols. (Westminster, Md., 1960–1961). *De doctrina christiana*, "Christian Doctrine," written 395–426; ed. J. Martin, CCSL 32 (1962); D. W. Robertson, Jr., trans., *On Christian Doctrine* (New York, 1958). *Confessiones*, "Confessions," written 397, ed. M. Skutella, 2d ed. (Stuttgart, 1969); F. J. Sheed, trans., *The Confessions of Saint Augustine* (London and New York, 1943). *De Trinitate*, "The Trinity," written 399–419, ed. W. J. Mountain, 2 vols., CCSL 50–50A (1968); S. McKenna, trans., *The Trinity* (New York, 1963). *De Genesi ad litteram*, "Commentary on Genesis," written 401–444, CSEL 28:1 (1894). *De divinatione daemonum*, "Demonic Divination," written 406, CSEL 41 (1901); R. W. Brown, trans., *The Divination of Demons* (Washington, 1955). *De natura boni contra Manichaeos*, "The Nature of Good," written 399, CSEL 25:2 (1892); J. H. S. Burleigh, trans., *Augustine: Earlier Writings* (London, 1953). *Contra Faustum Manichaeum*, "Against Faustus," written 397, CSEL 25 (1891). See C. P. Mayer, "Die antimanichäischen Schriften Augustins," *Augustinianum* 14 (1974), 277–313. *Contra Maximum Arianum*, "Against Maximus the Arian," written 428, MPL 42. *De sancta virginitate*, "On Holy Virginity," written 401, MPL 40. *De civitate Dei*, "The City of God," written 413 (Books 1–5), 415–418 (Books 6–16), 420 (Book 17), 425 (Books 18–22), ed. B. Dombaert and A. Kalb, CCSL 47–48 (1955); P. Levine, ed. and trans., *The City of God*, 7 vols. (London, 1966). *Contra Julianum*, "Against Julian," written 421, MPL 44, M. A. Schumacher, trans., *Against Julian* (New York, 1957). *Enchiridion ad Laurentium*, "Enchiridion," written 421, MPL 40; A. C. Outler, trans., *Confessions and Enchiridion* (London, 1955). *De correptione et gratia*, "Admonition and grace," MPL 44; J. C. Murray, trans., *Admonition and Grace* (Washington, 1947). *Epistulae*, "Letters," CSEL 34:1–2; 44; 57–58 (1904–1923); Sister W. Parsons, trans., 5 vols. (Washington, 1955–1956). *Sermones*, "Sermons," MPL 38–39. *Retractionum libri duo*, "Retractions," CSEL (1902); M. I. Bogan, trans., *The Retractations* [*sic*] (Washington, 1968).

Pelagius' works include the *Expositiones xiii epistularum Pauli*, A. Souter, ed., 3 vols. (Cambridge, 1922–1931); translated in part by R. F. Evans, *Four Letters of Pelagius* (New York, 1968); *De induratione cordis Pharaonis*, G. Morin, ed., in G. de Plinval, *Essai sur le style et la langue de Pélage* (Fribourg, 1947), pp. 135–203. On Pelagius see J. Ferguson, *Pelagius: A Historical and Theological Study* (Cambridge, 1956).

Bibliography

Ahern, Dennis M. "Foreknowledge: Nelson Pike and Newcomb's Problem." *Religious Studies*, 15 (1979), 475–490.

Aland, B. "Gnosis und Kirchenväter: Ihre Auseinandersetzung um die Interpretation des Evangeliums." *Gnosis*, no. 8134, pp. 158–215.

Andres, Friedrich. *Die Engellehre der griechischen Apologeten des zweiten Jahrhunderts und ihr Verhältnis zur griechisch-römischen Dämonologie*. Paderborn, 1914.

——. "Die Engel- und Dämonenlehre des Klemens von Alexandrien." *Römische Quartalschrift*, 34 (1926), 13–37; 129–140; 307–329.

Arbesmann, Rudolf. "The 'Daemonium Meridianum' and Greek and Latin Patristic Exegesis." *Traditio*, 14 (1958), 17–31.

Attwater, Donald. *Saint John Chrysostom*. London, 1959.

Audet, Jean-Paul. *La Didachè, instruction des apôtres*. Paris, 1958.

Aulén, Gustave. *Christus victor: La notion chrétienne de Rédemption*. Paris, 1949.

Baaren, Th. P. van. "Towards a Definition of Gnosticism." In Ugo Bianchi, ed., *Le origini dello gnosticismo*. Leiden, 1970.

Bamberger, Bernard J. *Fallen Angels*. Philadelphia, 1952.

Barb, A. A. "The Survival of Magic Arts." In Arnaldo Momigliano, ed., *The Conflict between Paganism and Christianity in the Fourth Century*. Oxford, 1963. Pp. 100–125.

Barnard, Leslie W. *Justin Martyr: His Life and Thought*. Cambridge, 1967.

——. *Studies in the Apostolic Fathers and Their Background*. Oxford, 1966.

Barnes, Timothy David. *Tertullian: A Historical and Literary Study*. Oxford, 1971.

Bartelink, G. J. M. "Les démons comme brigands." *Vigiliae Christianae*, 21 (1967), 12–24.

——. "Μισόκαλος, épithète du diable." *Vigiliae Christianae*, 12 (1958), 37–44.

Barton, G. A. "The Origin of the Names of Angels and Demons in the Extra-canonical Apocalyptic Literature to 100 A.D." *Journal of Biblical Literature*, 31 (1912), 156–167.

Basinger, David. "Human Freedom and Divine Providence: Some New Thoughts on an Old Problem." *Religious Studies*, 15 (1979), 491–510.

Benoit, André. *Le baptême chrétienne au second siècle: La théologie des pères.* Paris, 1953.

Berge, Reinhold. "Exegetische Bemerkungen zur Dämonenauffassung des M. Minucius Felix." Diss. University of Freiburg im Breisgau, 1929.

Bettencourt, Etienne. *Doctrina ascetica Origenis seu quid docuit de ratione animae humanae cum daemonibus.* Studia Anselmiana, XVI. Rome, 1945.

Bettenson, Henry. *The Later Christian Fathers.* London, 1970.

Beyschlag, Karl. *Clemens Romanus und der Frühkatholizismus.* Tübingen, 1966.

———. *Simon Magus und die christliche Gnosis.* Tübingen, 1974.

Bianchi, Ugo. *Le origini dello gnosticismo: Colloquo di Messina 13–18 Aprile 1966.* Leiden, 1970.

———. "Le problème des origines du gnosticisme." In Bianchi, ed., *Le origini.* Pp. 1–27.

Bieder, Werner. *Die Vorstellung der Höllenfahrt Jesu Christi.* Zurich, 1949.

Bietenhard, Hans. *Die himmlische Welt im Urchristentum und Spätjudentum.* Tübingen, 1951.

Blackman, Edwin C. *Marcion and His Influence.* London, 1948.

Bloomfield, Morton W. "The Origin of the Concept of the Seven Cardinal Sins." *Harvard Theological Review,* 34 (1941), 121–128.

———. *The Seven Deadly Sins.* East Lansing, Michigan, 1952.

Boer, S. de. *De anthropologie van Gregorius van Nyssa.* Assen, 1968.

Borchert, D. M. "Beyond Augustine's Answer to Evil." *Canadian Journal of Theology,* 8 (1962), 237–243.

Bousset, Wilhelm. "Zur Dämonologie der späteren Antike." *Archiv für Religionswissenschaft,* 18 (1915), 134–172.

Boyd, James W. *Satan and Mara: Christian and Buddhist Symbols of Evil.* Leiden, 1975.

Brandon, Samuel G. F., "The Gnostic Problem in Early Christianity." *History Today,* 10 (1960), 415–423.

Brown, Milton Perry. *The Authentic Writings of Ignatius: A Study of Linguistic Criteria.* Durham, N.C., 1963.

Brown, Patterson. "God and the Good." *Religious Studies,* 2 (1967), 269–276.

Brown, Peter. *Augustine of Hippo.* London, 1967.

———. "Sorcery, Demons, and the Rise of Christianity." In Brown, *Religion and Society in the Age of Saint Augustine.* New York, 1972. Pp. 119–146.

Brown, Robert R. "The First Evil Will Must Be Incomprehensible: A Critique of Augustine." *Journal of the American Academy of Religion,* 46 (1978), 315–330.

Bruno de Jésus-Marie, ed. *Satan.* New York, 1952.

Bussell, Frederick W. "The Purpose of the World-Process and the Problem of Evil as Explained in the Clementine and Lactantian Writings in a System of Subordinate Dualism." *Studia Biblica et Ecclesiastica,* 4 (1896), 133–188.

Buttrick, George A. *God, Pain, and Evil.* Nashville, 1966.

Caillois, Roger. "Les démons de midi." *Revue de l'histoire des religions,* 115 (1937), 142–173; 116 (1937), 54–83; 143–186.

Campenhausen, Hans von. *Die Idee des Martyrium in der alten Kirche.* Göttingen, 2d ed., 1964.

Canévet, Maurice. "Nature du mal et économie du salut chez Grégoire de Nysse." *Recherches de science religieuse*, 56 (1968), 87–95.

Capitani, Franco de. "Studi recenti sul manicheismo." *Rivista di filosofia neoscolastica*, 65 (1973), 97–118.

Carcopino, Jérome. "Survivances par substitution des sacrifices d'enfants dans l'Afrique romaine." *Revue de l'histoire des religions*, 106 (1932), 592–599.

Cavendish, Richard. *The Powers of Evil*. New York, 1975.

Chadwick, Henry. *Alexandrian Christianity*. Philadelphia, 1954.

———. *Early Christian Thought and the Classical Tradition: Studies in Justin, Clement, and Origen*, New York, 1966.

Chadwick, Owen. *John Cassian*. 2d ed. Cambridge. 1968.

Church, F. Forrester. "Sex and Salvation in Tertullian." *Harvard Theological Review*, 68 (1975), 83–101.

Clark, Elizabeth A. *Clement's Use of Aristotle: The Aristotelian Contribution to Clement of Alexandria's Refutation of Gnosticism*. New York, 1977.

Clark, Thomas. "The Problem of Evil: A New Study." *Theological Studies*, 28 (1967), 119–128.

Cooper, Robert M. "Saint Augustine's Doctrine of Evil." *Scottish Journal of Theology*, 16 (1963), 256–276.

Corte, Nicolas. *Who Is the Devil?* New York, 1958.

Corwin, Virginia. *Saint Ignatius and Christianity in Antioch*. New Haven, 1960.

Crouzel, Henri. *Bibliographie critique d'Origène*. The Hague, 1971.

———. "Chronique Origenienne." *Bulletin de la littérature ecclésiastique*, 80 (1979), 109–126.

———. "L'Hadès et la Géhenne selon Origène." *Gregorianum*, 59 (1978), 291–331.

Dammig, Johannes. *Die Divinae Institutiones des Laktanz und ihre Epitome*. Diss. Münster, 1957.

Daniélou, Jean. "L'apocatastase chez Saint Grégoire de Nysse." *Recherches de science religieuse*, 30 (1940), 328–347.

———. "Les démons de l'air dans la 'Vie d'Antoine.'" *Studia Anselmiana*, 38 (1956), 136–147.

———. *Gospel Message and Hellenistic Culture*. Philadelphia, 1973.

———. "Le mauvais gouvernement du monde d'après le gnosticisme." In Ugo Bianchi, ed., *Le origini dello gnosticismo*. Pp. 448–459.

———. *Origen*. New York, 1955.

———. *The Origins of Latin Christianity*. London, 1977.

———. "Les sources juives de la doctrine des anges des nations chez Origène." *Recherches de science religieuse*, 38 (1951), 132–137.

———. *The Theology of Jewish Christianity*. Chicago, 1964.

Davids, Adelbert. "Irrtum und Häresie: 1 Clem.; Ignaz von Antiochen; Justinus." *Kairos*, n.s. 15 (1973), 165–187.

Decret, François. *Mani et la tradition manichéenne*. Paris, 1974.

Dekkers, Eligius, ed. *Clavis patrum latinorum*. 2d ed. Steenbrugge, 1961.

"Démon." *Dictionnaire de spiritualité ascétique et mystique*, vol. 3. Pp. 142–238.

Diepen, H. M., and Jean Daniélou. "Théodoret et le dogme d'Ephèse." *Recherches de science religieuse*, 44 (1956), 243–248.

Dix, Gregory. *The Shape of the Liturgy*. London, 1945.

Doig, D. H. "The Question of Evil Re-Examined." *Theology,* 69 (1966), 485–492.

Dölger, Franz. *Der Exorzismus im altchristlichen Taufritual: Eine religionsgeschichtliche Studie.* Paderborn, 1969.

Dölger, Franz-Josef. "Der Kampf mit dem Ägypter in der Perpetua-Vision: Das Martyrium als Kampf mit dem Teufel." In Dölger, *Antike und Christentum,* 4 vols. Münster, 1929–1934. 3: 177–188.

Doresse, Jean. *The Secret Books of the Egyptian Gnostics: An Introduction to the Gnostic Coptic Manuscripts Discovered at Chenoboskion.* New York, 1960.

Douglas, Mary. "The Problem of Evil." In Douglas, *Natural Symbols: Explorations in Cosmology.* London, 1970. Pp. 136–152.

Draguet, R. "L'histoire lausiaque, une oeuvre écrite dans l'esprit d'Evagre." *Revue d'histoire ecclésiastique,* 41 (1946), 321–364.

Dukes, Eugene. "Magic and Witchcraft in the Writings of the Western Church Fathers." Diss., Kent State University, 1972.

Elze, Martin. *Tatian und seine Theologie.* Göttingen, 1960.

Erich, Oswald A. *Die Darstellung des Teufels in der christlichen Kunst.* Berlin, 1931.

Evans, John M. *Paradise Lost and the Genesis Tradition.* Oxford, 1968.

Evil. Ed. the Curatorium of the C. G. Jung Institute. Evanston, Ill., 1967.

Fitch, William. *God and Evil: Studies in the Mystery of Suffering and Pain.* Grand Rapids, Mich., 1967.

Floyd, William E. G. *Clement of Alexandria's Treatment of the Problem of Evil.* New York, 1971.

Foerster, Werner. *Gnosis: A Selection of Gnostic Texts.* 2 vols. Oxford, 1972–1974.

Fontaine, Jacques. "Sur un titre de Satan chez Tertullien: *Diabolus interpolator.*" *Studi e materiali di storia delle religioni,* 38 (1967), 197–216.

———, and M. Perrin, eds. *Lactance et son temps: Recherches actuelles.* Paris, 1978.

Frend, W. H. C. *Martyrdom and Persecution in the Early Church: A Study of a Conflict from the Maccabees to Donatus.* Garden City, N.Y., 1965.

———. *The Rise of the Monophysite Movement: Chapters in the History of the Church in the Fifth and Sixth Centuries.* Cambridge, 1972.

Frère, Jean-Claude. "Le démon: Évolution de l'idée du mal à travers quelques personnifications." *Cahiers d'études cathares,* 27, no. 70 (1976), 3–14.

Garitte, Gérard. *Un témoin important du texte de la Vie de S. Antoine par S. Athanase: La version latine inédite des Archives du Chapitre de S. Pierre à Rome.* Brussels, 1939.

Geach, Peter T. *Providence and Evil.* Cambridge, 1977.

Geerlings, Hermanus Jacob. *De antieke daemonologie en Augustinus' geschrift De divinatione daemonum.* The Hague, 1953.

Gellner, Ernest. *The Devil in Modern Philosophy.* London, 1974.

Ginzberg, Louis. *The Legends of the Jews.* 7 vols. Philadelphia, 1938.

Gokey, Francis X. *The Terminology for the Devil and Evil Spirits in the Apostolic Fathers.* Washington, 1961.

Gonzalez, Gonzalo. "Dios y el diablo: superación cristiana del dualismo." *Ciencia tomista,* 104 (1977), 279–301.

Goodenough, Erwin R. *The Theology of Justin Martyr*. Jena, 1923.

Grant, Robert M. "The Chronology of the Greek Apologists." *Vigiliae Christianae*, 9 (1955), 25–33.

———. *Gnosticism and Early Christianity*. 2d ed. New York, 1966.

———. "Manichees and Christians in the Third and Early Fourth Centuries." In *Ex orbe religionum: studia Geo Widengren*. Leiden, 1972. Pp. 430–439.

———, ed. *Gnosticism: A Source Book of Heretical Writings from the Early Christian Period*. New York, 1962.

Greenfield, Jonas C., and Michael E. Stone. "The Books of Enoch and the Tradition of Enoch." *Numen*, 26 (1979), 89–103.

Griffin, David Ray. *God, Power, and Evil: A Process Theology*. Philadelphia, 1976.

Grillmeier, Alois. "Der Gottessohn im Totenreich." *Zeitschrift für katholische Theologie*, 71 (1949), 1–53; 184–203.

Haag, Herbert. *Teufelsglaube*. Tübingen, 1974.

Haardt, Robert. *Gnosis: Character and Testimony: An Anthology of Hellenistic Gnosticism*. Leiden, 1971.

Haight, David, and Marjorie Haight. "An Ontological Argument for the Devil." *The Monist*, 54 (1970), 218–220.

Hallie, Philip P. "Satan, Evil, and Good in History." In Sherman M. Stanage, ed., *Reason and Violence: Philosophical Investigations*. Totowa, N.J., 1975.

Harnack, Adolf von. *History of Dogma*. 7 vols. London, 1894.

Hawthorne, Gerald F. "Tatian and his Discourse to the Greeks." *Harvard Theological Review*, 57 (1964), 161–188.

Hebblethwaite, Brian. *Evil, Suffering, and Religion*. New York, 1976.

———. "Some Reflections on Predestination, Providence, and Divine Foreknowledge." *Religious Studies*, 15 (1979), 433–448.

Heck, Eberhard. *Die dualistischen Zusätze und die Kaiseranreden bei Lactantius*. Heidelberg, 1972.

Hefner, Philip. "Is Theodicy a Question of Power?" *Journal of Religion*, 59 (1979), 87–93.

Henning, W. B. "The Book of the Giants." *Bulletin of the School of Oriental and African Studies*, 11 (1943–46), 52–74.

Hick, John. *Evil and the God of Love*. New York, 1966.

Hinchliff, Peter. *Cyprian of Carthage and the Unity of the Christian Church*. London, 1974.

Holl, Adolf. *Death and the Devil*. New York, 1976.

Horn, Hans-Jürgen. "Die 'Hölle' als Krankheit der Seele in einer Deutung des Origenes." *Jahrbuch für Antike und Christentum*, 11/12 (1968–1969), 55–64.

Hughes, Robert. *Heaven and Hell in Western Art*. New York, 1968.

Huhn, Josef. *Ursprung und Wesen des Bösen und der Sünde, nach der Lehre des Kirchenvaters Ambrosiens*. Paderborn, 1933.

Hummel, Edelhard. *The Concept of Martyrdom According to Saint Cyprian of Carthage*. Washington, 1946.

Huppenbauer, Hans W. "Belial in den Qumrantexten." *Theologische Zeitschrift*, 15 (1959), 81–89.

James, Montague Rhodes, ed. *The Apocryphal New Testament*. Oxford, 1924.

Janssens, Yvonne. "Le thème de la fornication des anges." In Bianchi, ed., *Le origini dello gnosticismo*. Pp. 488–495.

Jensen, Søren S. *Dualism and Demonology: The Function of Demonology in Pythagorean and Platonic Thought*. Copenhagen, 1966.

Jolivet, Régis. *Le problème du mal d'après Saint Augustin*. Paris, 1936.

Jonas, Hans. "Delimitation of the Gnostic Phenomenon—Typological and Historical." In Bianchi, ed., *Le origini dello gnosticismo*. Pp. 90–108.

——. *The Gnostic Religion: The Message of the Alien God and the Beginnings of Christianity*. Boston, 1958.

Jung, Leo. *Fallen Angels in Jewish, Christian, and Mohammedan Literature*. Philadelphia, 1926.

Kallis, Anastasios. "Geister (Dämonen): Griechische Väter." *Reallexikon für Antike und Christentum*, 9, 700–715.

Kannengiesser, Charles, ed. *Politique et théologie chez Athanase d'Alexandrie*. Actes du Colloque de Chantilly. Paris, 1974.

Keller, Carl-A. "Das Problem des Bösen." In Martin Krause, ed., *Gnosis and Gnosticism*. Leiden, 1977. Pp. 70–90.

Kelly, Henry Ansgar. *The Devil, Demonology, and Witchcraft*. 2d. ed. New York, 1974.

——. "The Devil in the Desert." *Catholic Biblical Quarterly*, 26 (1964), 190–220.

——. "The Metamorphoses of the Eden Serpent during the Middle Ages and Renaissance." *Viator*, 2 (1971), 301–328.

——. "The Struggle against Satan in the Liturgies of Baptism and Easter." *Chronica*, 24 (Spring, 1979), 9–10.

Kelly, John N. D. *Early Christian Creeds*. London, 1958. 3d. ed.: 1972.

——. *Early Christian Doctrines*. London, 1958.

——. *Jerome: His Life, Writings, and Controversies*. London, 1975.

Kelsey, Morton. "The Mythology of Evil." *Journal of Religion and Health*, 13 (1974), 7–18.

Khatchadourian, Haig. "God, Happiness, and Evil." *Religious Studies*, 2 (1960), 109–119.

Krause, M., ed. *Gnosis and Gnosticism: Papers Read at the Seventh International Conference on Patristic Studies (Oxford)*. Leiden, 1977.

Krieger, Leonard. "The Autonomy of Intellectual History." *Journal of the History of Ideas*, 34 (1973), 499–516.

Kruse, Heinz. "Das Reich Satans." *Biblica*, 58 (1977), 29–61.

Kyrilliana: spicilegia edita Sancti Cyrilli Alexandrini XV recurrente saeculo. Cairo, 1947.

Ladner, Gerhart. *The Idea of Reform: Its Impact on Christian Thought and Action in the Age of the Fathers*. Cambridge, Mass., 1959.

Langston, Douglas. "The Argument from Evil: Reply to Professor Richman." *Religious Studies*, 16 (1980), 103–113.

Langton, Edward. *Satan: A Portrait: A Study of the Character of Satan Through All the Ages*. London, 1945.

Laporte, Jean. "La Chute chez Philon et Origène." *Kyriakon: Festschrift Johannes Quasten* (Münster, 2 vols.) 1 (1970), 320–335.

Leisegang, Hans. *Die Gnosis*. 4th ed. Stuttgart, 1955.

Lenz, C. "Apokatastasis." *Reallexikon für Antike und Christentum*, 1, 510–516.

Liébaert, Jacques. "Saint Cyrille d'Alexandrie et la culture antique." *Mélanges de science religieuse*, 12 (1955), 5–26.

Lienhard, Joseph T. *Paulinus of Nola and Early Western Monasticism*. Bonn, 1977.

Lilla, Salvatore R. C. *Clement of Alexandria: A Study in Christian Platonism and Gnosticism*. London, 1971.

Loi, Vincenzo. "Problema del male e dualismo negli scritti di Lattanzio." *Annali delle facoltà di lettere filosofia e magistero dell'Università di Cagliari*, 29 (1961–1965), 37–96.

Lortz, Joseph. *Tertullian als Apologet*. 2 vols. Münster, 1927–1928.

Lovejoy, Arthur O. *The Great Chain of Being*. Cambridge, Mass., 1936.

Lukken, G. M. *Original Sin in the Roman Liturgy*. Leiden, 1973.

Maag, Victor. "The Antichrist as Symbol of Evil." In *Evil*, Curatorium of the C. G. Jung Institute, above. Pp. 57–82.

MacCulloch, John A. *The Harrowing of Hell: A Comparative Study of an Early Christian Doctrine*. Edinburgh, 1930.

Mackie, J. L. "Evil and Omnipotence." *Mind*, 64 (1955), 200–212.

Macquarrie, J. "Demonology and the Classical Idea of Atonement." *The Expository Times*, 68 (1956), 3–6; 60–63.

Maier, Johann. "Geister (Dämonen): Talmudisches Judentum." *Reallexikon für Antike und Christentum*, 9, 668–688.

Manselli, Raoul. *L'eresia del male*. Naples, 1963.

Maple, Eric. *The Domain of Devils*. London, 1966.

Maquart, Francis X. "Exorcism and Diabolical Manifestation." In Bruno de Jésus-Marie, ed., *Satan*, above. Pp. 178–203.

Marcovich, Miroslav. "On the Text of Athenagoras *De resurrectione*." *Vigiliae Christianae*, 33 (1979), 375–382.

Maritain, Jacques. *God and the Permission of Evil*. Milwaukee, 1966.

Martikainen, J. *Das Böse und der Teufel in der Theologie Ephraems des Syrers: Eine systematisch-theologische Untersuchung*. Aabo, 1978.

May, Harry S. "The Daimonic in Jewish History; or, the Garden of Eden Revisited." *Zeitschrift für Religions- und Geistesgeschichte*, 23 (1971), 205–219.

Mayer, C. P. "Die antimanichäischen Schriften Augustins." *Augustinianum*, 14 (1974), 277–313.

McCue, James F. "Orthodoxy and Heresy: Walter Bauer and the Valentinians." *Vigiliae Christianae*, 33 (1979), 118–130.

McHugh, Michael P. "The Demonology of Saint Ambrose in Light of the Tradition." *Wiener Studien*, 91 (1978), 205–231.

——. "Satan and Saint Ambrose." *Classical Folia*, 26 (1972), 94–106.

Michl, Johann. "Katalog der Engelnamen." *Reallexikon für Antike und Christentum*, 5 (1962), 200–239.

Micka, Ermin F. *The Problem of Divine Anger in Arnobius and Lactantius*. Washington, 1943.

Mitros, Joseph. "Patristic Views of Christ's Salvific Work." *Thought*, 42 (1967), 421–426.

Moore, George Foot. *Judaism in the First Centuries of the Christian Era*. 3 vols. Cambridge, Mass., 1955–1958.

Moreschini, Claudio. "Influenze di Origene su Gregorio di Nazianzo." *Atti e memorie dell'Accademia Toscana di scienze e lettere*, 44 (1979), 33–57.
——. "La polemica di Agostino contro la demonologia di Apuleio." *Annali della Scuola Normale Superiore di Pisa*, ser. 3, v. 2 (1972), 583–596.
Moulard, Anatole. *Saint Jean Chrysostome: Sa vie, son oeuvre*. Paris, 1941.
Müller, Gotthold. "Origenes und die Apokatastasis," *Theologische Zeitschrift*, 14 (1958), 174–190.
Munz, Peter. *The Shapes of Time*. Middletown, Conn., 1977.
Muyldermans, J. *A travers la tradition manuscrite d'Evagre le Pontique*. Louvain, 1932.
Nash, Victor Thomas. "The Other Satan: A Study of the Watcher Devil in Patristics, Folklore, and English Literature; Diss., University of Oregon, 1977.
Nautin, B. *Origène: Sa vie et son oeuvre*. Paris, 1977.
Newman, John Henry. *An Essay on the Development of Christian Doctrine*. London, 1845.
Oesterreich, Traugott K. *Possession: Demoniacal and Other among Primitive Races, in Antiquity, the Middle Ages and Modern Times*. New Hyde Park, N.Y., 1966.
Ogilvie, R. M. *The Library of Lactantius*. Oxford, 1978.
Olson, Alan M., ed. *Disguises of the Demonic: Contemporary Perspectives on the Power of Evil*. New York, 1975.
Orbe, Antonio. "La trinidad maléfica (a proposito de l' 'Excerpta ex Theodoto' 80.3)." *Gregorianum*, 49 (1968), 726–761.
Ort, L. J. M. *Mani: a Religio-historical Description of His Personality*. Leiden, 1967.
Osborn, Eric F. *Ethical Patterns in Early Christian Thought*. Cambridge, 1976.
——. *Justin Martyr*. Tübingen, 1973.
Pagels, Elaine. *The Gnostic Gospels*. New York, 1979.
Paterson, R. W. K. "Evil, Omniscience, and Omnipotence." *Religious Studies*, 15 (1979), 1–23.
Patrides, C. A. "The Salvation of Satan." *Journal of the History of Ideas*, 28 (1967), 467–478.
Peel, Malcolm L. "The 'Descensus ad Inferos' in 'The Teachings of Silvanus.'" *Numen*, 26 (1979), 23–49.
Pelikan, Jaroslav. *The Christian Tradition*. 3 vols. to date. Chicago, 1971–1978.
——. *Development of Christian Doctrine: Some Historical Prolegomena*. New Haven, 1969.
Penelhum, Terence. "Divine Goodness and the Problem of Evil." *Religious Studies*, 2 (1966), 95–107.
Pétrement, Simone. *Le dualisme chez Platon, les gnostiques, et les manichéens*. Paris, 1947.
——. "Le mythe des sept archontes créateurs peut-il s'expliquer à partir du christianisme?" In Bianchi, ed., *Le origini dello gnosticismo*, above. Pp. 460–487.
Philippou. A. J. "The Doctrine of Evil in Saint Gregory of Nyssa." *Studia Patristica*, 9 (1966), 251–256.
Pike, Nelson. "Plantinga on Free Will and Evil." *Religious Studies*, 15 (1979), 449–473.

Plantinga, Alvin. *God, Freedom, and Evil.* Grand Rapids, Mich., 1978.
Poteat, William H. "Foreknowledge and Foreordination: A Critique of Models of Knowledge." *Journal of Religion,* 40 (1960), 18–26.
Puech, Henri-Charles. *En quête de la gnose.* 2 vols. Paris, 1978.
——. *Le manichéisme.* Paris, 1949.
——. "The Prince of Darkness in His Kingdom." In Bruno de Jésus-Marie, ed., *Satan,* above. Pp. 127–157.
Quispel, Gilles. *De bronnen van Tertullianus' Adversus Marcionem.* The Hague, 1943.
——. *Gnosis als Weltreligion.* Zurich, 1951.
——. "Mani the Apostle of Jesus Christ." In *Epektasis: Mélanges patristiques offerts au cardinal Jean Daniélou* (Paris, 1972), pp. 667–672.
Ranke-Heinemann, Uta. "Der Kampf gegen die Dämonen und die Sünde." *Das frühe Mönchtum: Seine Motive nach den Selbstzeugnissen.* Essen, 1964. Pp. 50–64.
Recheis, Athanas. *Engel, Tod, und Seelenreise: Das Wirken der Geister beim Heimgang des Menschen in der Lehre der Alexandrinischen und Kappadokischen Väter.* Rome, 1958.
Rehm, Bernhard. *Die Pseudoklementinen.* 2 vols. Berlin, 1965–1969.
Reicke, Bo. *The Disobedient Spirits and Christian Baptism.* Copenhagen, 1946.
Richman, Robert J. "The Argument from Evil." *Religious Studies,* 4 (1969), 203–211.
Rist, John M. "Augustine on Free Will and Predestination." *Journal of Theological Studies,* ser. 2, 20 (1969), 420–447.
Rivière, Jean. "Le démon dans l'économie rédemptrice d'après les apologistes et les premiers Alexandrins." *Bulletin de littérature ecclésiastique,* 31 (1930), 5–20.
——. "La doctrine de Saint Irénée sur le rôle du démon dans la rédemption." *Bulletin d'ancienne littérature et d'archéologie chrétienne,* 1 (1911), 169–200.
——. "Rôle du démon au jugement particulier chez les pères." *Revue des sciences religieuses,* 4 (1924), 43–64.
Robinson, James M. *The Nag Hammadi Library: in English.* New York, 1977.
Roskoff, Gustav. *Geschichte des Teufels.* 2 vols. Leipzig, 1869.
Rousseau, Hervé. *Le dieu du mal.* Paris, 1963.
Rousseau, Philip. *Ascetics, Authority, and the Church in the Age of Jerome and Cassian* (Oxford, 1978).
Rudolph, Kurt. *Die Gnosis: Wesen und Geschichte einer spätantiken Religion.* Göttingen, 1977.
Rudwin, Maximilian. *The Devil in Legend and Literature.* La Salle, Ill., 1931.
Ruether, Rosemary Radford. *Gregory of Nazianzenus: Rhetor and Philosopher.* Oxford, 1969.
Ruhbach, G. "Zum Begriff ἀντίθεος in der alten Kirche." *Texte und Untersuchungen,* 92 (1966), 372–384.
Russell, Jeffrey Burton. *The Devil: Perceptions of Evil from Antiquity to Primitive Christianity.* Ithaca, N.Y., 1977.
Sage, Michael M. *Cyprian.* Cambridge, Mass., 1975.
Sagnard, François. *La gnose valentinienne et le témoignage de saint Irénée.* Paris, 1947.

Sans, Isidoro M. *La envidia primigenia del diablo según la patrística primitiva.* Madrid, 1963.

Schade, Herbert. *Dämonen und Monstren.* Regensburg, 1962.

Schlesinger, George. "The Problem of Evil and the Problem of Suffering." *American Philosophical Quarterly,* 1 (1964), 244–247.

Schmithals, Walter. *Gnosticism in Corinth: An Investigation of the Letters to the Corinthians.* 2d ed. Nashville, 1971.

———. *Paul and the Gnostics.* Nashville, 1972.

Schneweis, Emil. *Angels and Demons according to Lactantius.* Washington, 1944.

Schüle, Ernst U. "Der Ursprung des Bösen bei Marcion." *Zeitschrift für Religions- und Geistesgeschichte,* 16.1 (1964), 23–42.

Schweitzer, E. "Geister (Dämonen): Neues Testament." *Reallexikon für Antike und Christentum,* 9, 688–700.

Simon, Marcel. "Remarques sur l'angélologie juive au début de l'ère chrétienne." *Comptes-rendus des séances de l'académie des inscriptions et belles-lettres* (Paris), 1 (1971), 120–134.

Siwek, Paul. "The Problem of Evil in the Theory of Dualism." *Laval théologique et philosophique* (1955), 67–80.

Skinner, Quentin. "Meaning and Understanding in the History of Ideas." *History and Theory,* 8 (1969), 3–53.

Smith, Morton. *Clement of Alexandria and a Secret Gospel of Mark.* Cambridge, Mass., 1973.

Sontag, Frederick. *The God of Evil: An Argument from the Existence of the Devil.* New York, 1970.

Soury, Guy. *La démonologie de Plutarque: Essai sur les idées religieuses et les mythes d'un platonicien éclectique.* Paris, 1942.

Strack, Hermann. *Introduction to the Talmud and Midrash.* New York, 1959.

Tardieu, M. "Le Congrès de Yale sur le gnosticisme (28–31 mars 1978)." *Revue des études augustiniennes,* 24 (1978), 188–209.

Teichtweier, Georg. *Die Sündenlehre des Origenes.* Regensburg, 1958.

Te Selle, Eugene. *Augustine the Theologian.* New York, 1970.

Trachtenberg, Joshua. *The Devil and the Jews.* New Haven, 1943.

———. *Jewish Magic and Superstition.* New York, 1939.

Turmel, Joseph. *The Life of the Devil.* London, 1929.

Van der Hart, Rob. *The Theology of Angels and Devils.* Notre Dame, Ind., 1973.

Van der Nat, Pieter G. "Geister (Dämonen): Apologeten und lateinische Väter." *Reallexikon für Antike und Christentum,* 9 (1975), 715–761.

Völker, Walther. *Das Vollkommenheitsideal des Origenes.* Tübingen, 1931.

Wainwright, William J. "The Presence of Evil and the Falsification of Theistic Assertions." *Religious Studies,* 4 (1969), 213–216.

Wall, George B. "A New Solution to an Old Problem." *Religious Studies,* 15 (1979), 511–530.

Waltzing, J.-P. "Le crime rituel reproché aux chrétiens du IIe siècle." *Bulletin de l'Académie royale des sciences, des lettres, et des beaux-arts de Belgique.* Brussels, 1925.

Waszink, J. H. "*Pompa diaboli.*" *Vigiliae Christianae,* 1 (1947), 13–41.

Webster, Sister Gertrude. "Satan and Angels in Art and Literature." *Horizontes: Revista de la Universidad Católica de Puerto Rico*, 18 (October 1974), 19–41.

Weinel, Heinrich. *Die Wirkungen des Geistes und der Geister im nachapostolischen Zeitalter bis auf Irenäus*. Freiburg, 1899.

Wenzel, Siegfried. "The Seven Deadly Sins: Some Problems of Research." *Speculum*, 43 (1968), 1–22.

——. *The Sin of Sloth*. Chapel Hill, N.C., 1960.

Wey, Heinrich. *Die Funktionen der bösen Geister bei den griechischen Apologeten des zweiten Jahrhunderts nach Christus*. Winterthur, 1957.

Wickham, L. R. "The Sons of God and the Daughters of Men: Genesis vi:2 in Early Christian Exegesis." *Oudtestamentische Studien*, 19 (1974), 135–147.

Widengren, Geo. *The Gnostic Attitude*. Santa Barbara, 1973.

——. *Mani and Manichaeism*. London, 1965.

Williams, Norman Powell. *The Ideas of the Fall and of Original Sin*. London, 1927.

Wilson, Robert McL. *Gnosis: A Selection of Gnostic Texts*. 2 vols. Oxford, 1973–1974.

——. "Gnosticism in the Light of Recent Research." *Kairos*, n.s. 13 (1971), 282–288.

——. *The Gnostic Problem*. London, 1958.

Windisch, Hans. *Der Barnabasbrief*. Tübingen, 1920.

Wlosok, Antonie. *Laktanz und die philosophische Gnosis: Untersuchungen zu Geschichte und Terminologie der gnostischen Erlösungsvorstellung*. Heidelberg, 1960.

Wolfson, Harry A. *Philo*. 2 vols. Cambridge, Mass., 1947.

——. *The Philosophy of the Church Fathers: Faith, Trinity, Incarnation*. Cambridge, Mass., 1956.

Woods, Richard. *The Devil*. Chicago, 1973.

Yamauchi, Edwin M. *Pre-Christian Gnosticism: A Survey of the Proposed Evidences*. Grand Rapids, Mich., 1973.

Yates, Roy. "The Antichrist." *Evangelical Quarterly*, 46 (1974), 42–50.

Young, Frances M. "Insight or Incoherence: The Greek Fathers on Good and Evil." *Journal of Ecclesiastical History*, 24 (1973), 113–126.

Index

SATAN

Designed by Richard E. Rosenbaum.
Composed by Eastern Graphics
in 11 point Janson, 2 points leaded,
with display lines in Palatino and Palatino Bold.
Printed offset by R. R. Donnelley & Sons Company on
Warren's Sebago, 50 pound basis.
Bound by R. R. Donnelley
in Joanna book cloth.

Library of Congress Cataloging in Publication Data

Russell, Jeffrey Burton.
  Satan: the early Christian tradition.

  Bibliography: p.
  Includes index.
  1. Devil—History of doctrines—Early church, ca. 30–600. I. Title.
BT981.R87   235'.47'09015   81-66649
ISBN 0-8014-1267-6   AACR2